THE ABSENCE OF JUSTICE

THE ABSENCE OF JUSTICE

AN ANALYSIS OF THE BOOK OF JOB

AND

THE PROBLEM OF EVIL

BY

PAUL E. LEIGHTNER

Wipf and Stock Publishers
Eugene, Oregon

Unless otherwise indicated, Scripture quotations used in this book are from the Holy Bible, New International Version (NIV). Copyright 1973, 1978, 1984 International Bible Society. Used by permisssion of Zondervan Bible Publishers.

Scriptures indicated KJV are from the King James Version of the Bible.

Scriptures indicated NAS are from the New American Standard Bible.

Wipf and Stock Publishers
199 West 8th Avenue, Suite 3
Eugene, Oregon 97401

The Absence of Justice
An Analysis of the Book of Job
    And the Problem of Evil
Copyright©2003 by Paul E. Leightner
ISBN: 1-59244-252-8
Publication Date: July 2003

10   9   8   7   6   5   4   3   2   1

*Dedicated to my dear wife, Lois,
who endured much yet encouraged much
during the writing of this book.*

Table of Contents

	Introduction	1
Chapter 1	The Wager	3
Chapter 2	The Discourses	21
Chapter 3	The Lamentations of Job	24
Chapter 4	Dialogues, Round 1	29
Chapter 5	Dialogues, Round 2	53
Chapter 6	Dialogues, Round 3	69
Chapter 7	The Wisdom Chapter	81
Chapter 8	Job Presents His Case to God	84
Chapter 9	Elihu, the Brash Young Man	96
Chapter 10	God's Answer, Part 1	112
Chapter 11	Job's Responses & God's Answer, Part 2	138
Chapter 12	The Happy Ending	154
Chapter 13	The Problem of Evil	158
Chapter 14	There Is a Balm	190
	Appendix	210
	Bibliography	216

FOREWORD

Paul Leightner has written an extraordinarily incisive, beautifully expressed analysis of the Book of Job. His book has the merit of covering every aspect of the book in great detail and presenting clear-cut decisions on the many problems that scholars have raised in interpreting it. The discussion of the Prologue and Epilogue as well as the numerous speeches is stimulating and very carefully done.

His book has the merit of conclusively demonstrating that the common interpretation of the Book of Job—that which Job experiences and the experience itself is an answer to the problem posed by the book—is unwarranted. On the contrary he shows that the meaning of God's intervention out of the whirlwind contains an answer to the question posed by Job.

As bold as Leightner's interpretation is, and helpful to anyone wishing to make a study of the book, perhaps it does not go far enough.

It seems to me that the issue between Job and the friends is that they are judging him without in any way taking into consideration the agony of his suffering. They refuse to put themselves in his place. They immediately judge his suffering as the consequence of sin, indeed of blasphemy. They are convinced that there is no suffering without sin and that all who suffer must be sinful.

The great merit of the Book of Job is to conclusively demonstrate that there is no mechanical connection between suffering and sin; on the contrary, there may be great suffering as the result of doing good. The Prophets testify to this.

But it seems that Job is guilty with respect to God of the same deficiency as the friends. He is judging God by his standard of what the universe must be like, and I believe that one of the great teachings that comes out of the Voice on the Whirlwind is God's substantially asking Job, "When was the last time you created a world? Do you have any idea what is involved in creating this vast cosmos and all its diversity where human beings are merely an element within it?"

Justice is not a fact but rather an accomplishment that human beings must take upon themselves; that is why God in his speaking directly to Job goes from the Interrogative to the Imperative and says that he must take upon himself the burden of making the world better. This additional way of looking at the book in no way conflicts with Paul Leightner's interpretation. It is a tribute to his hard work and learning and I enthusiastically endorse it for classes and individual studies.

Rabbi Jack Bemporad,
Director of the Center for Interreligious Understanding
(For more information, visit his website at Ciuorg@aol.com.)

Acknowledgments

I owe a great debt of gratitude to Rabbi Jack Bemporad for his insights and encouragement. His lectures on the Book of Job gave me my first insights into the meaning and flow of the dialogues between Job and his friends. He had a way of condensing the long poetic passages down to a concise statement in the vernacular that made the conversations understandable. It was his style that prompted me to try to present the dialogues in a more understandable format. I have used a few of the condensations he used in his lectures almost verbatim. I simply couldn't think of a better, different, or more concise way to state them. Thank you, Dr. Bemporad, for getting me started and also for getting me "hooked" on Job.

To those who gave their suggestions and encouragement during the years I was struggling with the problems of the Book of Job and the problem of evil, I also owe a debt of gratitude. First of all, my wife, Lois, endured many years of my mental and emotional struggles with the meanings and interpretations presented in this book. My son, Dr. Jonathan Leightner, provided many insights gleaned from his undergraduate studies in philosophy. Dr. Blair Ritchie, Dr. William Hasker, and Dr. Kenn Gangel each contributed much needed encouragement at critical times.

My heartfelt thanks to these and others who contributed to this work must also include Mrs. Nora Calloway, who typed many pages of early drafts before we got our first computer. Susan Snowden, my editor, also contributed greatly to the finished product and was very kind in pointing out the many flaws in my manuscript.

INTRODUCTION

In January of 1975, my family and I were enjoying a long awaited vacation in Hawaii. We were guests of our dear friends Gilbert and Molly Williams on the island of Kauai. Our sons, Tim, Jon, and Dan, my wife, Lois, and I were swimming one day at Anahola Beach. On that particular day, an exceptionally high tide was predicted. Gilbert was pleased to hear this, as it meant the riptide would also be strong. Surfers love this, as the riptide can be counted on to carry them out to where they can catch the waves and surf back in. He failed to reckon on the fact that we were such landlubbers. Lois and I were together in water about up to our waists. We waded over to where our son Jon was trying to surf, not realizing that we were heading right into the riptide. Suddenly, there was no bottom. Being the landlubbers we were, we did not know that all we had to do was swim a few feet in the direction from which we had come, and we would have gotten out of danger. Instead, we began to struggle toward shore against the tide.

Lois began to panic, so I instructed Jon to get her up to the beach. I tried to follow, but my lack of buoyancy kept me too low in the water where the riptide kept pulling me out. I got nowhere, but seemed stuck at that part of the surf where the waves were continually breaking over me. I would just catch my breath when another wave would crash over my head. By the time Lois and Jon finally reached shore, I knew I was in trouble. I had gone through all the tricks I had learned as a boy scout and none of them helped. I was foundering, unable to make any headway toward the beach.

I distinctly remember having the strong impression that I was at the threshold of a definite "place" that had nothing to do with this physical world. I sensed that I was about to enter that "place." I glanced in to shore and Lois was lying on the beach, exhausted, tended to by my son. I did not panic, strangely enough. But I did say to God, "If you want me around, you are going to have to do something real quick because I am not going to make it!" As I said that, I was looking toward the shore at my wife and son.

Suddenly, my wife sat up and began gesticulating wildly, pointing in my direction. My son was very nearsighted and couldn't even see me. He started out in my direction, then after more gesticulating from my wife, turned back, got his surfboard, and headed out in my direction. When he got to me, I clung to the surfboard, but since I was so exhausted, the first wave jerked it out of my grasp. I told Jon, "Get it." Amazingly, it had not been swept more than twenty yards away, and he was able to retrieve it shortly. We then, both clinging to the board, slowly made our way to the beach, where I collapsed with a mass of jellied muscles.

The doctor at the hospital in Lihue where they took me for evaluation, informed me that I had been within seconds of passing out. I would have regained consciousness under water, taken a deep "breath," and that would have been the end.

Molly marched into my bedroom as I rested that evening and stated as only Molly could, "You know that you are living on borrowed time!" I didn't think much of it at the time. Certainly I was glad to be alive. We returned to the mainland, back to our home in Texas. Then things began happening that, in retrospect, formed a pattern. In the next few years, Satan tried to destroy my business, my marriage, my reputation, and my faith. I began to suspect that he was also behind the incident in Hawaii. It was at this time of personal turmoil that my pastor, Rev. Dave Reimer, turned me on to the Book of Job. He commented that most seminary professors were "scared to death" of that book. That was just like saying "sic em" to me, even though I am not a theologian.

I was puzzled greatly by the Book of Job. It just didn't make any sense to me. I began sharing my frustration with my friends. My dentist, Dr. Robert Schroeder, lent me some tapes on Job by another of his patients, Rabbi Jack Bemporad of Temple Emmanuel in Dallas. Later, I personally heard Rabbi Bemporad lecture on the Book of Job and the problem of evil. His teaching helped to solve many problems, and started me on the track of finding satisfying answers to others. However, there was still the central, troubling question, "What did God say?"

One day as I pondered the questions God asked Job, my engineering education entered the picture. I suddenly realized that I knew the answers to several of the questions God had asked. As I studied more, I came to the realization that I knew (or could find in books) the answers to just about all of God's questions. From that realization I put together an interpretation that could encompass Job in his world and me in the modern world. And I began to plan to write this book.

I want to make it clear that I am an engineer, not a theologian. I cannot read Hebrew. But I believe that my perspective as an engineer and businessman adds a new dimension to the literature on Job.

I have also found that there are many people who are not prepared to face tragedy when it strikes. When it does, they feel double-crossed by God because they think God is doing this or allowing it to happen, and they don't know why. They end up bitter, blaming God for their suffering. This feeling of betrayal is not necessary. A more thorough understanding about what God is up to in this world can free us from resentment and make it possible to live meaningful, productive lives in spite of intense pain and suffering. This is what freed Job from his quandary in the final analysis.

After the 9/11 terrorist attack, I noticed a number of articles that tried to deal with the question, "Where was God on 9/11?" Many wonderful and inspiring stories came out of that tragedy, but none adequately explained why so many people had to go on without a husband, wife, mother, or father. It is my prayer that many hurting people will gain a better understanding of the phenomenon of evil in this world through this book, and will be better able to bear it without damage to their faith in a loving and caring God.

CHAPTER 1

THE WAGER

The Book of Job is the story of a righteous man who, contrary to our sense of fairness, experienced great loss and suffering. We can all relate to Job because in this life we will either experience suffering ourselves, or we will encounter it in friends or relatives. We are also aware of the situation in which evil people prosper. Throughout history, theologians and philosophers have written volumes trying to explain these phenomena.

Scripture is not silent on this issue. The theme of the righteous suffering servant is found throughout Scripture, from Abel to the tribulation saints described in Revelation. Christians see Jesus as the culmination of this theme. Jews see themselves and their experience as the culmination. A prototype of the suffering servant in Scripture is Job.

> **Job 1:1-5 In the land of Uz there lived a man whose name was Job. This man was blameless and upright; he feared God and shunned evil. ²He had seven sons and three daughters, ³and he owned seven thousand sheep, three thousand camels, five hundred yoke of oxen and five hundred donkeys, and had a large number of servants. He was the greatest man among all the people of the East.**
> **⁴His sons used to take turns holding feasts in their homes, and they would invite their three sisters to eat and drink with them. ⁵When a period of feasting had run its course, Job would send and have them purified. Early in the morning he would sacrifice a burnt offering for each of them, thinking, "Perhaps my children have sinned and cursed God in their hearts." This was Job's regular custom.**

The Book of Job begins with a simple statement: "There lived a man." That Job existed in history cannot be disputed scripturally. The book does not begin "Once upon a time." Perhaps because the book is written in poetry and is located in the poetry section of our Bible, it is easy to conjure up mental images of the Ancient Mariner or Hiawatha and place Job among the legendary figures of literature. Yet as we study Scripture we find that Ezekiel believed that Job existed:

> **Ezekiel 14:14 Even if these three men Noah, Daniel and Job were in it, they could save only themselves by their righteousness, declares the Sovereign LORD.**

The Absence of Justice

And so did James.

> **James 5:11 As you know, we consider blessed those who have persevered. You have heard of Job's perseverance and have seen what the Lord finally brought about. The Lord is full of compassion and mercy.**

Therefore, we must conclude that Job did exist in history.

Exactly when he lived is not clear. Some think that the book was written during or after the exile to explain the suffering of righteous people such as Jeremiah at the fall of Judah and during the captivity. But these people also see Job as a legendary figure as mentioned above. Several observations would indicate that Job belongs in the patriarchal age:

1. No mention of the law is made in the book. This would indicate that it predates the time of Moses.
2. Job's wealth is counted in animals and children, a patriarchal custom.
3. A very ancient court procedure is used (Job 13:22).
4. An ancient style of poetry is used.
5. Characters define their lineage from very ancient people (Job 2:11 & 32:2).
6. Job's age at death could have been approximately two hundred, since he lived one hundred forty years after the events of this book (Job 42:16). This places his life span in the same range as the patriarchs'.
7. The Chaldean culture is depicted as a nomadic, raiding culture, not the urban society we see later in history.

Therefore, it seems reasonable to place Job at the time of the patriarchs. He could have been a contemporary of Abraham, Isaac, or Jacob. Many scholars consider Job to be the oldest book in the Bible.

The location of the land of Uz has been lost in antiquity. However, it must have been located somewhere in the Near East where the other ancient books of the Old Testament originated. Also, it was located where there were camels and ample grazing. Job is also called a "man of the east" (v 3), which would suggest a location to the east of Israel.

Verse one, besides identifying a real man named Job who lived in a real land named Uz, establishes our first basic principle for understanding the Book of Job:

Principle 1: Job was blameless and upright.

Some expositors portray Job as an inordinately proud man who needed humbling through suffering. But any attempt to cast Job as proud or wickedly self-righteous will not stand. The first verse establishes this principle quite forcefully. He was blameless, upright, God-fearing, and he turned away from evil. God himself confirms this fact in 1:8 and 2:3. Job 1:22 declares that in all his trials, Job did not sin, nor did he blame God, a fact we must remember as we listen to Job's statements throughout the book.

If Job indeed were proud, we would have a serious problem. Lucifer, who also had once been declared blameless, yielded to pride and became Satan (Isa 14:12-14) and now stands condemned before God. If Job were being punished for the sin of pride, how then could he be declared blameless? So, whatever the cause of Job's suffering, it did not come as the result of any sin including pride or sinful self-righteousness.

We will come to see Job as self-righteous, but not in a vain, egotistical way. It is very possible to be right and to know one is right. Sometimes that can make us hard to live with. Peter Marshall prayed, "Lord, where we are wrong, make us willing to change. And where we are right make us easy to live with."[1] Job's friends found him resolute as he steadfastly maintained his innocence. From the sarcasm and innuendos copiously sprinkled throughout the discourses of the friends, one can almost hear them raising their voices and shouting in frustration because of Job's adamant stand. Yet verse one categorically states that he was blameless.

Job was one of a unique group of people in Scripture described as blameless or righteous, either directly or by inference.

Enoch	Genesis 5:23-24
Noah	Genesis 6:9
Joseph	Genesis 39 through 50
Job	Job 1:8 & 2:3
Daniel	Ezekiel 14:14 & 20
Zecharias and Elizabeth	Luke 1:6
Mary and Joseph	Luke 1:28 & Matthew 1:19

These passages could be taken as confirmation of God's statement regarding the law in Deuteronomy 30:11 where he says, "Now what I am commanding you today is not too difficult for you or beyond your reach." However, Romans 3:23 states that "all have sinned." The Book of Job gives us insight into this matter because Job never claimed to be sinless. In fact, he acknowledged the "sins of his youth" (13:26). Therefore we must conclude that the blamelessness or righteousness of these people, along with a host of other Old and New Testament saints, is a righteousness that is credited to their accounts because of their faith. (Genesis 15:6)

JOB & COMPANY

In verse three, Job is described as "the greatest man among all the people of the East." He had vast holdings in sheep, camels, oxen, and donkeys, and he had many employees. His wealth and reputation were such that he consorted and probably did business with kings and great men, as we will see

The Absence of Justice

when we meet his comforting friends. He may have been a king himself. (See 19:9 and 29:25)

It is easy for the modern urban reader to pass over verses one through four without grasping the full extent of Job's wealth. It is important that we comprehend how wealthy Job was in the light of Jesus' statement in Matthew:

> **Matthew 19:24-26** "... Again I tell you, it is easier for a camel to go through the eye of a needle than for a rich man to enter the kingdom of God."
> [25]When the disciples heard this, they were greatly astonished and asked, "Who then can be saved?"
> [26]Jesus looked at them and said, "With man this is impossible, but with God all things are possible."

Job seems to be the exception to the typical characterization of the rich as arrogant and even wicked. Job himself addresses this issue in Chapter 21. The message to us is that if a very wealthy Job could please God, then this goal is not beyond the realm of possibility for anyone.

We are not given a great deal to work with, but enough of the assets of "Job & Co." are listed to provide a framework which we can flesh out. His assets are listed as:

> 7000 sheep (1:3)
> 3000 camels (1:3)
> 500 yoke of oxen (1:3)
> 500 donkeys (1:3)
> Eleven houses (1:4)
> The land for his operations (31:38)

From the perspective of a businessman, there were certainly other ventures in which Job would have been involved. There are hints in the book that would suggest some of these. They include:

> Dairy operation (29:6)
> Olive orchards (29:6)
> Weaving operation and tannery (31:20)
> Import/export business with the necessary warehouses

In addition, 1:3 states that he had "many servants" or employees. Referenced in 31:39 are tenant farmers. His assets, less cash, would have been between $11.28 million and $91.68 million, with a possible annual income of $12.6 billion! (An analysis of how these figures were derived is given in the Appendix.)

Further insight as to his wealth is seen in the lifestyle of his children. There is no mention that they worked or even helped Job manage his businesses, although I suspect that they did. Verse 4 describes their lifestyle. They partied a lot. They could be described as the camel set, predecessors of our modern day jet set, going from place to place and partying wherever they went.

Some, like Job's three friends who saw wickedness as the root cause of every calamity, may see here a justification for the death of Job's children. The text (v 4) is not explicit and in no way does it declare that his children were wicked. But even if they were wicked, Scripture does not allow us the privilege of making such cause-effect linkages. C. S. Lewis calls such thinking "historicism."[2] Jesus conclusively discards this thinking when he speaks of the disaster at the tower of Siloam (Luke 13:4) and the man born blind (John 9:3). The context of this passage in Job is recorded simply to demonstrate Job's sensitive, righteous heart as he continually prayed for his children.

The number of Job's children presents an interesting picture. There were ten. Seven were sons and three were daughters. In ancient numerology, the number ten was considered the complete number. Number seven was the perfect number. Therefore, the picture is that of a man who had a perfect number of sons and a complete family. These verses present Job as a man who "had it made" with a perfect family and almost unlimited wealth.

JOB'S SOCIAL VALUES

Verse three also gives us insight into Job's basic attitudes about other human beings. It is interesting that while we are given a head count of his sheep, camels, oxen, and donkeys, his servants are placed in another category and not numbered. In his age this is remarkable since up to very recent times, servants and slaves were considered mere chattel, and the property of their owners. One hundred fifty years ago, plantation owners in the United States listing their property counted horses, cattle, and slaves. But not Job. He recognized the dignity of being human and refused to include his servants in the same category with his animals. In fact Job directly addresses this issue when he makes his defense before God:

> **Job 31:13-15 "If I have denied justice to my menservants and maidservants when they had a grievance against me,**
> **[14]what will I do when God confronts me?**
> **What will I answer when called to account?**
> **[15]Did not he who made me in the womb make them?**
> **Did not the same one form us both within our mothers?..."**

So we find in Job a man who is centuries before his time in his attitudes about human dignity and rights. Actually, this reference proves that it has always been right to think and act this way; subsequent generations who violated the rights of others were defying God's principle of the dignity of being human.

The Absence of Justice
JOB'S RELIGION

As we have said, there is no indication whether Job's children were blameless or not, but Job was not taking any chances. Job stood as priest in behalf of his family and felt an obligation to his God to answer for the actions of his children. He also probably felt an obligation to his children to intercede for them. He obviously loved them very much and wanted them to have the same kind of personal relationship with God that he enjoyed. He demonstrated his love and devotion by continually fulfilling his perceived responsibilities before God in behalf of his children. Their "partying" lifestyle evidently troubled him and he never ceased to pray for them in the event their actions were offensive to God.

We notice that Job was not in attendance at his eldest son's birthday party. It may be that he was not invited to these parties at all, although he was well aware that they took place and took pains to intercede with God for his children after the festivities were over. I am not sure that we can infer anything from the absence of Job and his wife, but it does raise questions.

A LOOK BEHIND THE SCENES: WHAT JOB DIDN'T KNOW

> **Job 1:6-12 One day the angels came to present themselves before the LORD, and Satan also came with them. ⁷The LORD said to Satan, "Where have you come from?"**
>
> **Satan answered the LORD, "From roaming through the earth and going back and forth in it."**
>
> **⁸Then the LORD said to Satan, "Have you considered my servant Job? There is no one on earth like him; he is blameless and upright, a man who fears God and shuns evil."**
>
> **⁹"Does Job fear God for nothing?" Satan replied. ¹⁰"Have you not put a hedge around him and his household and everything he has? You have blessed the work of his hands, so that his flocks and herds are spread throughout the land. ¹¹But stretch out your hand and strike everything he has, and he will surely curse you to your face."**
>
> **¹²The LORD said to Satan, "Very well, then, everything he has is in your hands, but on the man himself do not lay a finger."**
>
> **Then Satan went out from the presence of the LORD.**

At this point we get a rare glimpse into the unseen realm of the spirits and the protocol of heaven. We observe the heavenly convocation of the sons of God. It must have been a great assembly. But before we have time to look around for Gabriel or Michael, our attention is drawn to an unusual visitor. He is listed separately from the sons of God. The original text calls him "The Satan," more of a title than a name. It means "The Accuser" or "The Adversary." This reminds us that he is described in the New Testament as the accuser of the brethren (Rev 12:10) and as a roaring lion seeking someone to

The Wager

devour (1 Peter 5:8). Here we see him accusing Job. Later he will attempt to devour him.

The description of "The Satan" in this passage reminds us of Khomeini's name for the United States when he took over Iran as a fundamentalist Muslim dictator. The United States was called "The Great Satan" and Americans were incensed regarding the implications. Yet in perhaps a narrow sense, Khomeini was right in using this term. America was indeed an adversary, and America did accuse him and his regime of (what to Americans were) atrocities.

In other usage in the Scriptures, Satan seems to have become less of a title and more of a name, although the implications of accuser and adversary have stuck. We will expand on the different aspects of Satan in Chapter 11.

Certainly Job is not the only person in history so accused by Satan. Anyone who claims to trust in God is assuredly accused before God. However, 1 John 2:1 says:

> **1 John 2:1 My dear children, I write this to you so that you will not sin. But if anybody does sin, we have one who speaks to the Father in our defense — Jesus Christ, the Righteous One.**

While Job did not see or know what was going on behind the scenes, he expresses the same kind of faith in Job 16:19:

> **Job 16:19 Even now my witness is in heaven;
> my advocate is on high.**

All believers have a heavenly defense attorney pleading our case before the Father even as Satan accuses us.

Satan's abode is commonly thought of as hell, where he is pictured with his trident and horns in a red suit presiding over the regions of torment. Here we see him in the very presence of God, conversing with him. While Scripture predicts the ultimate destiny of Satan to be the lake of fire (Revelation 20:10) he now has access to heaven as well as earth. I suspect that he rarely, if ever, visits the place where we most commonly imagine him to be, and will not go there until God finally binds him and confines him there.

THE POINT OF DIFFERENCE

God opens the conversation by asking, "Where have you come from?" The universe is full of places where Satan might have been. When Satan responds that he had been on the earth, God immediately thinks of Job. Note that God, not Satan, first mentions Job. He holds Job up as an example of integrity and righteousness. The dynamics of the mysterious relations and conflict between God and Satan will probably never be fully revealed to us. It is almost as if there had been a running argument between God and Satan

The Absence of Justice

since the initial break between the two (see Ezekiel 28:12-17). God takes this opportunity to make another point for his argument. God's point is simply that Job is righteous and blameless. Satan counters that Job is righteous because it happens to be profitable. He claims Job's righteousness is for reward. Satan's reply implies that his position in the argument is that there is no such thing as righteousness for righteousness' sake alone, and therefore there is no such thing as a righteous man. Perhaps Satan's argument is his attempt to justify himself and prove God wrong in having condemned Satan for his sinful pride. God contends that Job will do right whether he profits from it or not. Satan contends that Job will quickly lose his integrity if tragedy should strike his business or wealth, and challenges God to allow Job's integrity to be challenged.

The nature of this controversy is difficult to understand. Why didn't God just tell Satan to get lost? Why does God find it necessary to prove his point at Job's (and our) expense? This controversy is alluded to in numerous biblical passages, and reached its spiritual climax at the cross when Jesus was crucified. It will reach its physical and political climax in the future as described in the books of Daniel and the Revelation.

SATAN ON TRIAL

Perhaps the relationship between God and Satan is that of judge and defendant. Ezekiel 28:12-17 and Isaiah 14:12-15 describe Satan before and at the time of his great sin resulting in his fall. Note that Satan was once called blameless also (Ezekiel 28:15). Revelation 20:1-10 describes the sentencing and eternal penalty for his sin. Since we live between these events, could it be that Satan's trial is in progress now, and has been since he fell? If this scenario is correct, then Job was introduced as evidence for the prosecution and Satan would try to discredit this evidence. God's justice would oblige him to grant Satan the right to challenge and cross-examine God's evidence. Of course this would leave us still wondering why we are required to defend God's point at our expense, but perhaps this is one of the consequences of the fall of the human race. I doubt that we will ever fully understand this relationship between God and Satan, at least this side of heaven, but for some of us it is fascinating to ponder these mysteries. What is certain is that many of us will find ourselves joining the company of the righteous, suffering servants along with Job.

This passage implies that somehow Satan has the right to challenge the integrity of God's followers, and for some reason God seems to be obliged to expose his children to the test. One other passage in Scripture presents another example of this mystery. Jesus says in Luke:

> **Luke 22:31-32** "Simon, Simon, Satan has asked to sift you as wheat. [32]But I have prayed for you, Simon, that your faith may not fail. And when you have turned back, strengthen your brothers."

The Wager

Satan, hoping to cause Peter's permanent downfall, demanded permission to test him (NAS). And it was evidently granted. Satan, knowing human nature, attacked Peter where he was most vulnerable. Peter was a loud, blustery type of man who didn't like to be ridiculed, so Satan utilized this knowledge in his attack.

An amazing thing this passage in Job reveals is that God stoops to stake his reputation on humans. Remember that all the hosts of heaven were there—and probably listening to every word. In Hebrews 12:1 the faithful dead are described as a great cloud of witnesses. In Daniel 4:13, 17, and 23 angels are described as "watchers." They are still watching today (Ps 91:11). God is also staking his reputation on all of us who follow him. Job came through with flying colors as we will see. The question is, how are you and I doing?

Satan knows human nature well. Most of us are very jealous about our possessions, so Satan attacked where he thought it would hurt the most. Where our "things" are involved, our moral principles become foggy. Peter Marshall prayed: "Help us to stand for what is right, not because it may yield dividends later, but because it is right now."[3] Job was the kind of man whose actions and thoughts were determined by what was right and nothing else.

In verse ten, Satan reminds God of the hedge placed around Job. The nature of Satan, who is described as a "murderer from the beginning" (John 8:44), is such that if God did not protect his children it is doubtful that Satan would let them live at all in a world where he is in control (1 John 5:19). However, we are given ample assurances of God's protection in God's Word:

> **Psalm 91:11 For he will command his angels**
> **concerning you to guard you in all your ways;**
>
> **Numbers 6:24 "The LORD bless you and keep you..."**
>
> **Deuteronomy 7:15 The LORD will keep you free from every disease. He will not inflict on you the horrible diseases you knew in Egypt, but he will inflict them on all who hate you.**
>
> **Psalm 12:7 O LORD, you will keep us safe**
> **and protect us from such people forever.**
>
> **Psalm 27:5 For in the day of trouble**
> **he will keep me safe in his dwelling;**
> **he will hide me in the shelter of his tabernacle**
> **and set me high upon a rock.**

And yet, we also know that trouble often overtakes good people when they do not deserve it. This became Job's dilemma and the subject of the arguments of this book.

The Absence of Justice

And so, at Satan's challenge, God's blessing and protection were partially removed, and Satan attacked Job in his most vulnerable areas. Job had fears. We have seen that his fears motivated him in his religious actions. Satan attacked him through the very things Job feared:

> **Job 3:25 What I feared has come upon me;**
> **what I dreaded has happened to me.**

We have seen that Job feared for his children and offered sacrifices continually for them. It is also likely that Job, a generous philanthropist (see Ch 29), feared any circumstance that would alter his ability to help others. And it is likely that he feared something could come between him and his God. So it was in these areas that Satan attacked.

It is a comfort to note from the New Testament example about Peter that Jesus said he had prayed for Peter. Although we do not fully understand why it is that some are exposed to Satan's ferocity more than others, we are assured of the prayers of the Son of God and this should give us courage.

> **Hebrews 7:25 Therefore he is able to save completely those**
> **who come to God through him, because he always lives to**
> **intercede for them.**

In Job 1:11, Satan challenges God regarding Job's integrity. He asserts that if Job loses his wealth and possessions, his integrity will disappear and Job will even curse God to his face. God acquiesces to this challenge, but places limits on the test. Evidently, in such a situation, while God seems honor-bound to participate, he can (and does) set limits. This is consistent with the New Testament promise:

> **1 Corinthians 10:13 No temptation has seized you except what**
> **is common to man. And God is faithful; he will not let you be**
> **tempted beyond what you can bear. But when you are tempted,**
> **he will also provide a way out so that you can stand up under it.**

The phrase "everything he has is in your hands" (Job 1:12) is interestingly quite true for all of us. We live in a world that is antagonistic to God. Satan is described as the prince of this world:

> **John 14:30 I will not speak with you much longer, for the prince**
> **of this world is coming. He has no hold on me,...**

> **1 John 5:19 We know that we are children of God, and that the**
> **whole world is under the control of the evil one.**

So in a literal sense, Job lived (and we live as well) in a world that is under the control of Satan. What happens to us here in this world which is domi-

The Wager

nated by Satan can be tragic and calamitous. However, as we follow Job through his suffering we will see that Satan cannot touch Job's spirit, which is unalterably committed to God. Job's (and our) ultimate spiritual destination can be turned over to God, who is ultimately sovereign. But because the human race chose contrary to God's will, our physical destination is the grave (Heb 9:27). We will see, however, that our physical circumstances can also be committed to God, who delights in salvaging good out of bad situations.

To carry this thought a bit further, Satan is then described as leaving the presence of the Lord (1:12). In leaving God's presence, he came to the earth. In the sense that God's will is not done in this world system that is controlled by Satan, God is not present on the earth, at least not in the same sense as he is present in heaven. This difference is evident in the prayer Jesus taught us:

> **Matthew 6:10 . . . your kingdom come,**
> **your will be done**
> **on earth as it is in heaven.**

We will develop this theme more fully later in the book. It is a key to understanding the problem of evil since Job, his friends, and many of us erroneously believe that God does everything that happens and is in total, immediate control of all that transpires on the earth.

TRAGEDY STRIKES

Job 1:13-19 One day when Job's sons and daughters were feasting and drinking wine at the oldest brother's house, [14]a messenger came to Job and said, "The oxen were plowing and the donkeys were grazing nearby, [15]and the Sabeans attacked and carried them off. They put the servants to the sword, and I am the only one who has escaped to tell you!"
[16]While he was still speaking, another messenger came and said, "The fire of God fell from the sky and burned up the sheep and the servants, and I am the only one who has escaped to tell you!"
[17]While he was still speaking, another messenger came and said, "The Chaldeans formed three raiding parties and swept down on your camels and carried them off. They put the servants to the sword, and I am the only one who has escaped to tell you!"
[18]While he was still speaking, yet another messenger came and said, "Your sons and daughters were feasting and drinking wine at the oldest brother's house, [19]when suddenly a mighty wind swept in from the desert and struck the four corners of the house. It collapsed on them and they are dead, and I am the only one who has escaped to tell you!"

The Absence of Justice

Satan had devised a strategy that would certainly stagger the best of men. He waited until the most opportune time—when the children were partying at the oldest brother's house. Then he attacked suddenly and swiftly. It will be noted that poor Job was hit again and again with hardly a chance to catch his breath between blows. The first report was of the loss of his oxen and donkeys to the raiding Sabeans. Without his beasts of burden, he was suddenly out of the farming business. The second report was of a tremendous electrical storm that wiped out all his flocks and shepherds. Job was suddenly out of the wool and mutton business. The third report came immediately after the second. It was news of the loss of his camels to the Chaldean raiders. Job was suddenly out of the import-export and transportation business. In each case all of Job's servants were lost except the lone survivors that Satan had spared to bear the bad news.

It is an interesting sidelight that both of these ancient cultures that gave Job so much grief are still causing grief and concern to Israel and the modern world today. The Sabean culture seems to have originated in the southern Arabian Peninsula and eventually spread to build cities in modern day Yemen as well as in Egypt and in Africa. Osama bin Laden could be a descendant of these peoples since he is reportedly a Saudi Arabian. The Chaldean raiders eventually settled down and built Babylon in the part of the world we know as Iraq. Saddam Hussein claimed to be a descendant of the Chaldeans.

Then there came the report that surely made Job forget all the others. A tornado had killed all his children. Now, suddenly Job, who had lost everything else, didn't even have a family!

Referring back to the statistics about Job & Company, we note that a large number of Job's employees were killed that day. There would have been five hundred ox drivers, a number of people herding the donkeys, perhaps a dozen or so herding the sheep, and as many as twelve hundred with the camel caravans. In addition, all the servants (save one) of the households of his children also died. This could total somewhere around two thousand people! This tragedy did not hit only Job. It was a major economic disaster for the land of Uz. It undoubtedly left many widows and orphans.

Someone might observe that a businessman like Job would surely have had a bank account, or a nest egg for a rainy day. Certainly he kept a reasonable amount of gold around to make business deals. We will see that Job was the kind of man who would have turned his bank account over to the widows and the orphans of his employees. We are not told this, but I believe that is just what Job did, leaving him penniless for all practical purposes.

Satan attacks us without warning. When things seem to be going great for us, he often destroys our equanimity in a matter of seconds. Job lived in a world where calamities could happen anytime and we live in the same world. But for the hedge God places around us and the prayers of our Lord Jesus and our friends, it is certain that we would be destroyed. But the limits God had

The Wager

placed on the wager held. We now find Job suddenly poverty stricken and suffering unfathomable grief over the loss of his children. How would we react to such a turn of events?

JOB RESPONDS

> **Job 1:20-22 At this, Job got up and tore his robe and shaved his head. Then he fell to the ground in worship ²¹and said:**
> **"Naked I came from my mother's womb,**
> **and naked I will depart.**
> **The LORD gave and the LORD has taken away;**
> **may the name of the LORD be praised."**
> **²²In all this, Job did not sin by charging God with wrongdoing.**

Job had no inkling about what had transpired behind the scenes in heaven. He could not know that God had staked his reputation on Job's reaction. Job, without his knowledge, must have been the focus of attention throughout heaven as Satan and the heavenly host waited in suspense for his response. Satan was so sure Job would curse and revile God. How would he react?

God had picked his man well. We can only stand in awe and respect as Job expresses his great grief in the traditional way by shaving his head and tearing his robe. Then he falls to the ground and—believe it or not—he worships! Most people would shake their fists at God and curse (as Satan well knows), but this was not Job's response. Job had retained his perspective. He realized that he had come into the world naked and that he would take nothing along when he died. He evidently viewed his possessions and the loss of them in the light of this inevitable truth.

He also made one of the most profound and classic utterances ever to come out of tragedy (v 21). No one could make such a statement at such a time unless he had arranged his priorities long beforehand. The words, "The Lord gave and the Lord has taken away. Blessed be the name of the Lord" are the words of a man who had committed not only himself, but everything he owned to God. Having committed everything he had to God, he considered it God's prerogative to do with them as he wished. So when Job lost all his possessions and also his children, he must have reckoned that he had really lost nothing since they were already God's. The only way any of us can be safe from disillusionment and despair due to material losses in this life is to give our possessions to God as Job did.

> **Matthew 6:21 For where your treasure is, there your heart will be also.**

Job's statement gives a clue to his theological position. It indicates that he believed that God had sent the tragedy. Job will come to question this position during the course of the arguments with his friends.

The Absence of Justice

The first chapter ends with victory for God. We are specifically told that in all this Job did not sin and that he did not blame God.

SATAN UPS THE ANTE

Job 2:1-6 On another day the angels came to present themselves before the LORD, and Satan also came with them to present himself before him. ²And the LORD said to Satan, "Where have you come from?"

Satan answered the LORD, "From roaming through the earth and going back and forth in it."

³Then the LORD said to Satan, "Have you considered my servant Job? There is no one on earth like him; he is blameless and upright, a man who fears God and shuns evil. And he still maintains his integrity, though you incited me against him to ruin him without any reason."

⁴"Skin for skin!" Satan replied. "A man will give all he has for his own life. ⁵But stretch out your hand and strike his flesh and bones, and he will surely curse you to your face."

⁶The LORD said to Satan, "Very well, then, he is in your hands; but you must spare his life."

Satan doesn't like to concede defeat. His tactics often consist of a hit and run strategy. In Matthew 12:43-45 an unclean spirit leaves a man for a time, but returns later with others "and the last state of that man becomes worse than the first." Here we see Satan attacking Job on a different level. He had lost the first round, but he had not given up.

As we are again permitted behind the scenes in heaven, we witness a scene that is similar to the first dispute regarding Job's integrity. God again holds up Job as a blameless and upright man (v 3). But here he adds, "...and he still holds fast his integrity, although you incited me against me, to ruin him without cause." One could almost say that God is bragging on Job in the same sense that we brag on our children. Without doubt God was greatly pleased with Job's performance.

It sounds as if God regretfully admits in verse 3 to having turned against Job resulting in Job's ruin. Here again we are confronted with the strange, inscrutable relations between God and Satan. Is it fair that Job should be exposed in this way to Satan's attack? Perhaps fairness is not the issue. As we will see time and again throughout the book, Job lived in a fallen world, exposed to all that any other man may experience. For his own reasons, God had placed a protective hedge around him. When it was removed, Job was helplessly exposed to the normal consequences of living in a fallen world. I suspect that without God's hedges, the whole human race would have long since perished. In the final analysis, it is not God who afflicted Job, but Satan. Satan challenged Job's integrity in the context of God's hedge and God, because of that strange, inscrutable reason, finds it necessary to prove Job's faithfulness—with or without the hedge.

If any doubt still lingers as to Job's innocence, the last three words of verse 3 should settle the matter. God himself declares that Job suffered without any reason.

Satan makes one more appeal. The first challenge was against Job's possessions. The second challenge was against Job's person, and his very life, for all that Job knew. Satan challenged God to extend the wager to include an attack on Job's body, asserting that Job would not value righteousness above health. "All that a man has he will give for his life." Satan had been observing human nature since the beginning, and he knew that self-preservation is man's strongest and most basic instinct. A drowning man will grasp anyone nearby, and even drag down his dearest loved ones in his attempt to save his own life. But God knew something Satan was not willing to accept. Job had put God first in his life. Absolutely first. Job had conquered all the lusts and temptations in life because of this commitment. Temptation to sexual impurity was manageable in Job's life because his sex drives were subjected to God's control. (31:1, 9, 10) The temptation of greed was subjected to God's control also (31:24, 25), as were all the other temptations. His instinct for self-preservation was also second to his commitment to God. It is this kind of commitment that makes it possible for martyrs to die at the stake singing praises. Their love of life has been made secondary to their love of God. Satan is not willing to admit that anyone would love God that much.

As a result, to prove his point, God took the challenge, but with the limiting condition that Job's life would be spared (v 6).

JOB IN MISERY

Job 2:7-10 So Satan went out from the presence of the LORD and afflicted Job with painful sores from the soles of his feet to the top of his head. [8]Then Job took a piece of broken pottery and scraped himself with it as he sat among the ashes.
[9]His wife said to him, "Are you still holding on to your integrity? Curse God and die!"
[10]He replied, "You are talking like a foolish woman. Shall we accept good from God, and not trouble?"
In all this, Job did not sin in what he said.

This is the last we hear of Satan (at least by that name) in this book. Later we will make a connection between the name Satan and "Leviathan."[4] We are not told whether God had the opportunity to say "I told you so." Perhaps the end of the matter, and all similar situations, will not be realized until the final judgment when God finally does tell Satan to "get lost." One thing is certain: Satan has not yet given up. His works producing suffering and tragedies are still seen all over the earth.

The Absence of Justice

Satan proceeds to throw everything in the book at Job. Although it is impossible to accurately diagnose Job's affliction, some have tried to identify his illness. Some suggest leprosy. Some see in the open, suppurating sores an evidence of elephantiasis. Cancer or tropical fungal infections are also indicated. Some simply accept the account literally. He was covered with boils from head to toe. Perhaps he had all these diseases simultaneously! His symptoms were:

1. Painful suppurating sores which covered his body. (2:7)
2. Appearance was disfigured or distorted. (2:12)
3. Nausea. (3:24)
4. Restlessness. (3:26)
5. Sleeplessness. (7:4)
6. Infection in the sores which was attacked by worms (maggots). (7:5)
7. Hallucinations and nightmares. (7:14)
8. Flushed face with bags under his eyes. (16:16)
9. Drastic loss of weight. (16:8, 17:7, 19:20)
10. Bad breath. (19:17)
11. Discoloration of the skin with peeling. (30:28 & 30)
12. Fever. (30:30)
13. Depression. (30:31)

Whatever the technical name and diagnosis of his affliction, we can be certain that Satan would not stop short of total misery. Job's treatment consisted of sitting in the ashes and scraping himself with a shard of broken pottery. The Septuagint records that "the ashes" were in the dunghill outside the city. Why did he not stay in his house, tended by his wife? It was the custom in this culture that people with communicable diseases, such as leprosy, dwell apart from society. They were not permitted to mingle with healthy people. The village dump provided a place where such wretches could sort through the garbage for scraps to eat while maintaining minimal contact with society.

Chapter 19, verse 17 seems to confirm that he had been banished from his own home: "My breath is offensive to my wife and I am loathsome to my own brothers." Due to societal custom his wife would not allow him in the house. Her attitude in verse 9 does not show much compassion or love for him. On the other hand, we could give her the benefit of the doubt. She was, no doubt, very bitter. The children had been hers too, and she had shared Job's wealth. Since there was little or no belief in life beyond the grave (as we will see later), her reaction was "If cursing God will give you the relief of oblivion in the grave, do it and get it over with." Surely she would not have suggested such a thing if she believed in a hereafter. I believe she was spared by Satan precisely because he was planning to use her. She was encouraging Job to do exactly what Satan wanted. Bereft of children, penniless, avoided by his brothers and in constant pain, Job's integrity never faltered and he found strength of spirit to rebuke the foolishness of his wife (v 10).

The specific sin with the lips is mentioned here because that is the specific

The Wager

sin involved in the bet between God and Satan. Jesus made it abundantly clear that what comes out of the mouth comes from the heart. (Matt 12:34) Therefore, the fact that Job did not curse God proved the pureness of his heart.

Some people are mistaken in thinking that when they become Christians, all their troubles will go away. Job tells us that this is not so. We accept Christ expecting better, but from the hand of Satan we can be sure we will receive the worst. Satan is still trying to delude us into expecting reward in this life for right actions, and he is experiencing considerable success in his campaign.

ENTER JOB'S FRIENDS

Job 2:11-13 When Job's three friends, Eliphaz the Temanite, Bildad the Shuhite and Zophar the Naamathite, heard about all the troubles that had come upon him, they set out from their homes and met together by agreement to go and sympathize with him and comfort him. [12]When they saw him from a distance, they could hardly recognize him; they began to weep aloud, and they tore their robes and sprinkled dust on their heads. [13]Then they sat on the ground with him for seven days and seven nights. No one said a word to him, because they saw how great his suffering was.

The word quickly got out about Job's calamity. Businessmen of Job's stature develop many close associations and friendships. Job was no exception. His friends were outstanding. Who of us has friends who would leave their businesses and duties to sit with us seven days *and* seven nights plus all the time consumed in the debates reported in the rest of the book? They proved that they were sincerely concerned about Job and trying to help, although in a misguided way.

The Septuagint casts Eliphaz as a king, Bildad as a ruler, and Zophar as a tyrant. As they approached Job's city, they were appalled when they realized that the repulsive creature sitting on the ash heap in the city dump was their friend Job. They broke down and wept. Seeing his condition in person, they came to the erroneous conclusion on which they base all their arguments in the following chapters. No one could be afflicted like this in God's just world unless he had blasphemed God. Then they performed the traditional ritual appropriate for blasphemy cases. They each tore their robes and threw dust in the air (Mishna Sanhedrin 7:5).

We see this traditional ritual performed in the New Testament in Acts 22:23. Paul had been attacked by the Jews in Jerusalem, placed in protective custody by the Romans, then allowed to address the crowd. In his discourse he stated that God had sent him to the Gentiles. The Jews, considering this blasphemy, threw off their cloaks and tossed dust into the air, demanding his execution.

The Absence of Justice

Job's friends clearly demonstrated their conclusion by this act, although they held their peace for seven days and seven nights because they could see his pain was very great. Perhaps Job had miserable comforters, but they showed more compassion and concern than most of us would show under such trying circumstances. They even set up camp there in the city dump with their friend and waited.

The seven days and seven nights also had ritual significance. This was the traditional mourning period for a death. In Jewish tradition it is required that friends and family come to "sit shivah" to comfort the mourner for seven days. So, while Eliphaz, Bildad, and Zophar may have come to "sit shivah" as Job mourned for his children, it is obvious as we proceed through the dialogues that they refocused on Job himself. They were saying by their actions, "Job, you have blasphemed God; you are as good as dead!" At this point, they ceased to be friends. They became his accusers.

1. Marshall, Catherine, ed. *The Prayers of Peter Marshall.* Lincoln, Va: Chosen Books, 1949. p. 172
2. Lewis, C. S. *Christian Reflections.* Grand Rapids: Wm. B. Erdmans, 1967. p. 100
3. Marshall, Catherine, ed. *The Prayers of Peter Marshall.* Lincoln, Va: Chosen Books, 1949. p. 103
4. The connection between Satan and Leviathan is crucial to the wholeness of the Book of Job. If there is no connection, then Satan's appearance at the first of the book only, leaves the reader hanging. However, by connecting the two, there is closure to the book.

CHAPTER 2

THE DISCOURSES

While the prologue (Chapters 1 and 2) and the epilogue (Chapter 42) are written in prose, the heart of the book—the dialogues along with God's answer—is written in poetry. This is an ancient poetic style which consists of an intricate weaving of parallel statements. I understand that translation from the original language is quite difficult and at times the meanings are quite obscure. On the other hand, making a point by saying it in several different ways can assist us in understanding the original meaning of the text. When God answers Job, we will find that this form of writing will help as we try to understand just what it is that God is saying. However, it is also easy to get bogged down as we try to follow the flow of ideas between the speakers. The western reader prefers to get it straight and simple. Therefore, in the three rounds of dialogue between Job and his friends, and the monologue of Elihu, I have attempted to reduce the speeches to what the speakers would have said were they modern day people with average intelligence and education. I hope this will help the reader to comprehend the flow of the conversations more easily.

After the seven days and seven nights of silent mourning by Job's friends, the conversation opens with Job's lamentations. Thereafter, each friend in turn speaks and Job responds to each. Eliphaz, Bildad, and Zophar each try three times to convince Job that he is guilty of some sin. Their initial verdict does not change until Chapter 42. Job, however, in dealing with the dilemma he is facing, moves from a position where he essentially agrees with the philosophy of the friends to a point where he questions it, and finally sues God for an explanation.

Chapters 32 through 37 contain the discourse of a young man, Elihu, whose words merit neither recognition by God nor response from Job.

As we read through the discourses of Eliphaz, Bildad, Zophar, and Elihu's monologues, we encounter many statements that sound right, while many of Job's statements sound rash at best and cause us to raise our eyebrows. God has not left us without help in understanding this section. In the end of the book he gives us the basis for interpreting the dialogues. In Chapter 42, verses 7 and 8, God speaks to Job's three friends (ignoring Elihu) and categorically states "—you have not spoken of me what is right as my servant Job has." And for emphasis, he says it twice. We now have two more principles that help us to interpret and understand this book. We can now complete our little list of principles begun on page four:

The Absence of Justice

Principle 1: Job was blameless and upright.

Principle 2: What Job said was right.

Principle 3: What Job's friends said was wrong.

Although the friends' statements contain many truisms and clichés that might be true enough in a special context, they are improperly applied to Job and therefore are false by either implication or application.

It is disturbing and sometimes amusing how many "proof texts" are drawn by authors and speakers from Eliphaz's, Bildad's, Zophar's, and even Elihu's speeches. When a passage from Job is quoted, it is advisable to find out who said it. To use "proof texts" from the friends' speeches is to use a source God has declared *wrong!*

We will also note that Job's understanding of many things does not seem to agree with God's view (and ours, since we were privileged to see the situation from a vantage point in heaven). To cite one example, we have seen that God was actually protecting Job with a "hedge of goodness" before Satan's attack. However, Job in 3:23 says, "Why is light given to a man whose way is hidden and whom God has hedged in?" Job felt that in his suffering he was hedged in with evil by God, whereas we have seen that from God's point of view, the hedge of goodness had been removed. How then can God state that Job was right in what he said?

DIVINE VS. HUMAN PERSPECTIVES

The answer lies in the difference of perspectives. I believe God was saying, "Job, you are right from the human viewpoint. With your limited knowledge and understanding, you have stated what is right." I believe there are divine and human perspectives that seem contradictory for many Bible doctrines. The centuries-old conflict about the sovereignty of God and the free will of man is a classic example. The sovereignty of God is the divine perspective. Free will is the human perspective. Both are scriptural and both are right. Psalm 103:14 says, "For he himself knows our frame; he is mindful that we are but dust." This principle, illustrated in Job, is comforting to us because we see God willing to stoop to see man's point of view. This reaches its ultimate in Jesus Christ who, as God, became flesh to gain the human perspective and bring us salvation. (Heb 5:8 and Phil 2:5-8)

Great difficulty arises when we try to combine the two perspectives. They may seem contradictory. It is like trying to look at two sides of a coin at the same time. One method to accomplish this would be to hold it up in front of a mirror and see the far side in the mirror. The trouble is that you'll be seeing the far side backwards! Or, perhaps you could hold it edgewise on your nose and see one side with one eye and the other side with the other eye. But the trouble is that now

The Discourses

everything you see is blurred, and in addition, you look ridiculous! Attempts to synthesize the two perspectives are often just as ludicrous.

So as we remember that God has declared Job's statements right, Job is coming from the human perspective while we, the readers, have been privileged to see the divine perspective. The main emphasis of this book, however, will be the human perspective. After all, that's where we live and we are responsible for our actions, which are based on our perceptions. But we are also responsible to accept *by faith* the divine perspective to the extent that we can grasp it.

CHAPTER 3

THE LAMENTATIONS OF JOB

Job 3:1-10 After this, Job opened his mouth and cursed the day of his birth. ²He said:
³"May the day of my birth perish,
**   and the night it was said, 'A boy is born!'**
⁴That day—may it turn to darkness;
**   may God above not care about it;**
**   may no light shine upon it.**
⁵May darkness and deep shadow
**   claim it once more;**
**   may a cloud settle over it;**
**   may blackness overwhelm its light.**
⁶That night—may thick darkness seize it;
**   may it not be included among the days of the year**
**   nor be entered in any of the months.**
⁷May that night be barren;
**   may no shout of joy be heard in it.**
⁸May those who curse days curse that day,
**   those who are ready to rouse Leviathan.**
⁹May its morning stars become dark;
**   may it wait for daylight in vain**
**   and not see the first rays of dawn,**
¹⁰for it did not shut the doors of the womb on me
**   to hide trouble from my eyes.**

JOB: Why was I born?

Job's opening words (vs 3-10) erupt like a volcano from the depths of his anguished heart. From the pits of depression he can see no sense in his life, no meaning for his existence. He curses the day he was born and the poetic flow of words is filled with the horror and pathos of his condition. His birthday, instead of a day of rejoicing, should go down as a day of infamy, a day of darkness, the remembrance of which should bring shudders and dread. Verses 3-10 can be summed up in one word that is familiar to all who suffer. WHY?

"Why?" is the inevitable question that arises out of all tragedy. Why is this happening to me? Why me, God? Some ask this question from a wounded spirit that cries out to God for a reason for the suffering. Others shake their fists at God in defiance and demand an explanation for the injustice. But the fact that we ask "Why?" proves that we have a sense of how it "ought" to be,

The Lamentations of Job

that something indeed has gone wrong.

This is not the only passage in the Bible where God's righteous, suffering servants express their torment. The Book of Lamentations is the heart-wrenching cry of Jeremiah upon the occasion of the fall of Judah and the exile of its inhabitants. Chapter 3 in particular expresses Jeremiah's personal pain. Our Lord on the cross asked the question, "Why hast thou forsaken me?" This question will come from all of us at some time in our lives.

> **Job 3:11-12** "Why did I not perish at birth,
> and die as I came from the womb?
> ¹²Why were there knees to receive me
> and breasts that I might be nursed?

It is not uncommon to hear persons who have experienced tragedy say, "If only I had—" Critical introspection at times like these often brings a sense of inadequacy or guilt, and the person is consumed with regrets because the tragedy could have been avoided "if only—" In a more positive frame of mind, it is easy to see the futility of such thinking. We cannot go back and do it over. Job now expresses the ultimate "if only—"

JOB: Why didn't I die at birth?

Job considers his condition and cannot see any reason for his own existence. Men can usually justify their existence in terms of their offspring. But Job's children were all dead. Or men can justify their existence in terms of their service and contributions to their communities. But now Job finds himself sitting in the garbage dump of the city. He is held in contempt by the community as we will see later. He can see no reason whatsoever that he should have ever seen the light of day.

> **Job 3:13-19** For now I would be lying down in peace;
> I would be asleep and at rest
> ¹⁴with kings and counselors of the earth,
> who built for themselves places now lying in ruins,
> ¹⁵with rulers who had gold,
> who filled their houses with silver.
> ¹⁶Or why was I not hidden in the ground like a stillborn child,
> like an infant who never saw the light of day?
> ¹⁷There the wicked cease from turmoil,
> and there the weary are at rest.
> ¹⁸Captives also enjoy their ease;
> they no longer hear the slave driver's shout.
> ¹⁹The small and the great are there,
> and the slave is freed from his master.

The Absence of Justice

JOB: I long for the grave.

The language of verses 13-19 graphically expresses Job's intense longing for the release of death. If Job longed for death so much, why didn't he commit suicide? Suicide can be described as the final act of giving up on God. It has been said that suicide is the ultimate act of selfishness. While Job became extremely introspective and self-centered as a result of his pain, he never became selfish nor did he give up on God.

I believe there are at least three reasons why he didn't even consider suicide. Although Job had lost his children, his health, and his material wealth, what he did have left were of infinite value.

1. A **conviction** that he was innocent, that he didn't deserve this tragedy. His integrity would not let him give in to this thing. Job's friends could not understand the depth of this conviction and his wife certainly did not either. But Job knew that he was innocent, and he challenged first his friends and finally God to show him where he had erred.

2. **Curiosity** about why he was suffering. He seemed convinced that there was an answer somewhere. If the answer could not be given by his friends, and if it could not be found in nature, then certainly God knew the answer. But God had withdrawn from Job and Job couldn't find him. He seemed determined to get to the bottom of this and get the answer to the age-old question of "Why?" Experts on suicide say that in most cases of suicide, had the victim waited just twenty-four hours, circumstances would have changed so dramatically that the suicide would not have seemed necessary. Job's patience held in order to satisfy his curiosity.

3. Job had **confidence** in God in spite of the fact that God seemed to have abandoned him. His confidence and faith in God are beautifully expressed later in the book. He believed that somehow, sometime, God would make it clear.

> Job 3:20-23 "Why is light given to those in misery,
>   and life to the bitter of soul,
> [21] to those who long for death that does not come,
>   who search for it more than for hidden treasure,
> [22] who are filled with gladness
>   and rejoice when they reach the grave?
> [23] Why is life given to a man
>   whose way is hidden,
>   whom God has hedged in?

The Lamentations of Job

JOB: Why do the righteous suffer?

Now Job states his own version of "the problem of pain," which is a variant of the problem of evil. The problem of evil has been stated in various ways. A couple of variations are as follows:

If God is all powerful, he will be able to make us happy. If he is good, he will want us to be happy. But we are not happy. Therefore, God is not all-powerful, or he is not good, or both.

God <u>wants</u> us to be free from suffering but can't do anything about it in which case he is impotent. Or, he can relieve our suffering, but he won't, in which case he is malevolent.

Job and his friends believe that God is all-powerful. They also believe that God is just. The friends therefore come up with a simplistic answer for Job's suffering: Job has sinned. However, Job, knowing he has not sinned, is faced with "the problem of evil." And he doesn't know the answer. In verse 23 he describes himself as a man "whose way is hidden."

There were three characteristics that factored into the equation as they all pondered Job's suffering. God's power, God's justice, and Job's innocence. Since all three were not compatible, one had to go. For the friends, it was Job's innocence. But Job was in a real quandary because he could not legitimately eliminate any one of the three.

Verse 23 also indicates that Job really believed that these calamities had come from God. The reader is aware of the fact that Satan was the one who challenged Job's integrity and afflicted him with all his suffering. We are not told whether Job's perception was ever corrected, although I suspect it was at the end of the book where God described to Job the characteristics of Behemoth and Leviathan.

> Job 3:24-26 For sighing comes to me instead of food;
> my groans pour out like water.
> ²⁵What I feared has come upon me;
>   what I dreaded has happened to me.
> ²⁶I have no peace, no quietness;
>   I have no rest, but only turmoil."

JOB: My existence is nothing but pain and suffering.

The rest of Job's lamentation expresses his physical and emotional distress. He is nauseous. He cries out constantly with pain. He is filled with fear

The Absence of Justice

and dread. He can get no rest or ease from the pain. He is in emotional turmoil. He is certainly still grieving over his children. Satan's attack was enough to get to the bottom of anyone's reserves.

All of us have fears. There are diseases we dread. Satan knows this. However, few of us ever experience the worst of our fears. One way counselors have dealt with people's fears is to get them to imagine the worst thing that could happen to them, then decide what they would do in that circumstance, and go on from there, knowing that the issue is settled. Job was a man who experienced his worst fears and dreads, and the matter was far from settled.

It is obvious that Job expected some real comfort from his friends. We don't usually bare our souls to someone if we even suspect they might ridicule us. We will see that Job was to be bitterly disappointed.

Job also exhibits the beginning of anger. He becomes angry because what is happening to him is **not fair**. All humans have a sense of "fair." We got it from our ancestors, who partook of the fruit of the tree of the knowledge of good and evil. C. S. Lewis begins his book *Mere Christianity*[1] with a discussion of this point. So Job increasingly expresses anger because he knows he *ought not* be treated this way. The fact that Job expresses considerable anger in the book and God does not censure him for it or charge him with sin indicates that it is OK to be angry about injustice. However, anger is not to be allowed to consume us. There is to be an end to anger. (Eph 4:26)

1. Lewis, C. S. *Mere Christianity.* New York: Macmillan, 1943. Book 1, Chapter 1

CHAPTER 4

DIALOGUES, ROUND 1

> **Job 4:1-6** Then Eliphaz the Temanite replied:
> ²"If someone ventures a word with you, will you be impatient?
>   But who can keep from speaking?
> ³Think how you have instructed many,
>   how you have strengthened feeble hands.
> ⁴Your words have supported those who stumbled;
>   you have strengthened faltering knees.
> ⁵But now trouble comes to you, and you are discouraged;
>   it strikes you, and you are dismayed.
> ⁶Should not your piety be your confidence
>   and your blameless ways your hope?

ELIPHAZ: Excuse me, Job, but you should practice what you preach.

After Eliphaz's diplomatic beginning, he gives himself away with "...who can keep from speaking?" In the face of tragedy, the kindest people are often the ones who say the least. A firm handshake or a sympathetic arm around the shoulder can say volumes, but people who feel compelled to talk a lot in the presence of great sorrow are usually unfeeling, unthinking, and unwelcome.

Eliphaz reminds Job that he (Job) had counseled many in the past. He should now be consistent and apply that advice to himself. "Be objective. If you put your faith in God, he will see you through." It is interesting that while Eliphaz asserts that Job is impatient and dismayed, James 5:11 asserts that Job displayed endurance and patience.

> **Job 4:7-11** "Consider now: Who, being innocent, has ever perished?
>   Where were the upright ever destroyed?
> ⁸As I have observed, those who plow evil
>   and those who sow trouble reap it.
> ⁹At the breath of God they are destroyed;
>   at the blast of his anger they perish.
> ¹⁰The lions may roar and growl,
>   yet the teeth of the great lions are broken.
> ¹¹The lion perishes for lack of prey,
>   and the cubs of the lioness are scattered.

The Absence of Justice

ELIPHAZ: God is just. Therefore the righteous prosper and the wicked suffer. You are suffering. Therefore you are wicked.

Eliphaz here states his theological position. Verse 7 categorically states that he believes justice rules on the earth. From this point forward, justice is the main subject of the Book of Job. The three friends consistently maintain that the righteous get what they deserve: prosperity. The wicked also get what they deserve: suffering. Eliphaz takes it one step further in this passage by including the realm of nature. He insists that justice even reigns in the animal kingdom. His position is:

> God is omnipotent.
> God is just.
> God is sovereign.
> Since he is in control, justice prevails on the earth.

Eliphaz is overlooking a fundamental truth and is therefore totally wrong. We will see what his error was as we progress.

> **Job 4:12-21** "A word was secretly brought to me,
>   my ears caught a whisper of it.
> [13]Amid disquieting dreams in the night,
>   when deep sleep falls on men,
> [14]fear and trembling seized me
>   and made all my bones shake.
> [15]A spirit glided past my face,
>   and the hair on my body stood on end.
> [16]It stopped,
>   but I could not tell what it was.
> A form stood before my eyes,
>   and I heard a hushed voice:
> [17]Can a mortal be more righteous than God?
>   Can a man be more pure than his Maker?
> [18]If God places no trust in his servants,
>   if he charges his angels with error,
> [19]how much more those who live in houses of clay,
>   whose foundations are in the dust,
>   who are crushed more readily than a moth!
> [20]Between dawn and dusk they are broken to pieces;
>   unnoticed, they perish forever.
> [21]Are not the cords of their tent pulled up,

ELIPHAZ: God himself told me!

Eliphaz continues by stating the authority for his position. He has had a vision from God, he says. Eliphaz is on very thin ice here. Paul warns us in Colossians 2:18 (NAS) about people who take their stand on visions. Kurt Koch[1] points out that people who have had a real supernatural experience from God are usually reticent about it. Such an experience is too sacred to publish. He warns us to note a person who brags about such experiences. For such people, if the experience has occurred at all, it has likely come from Satan. It is a dangerous thing to base our theology on a mystical experience. Rather, it is always proper to judge such experiences on the basis of Scripture.

Eliphaz shows no restraint in bragging about his "experience." He relates his "experience" to establish his superiority and make him an authority on the subject. He tells about it in vivid detail, including that his hair stood on end. And then came the "voice," verse 17. The application of Eliphaz's vision to Job implies that Job is very wicked. In response to this implied allegation, we can only refer to God's statement that Job was blameless.

> Job 5:1-7 "Call if you will, but who will answer you?
> To which of the holy ones will you turn?
> ²Resentment kills a fool,
> and envy slays the simple.
> ³I myself have seen a fool taking root,
> but suddenly his house was cursed.
> ⁴His children are far from safety,
> crushed in court without a defender.
> ⁵The hungry consume his harvest,
> taking it even from among thorns,
> and the thirsty pant after his wealth.
> ⁶For hardship does not spring from the soil,
> nor does trouble sprout from the ground.
> ⁷Yet man is born to trouble
> as surely as sparks fly upward.

ELIPHAZ: Who's going to support your innocence? Suffering like yours surely has a cause. I think you are a fool to claim innocence.

Eliphaz casts aside all politeness, and his preconceptions are thinly veiled. The cruelty of his approach is evident in verses 2 through 5. He is really rubbing salt in the wounds, attacking Job regarding the loss of his wealth and children. He feigns citing an example from his experience, but he is really describing Job.

> Job 5:8-16 "But if it were I, I would appeal to God;
> I would lay my cause before him.
> ⁹He performs wonders that cannot be fathomed,
> miracles that cannot be counted.
> ¹⁰He bestows rain on the earth;
> he sends water upon the countryside.
> ¹¹The lowly he sets on high,

The Absence of Justice

>   and those who mourn are lifted to safety.
> ¹²He thwarts the plans of the crafty,
>   so that their hands achieve no success.
> ¹³He catches the wise in their craftiness,
>   and the schemes of the wily are swept away.
> ¹⁴Darkness comes upon them in the daytime;
>   at noon they grope as in the night.
> ¹⁵He saves the needy from the sword in their mouth;
>   he saves them from the clutches of the powerful.
> ¹⁶So the poor have hope,
>   and injustice shuts its mouth.

ELIPHAZ: You need to call on God. He will help you.

Here is Eliphaz's punch line. He will return to it more forcefully later. As if Job has forgotten or doesn't know, he reminds him of God's compassion for the needy and that because of it the needy and poor can have hope. "Injustice shuts its mouth" in the light of God's compassion.

> Job 5:17-27 "Blessed is the man whom God corrects;
>   so do not despise the discipline of the Almighty.
> ¹⁸For he wounds, but he also binds up;
>   he injures, but his hands also heal.
> ¹⁹From six calamities he will rescue you;
>   in seven no harm will befall you.
> ²⁰In famine he will ransom you from death,
>   and in battle from the stroke of the sword.
> ²¹You will be protected from the lash of the tongue,
>   and need not fear when destruction comes.
> ²²You will laugh at destruction and famine,
>   and need not fear the beasts of the earth.
> ²³For you will have a covenant with the stones of the field,
>   and the wild animals will be at peace with you.
> ²⁴You will know that your tent is secure;
>   you will take stock of your property
>   and find nothing missing.
> ²⁵You will know that your children will be many,
>   and your descendants like the grass of the earth.
> ²⁶You will come to the grave in full vigor,
>   like sheaves gathered in season.
> ²⁷"We have examined this, and it is true.
>   So hear it and apply it to yourself."

ELIPHAZ: Submit to God's discipline. God means this suffering for your good. He's trying to straighten you out.

Eliphaz speaks with the voice of inexperience. Notice the thoughtless barb

Dialogues, Round 1

again in verse 25. He is talking to a man who has just lost all his children. It is a wonder that Job even answers him. Eliphaz goes on and on describing the benefits of submitting to the discipline of the Almighty.

He concludes his first discourse with his own stamp of authority. Eliphaz may have investigated these things, but never experienced them. Job will throw this back to his friends before he is finished.

Job 6:1-7 Then Job replied:
²"If only my anguish could be weighed
    and all my misery be placed on the scales!
³It would surely outweigh the sand of the seas—
    no wonder my words have been impetuous.
⁴The arrows of the Almighty are in me,
    my spirit drinks in their poison;
    God's terrors are marshaled against me.
⁵Does a wild donkey bray when it has grass,
    or an ox bellow when it has fodder?
⁶Is tasteless food eaten without salt,
    or is there flavor in the white of an egg?
⁷I refuse to touch it;
    such food makes me ill.

JOB: The scales of justice have gone haywire.

"I am suffering more than I deserve," Job contends. "Do you think there is no reason for my complaint?" Verse 4 again indicates Job's belief that his suffering comes from God. Verses 6 and 7 indicate his loss of appetite. Food makes him nauseous.

Job 6:8-10 "Oh, that I might have my request,
    that God would grant what I hope for,
⁹that God would be willing to crush me,
    to let loose his hand and cut me off!
¹⁰Then I would still have this consolation—
    my joy in unrelenting pain—
    that I had not denied the words of the Holy One.

JOB: I wish God would put an end to me although I still maintain my integrity and innocence.

Job repeats his longing for death but also testifies to the consolation of knowing he has not denied God. This is the only consolation he has since none is forthcoming from his friends. It is ironic that the one hedge God had kept in place (preservation of Job's life) is the thing that Job now wishes away.

The Absence of Justice

> **Job 6:11-13** "What strength do I have,
>   that I should still hope?
>   What prospects, that I should be patient?
> [12]Do I have the strength of stone?
>   Is my flesh bronze?
> [13]Do I have any power to help myself,
>   now that success has been driven from me?

JOB: I doubt that I have enough strength to wait on God.

Job feels his strength ebbing away. He feels that he does not have much time left. There is little time for patience.

> **Job 6:14-23** "A despairing man should have the devotion of his friends,
>   even though he forsakes the fear of the Almighty.
> [15]But my brothers are as undependable
>   as intermittent streams, as the streams that overflow
> [16]when darkened by thawing ice
>   and swollen with melting snow,
> [17]but that cease to flow in the dry season,
>   and in the heat vanish from their channels.
> [18]Caravans turn aside from their routes;
>   they go up into the wasteland and perish.
> [19]The caravans of Tema look for water,
>   the traveling merchants of Sheba look in hope.
> [20]They are distressed, because they had been confident;
> they arrive there, only to be disappointed.
> [21]Now you too have proved to be of no help;
>   you see something dreadful and are afraid.
> [22]Have I ever said, 'Give something on my behalf,
>   pay a ransom for me from your wealth,
> [23]deliver me from the hand of the enemy,
>   ransom me from the clutches of the ruthless'?

JOB: All I want is a little kindness from my friends.

"I hoped for consolation when you came but I'm disappointed. You're like a stream bed without water to a man dying of thirst." This reminds us of the "clouds without water" of Jude 12; promise but no fulfillment. This was a plaintive cry that fell on insensitive ears. While Job's friends demonstrated their care and concern for him by sticking with him through his ordeal, their accusations of him and conclusions about him were anything but kind.

Dialogues, Round 1

> **Job 6:24-30** "Teach me, and I will be quiet;
> show me where I have been wrong.
> ²⁵How painful are honest words!
> But what do your arguments prove?
> ²⁶Do you mean to correct what I say, and treat the words of a despairing man as wind?
> ²⁷You would even cast lots for the fatherless and barter away your friend.
> ²⁸"But now be so kind as to look at me. Would I lie to your face?
> ²⁹Relent, do not be unjust; reconsider, for my integrity is at stake.
> ³⁰Is there any wickedness on my lips? Can my mouth not discern malice?

JOB: OK, cruel friends, show me where I have been wicked.

For contrast, refer to Psalm 25:11 where David prayed, "Pardon my iniquity for it is great." Job here says, "What have I done wrong? I'm not lying. Look me in the eye. You can tell when someone is lying."

> **Job 7:1-6** "Does not man have hard service on earth? Are not his days like those of a hired man?
> ²Like a slave longing for the evening shadows, or a hired man waiting eagerly for his wages,
> ³so I have been allotted months of futility, and nights of misery have been assigned to me.
> ⁴When I lie down I think, 'How long before I get up?' The night drags on, and I toss till dawn.
> ⁵My body is clothed with worms and scabs, my skin is broken and festering.
> ⁶"My days are swifter than a weaver's shuttle, and they come to an end without hope.

JOB: Life is hard, but this is ridiculous. Look at my condition.

Job's statement is full of despair. He describes his inner turmoil and fleshly corruption and sees his life melting away in misery. Under these circumstances, what reason would a man have to continue to deceive himself and others? What does he have to lose? Why should Job be anything but honest?

The condition of Job's body is gruesome indeed. Evidently his running sores were infected with maggots.

> **Job 7:7-10** Remember, O God, that my life is but a breath;

The Absence of Justice

> my eyes will never see happiness again.
> ⁸The eye that now sees me will see me no longer; you will look for me, but I will be no more.
> ⁹As a cloud vanishes and is gone, so he who goes down to the grave does not return.
> ¹⁰He will never come to his house again;
> his place will know him no more.

JOB: God, have you forgotten my mortality?

Job talks to God often during the discourses, although he gets no reply until Chapter 38. While God is nowhere to be found, Job seems concerned that his best friend has forgotten that men are mortal. There is no indication here that Job believed in a hereafter.

> Job 7:11-16 "Therefore I will not keep silent;
> I will speak out in the anguish of my spirit,
> I will complain in the bitterness of my soul.
> ¹²Am I the sea, or the monster of the deep,
> that you put me under guard?
> ¹³When I think my bed will comfort me
> and my couch will ease my complaint,
> ¹⁴even then you frighten me with dreams
> and terrify me with visions,
> ¹⁵so that I prefer strangling and death,
> rather than this body of mine.
> ¹⁶I despise my life; I would not live forever.
> Let me alone; my days have no meaning.

JOB: Because my time is short, I will not keep silent. Who am I that you are torturing me, God? Let me alone!

Job wonders if God considers him one with his worst enemy, the monster of the deep. We will discuss this entity when we deal with Leviathan later.

He also gives us more symptoms of his affliction, terrifying nightmares, and hallucinations. He states that he would prefer to be strangled rather than continue suffering in his horrible body. Only one in extreme pain could feel this way.

> Job 7:17-21 "What is man that you make so much of him,
> that you give him so much attention,
> ¹⁸that you examine him every morning
> and test him every moment?
> ¹⁹Will you never look away from me,
> or let me alone even for an instant?

Dialogues, Round 1

²⁰If I have sinned, what have I done to you,
O watcher of men?
Why have you made me your target?
Have I become a burden to you?
²¹Why do you not pardon my offenses
and forgive my sins?
For I will soon lie down in the dust;
you will search for me, but I will be no more."

JOB: God, why are you going to so much trouble to torment me? Why don't you just pardon whatever I've done because I don't have much time left?

Job voices one of the great philosophical questions in verse 17. "What is man that you make so much of him, that you give him so much attention?..." The same question occurs in Psalm 8:4-6 but a part of the answer is also included:

Psalm 8:4-6 ...what is man that you are mindful of him,
the son of man that you care for him?
⁵You made him a little lower than the heavenly beings
and crowned him with glory and honor.
⁶You made him ruler over the works of your hands;
you put everything under his feet:

The question is essentially the same, but verse 6 is part of the answer. God is mindful of man because he has commissioned man with the task of ruling over his creation. God is intensely interested in how well man performs his task. But Job didn't understand this from his bed of pain. He failed to see why God should focus so much painful attention on him.

Job 8:1-7 Then Bildad the Shuhite replied:
²"How long will you say such things?
Your words are a blustering wind.
³Does God pervert justice?
Does the Almighty pervert what is right?
⁴When your children sinned against him,
he gave them over to the penalty of their sin.
⁵But if you will look to God
and plead with the Almighty,
⁶if you are pure and upright,
even now he will rouse himself on your behalf
and restore you to your rightful place.
⁷Your beginnings will seem humble,
so prosperous will your future be.

The Absence of Justice

BILDAD: God does not pervert justice! He is not punishing you for nothing. If you repent, God will surely restore to you a bright future.

Bildad accuses Job of implying that God is unjust. He calls Job's speech "blustering wind." Then he comes right out and says what Eliphaz only hinted at. In verse 4 he categorically states that Job's children have sinned and have received the penalty of their sin. How callous can people be?

> Job 8:8-19 "Ask the former generations
>   and find out what their fathers learned,
> ⁹for we were born only yesterday and know nothing,
>   and our days on earth are but a shadow.
> ¹⁰Will they not instruct you and tell you?
>   Will they not bring forth words from their understanding?
> ¹¹Can papyrus grow tall where there is no marsh?
>   Can reeds thrive without water?
> ¹²While still growing and uncut,
>   they wither more quickly than grass.
> ¹³Such is the destiny of all who forget God;
>   so perishes the hope of the godless.
> ¹⁴What he trusts in is fragile;
>   what he relies on is a spider's web.
> ¹⁵He leans on his web, but it gives way;
>   he clings to it, but it does not hold.
> ¹⁶He is like a well-watered plant in the sunshine,
>   spreading its shoots over the garden;
> ¹⁷it entwines its roots around a pile of rocks
>   and looks for a place among the stones.
> ¹⁸But when it is torn from its spot,
>   that place disowns it and says, 'I never saw you.'
> ¹⁹Surely its life withers away,
>   and from the soil other plants grow.

BILDAD: Consult history and nature. Both will affirm that only the wicked suffer.

Bildad directs Job's attention to folklore. He claims it lends support to the position that the righteous prosper and the wicked suffer. Since Job is suffering, then certainly, according to tradition, he is wicked. He draws from nature to confirm that there is a cause-effect relationship working in Job's situation. The godless cannot prosper or even survive.

> Job 8:20-22 "Surely God does not reject a blameless man
>   or strengthen the hands of evildoers.
> ²¹He will yet fill your mouth with laughter
>   and your lips with shouts of joy.

Dialogues, Round 1

>²²Your enemies will be clothed in shame,
>>and the tents of the wicked will be no more."

BILDAD: If you really were righteous, God would bless you.

But, of course, Bildad doesn't believe that Job is righteous. Perhaps if Job repents, God will bless him, but so far, Job is not repenting.

>**Job 9:1-13** Then Job replied:
>²"Indeed, I know that this is true.
>>But how can a mortal be righteous before God?
>³Though one wished to dispute with him,
>>he could not answer him one time out of a thousand.
>⁴His wisdom is profound, his power is vast.
>>Who has resisted him and come out unscathed?
>⁵He moves mountains without their knowing it
>>and overturns them in his anger.
>⁶He shakes the earth from its place
>>and makes its pillars tremble.
>⁷He speaks to the sun and it does not shine;
>>he seals off the light of the stars.
>⁸He alone stretches out the heavens
>>and treads on the waves of the sea.
>⁹He is the Maker of the Bear and Orion
>>the Pleiades and the constellations of the south.
>¹⁰He performs wonders that cannot be fathomed,
>>miracles that cannot be counted.
>¹¹When he passes me, I cannot see him;
>>when he goes by, I cannot perceive him.
>¹²If he snatches away, who can stop him?
>>Who can say to him, 'What are you doing?'
>¹³God does not restrain his anger;
>>even the cohorts of Rahab cowered at his feet.

JOB: I know, but all the tricks are on God's side. Might is right! Besides, he's invisible and invincible.

He points to God's greatness and power with numerous examples. He cites God's omniscience (v 4), and his omnipotence (vs 5-10), stating that his might is operative on the earth as well as throughout the heavens. Besides, God is transcendent and not accountable to man.

>**Job 9:14-19** "How then can I dispute with him?
>>How can I find words to argue with him?
>¹⁵Though I were innocent, I could not answer him;
>>I could only plead with my Judge for mercy.

The Absence of Justice

¹⁶Even if I summoned him and he responded,
  I do not believe he would give me a hearing.
¹⁷He would crush me with a storm
  and multiply my wounds for no reason.
¹⁸He would not let me regain my breath
  but would overwhelm me with misery.
¹⁹If it is a matter of strength, he is mighty!
  And if it is a matter of justice, who will summon him?

JOB: Then how can I argue with God?

Even if Job were right and God wrong, God could out talk him. Even if God answered Job's call, Job does not believe that God would stoop to listen to him. Job couldn't make him reply; God is the strong one. Who could make God answer in court? No one.

Job 9:20-24 Even if I were innocent, my mouth would
  condemn me;
  if I were blameless,
  it would pronounce me guilty.
²¹"Although I am blameless,
  I have no concern for myself;
  I despise my own life.
²²It is all the same; that is why I say,
  'He destroys both the blameless and the wicked.'
²³When a scourge brings sudden death,
  he mocks the despair of the innocent.
²⁴When a land falls into the hands of the wicked,
  he blindfolds its judges.
  If it is not he, then who is it?

JOB: If God's justice reigns on the earth, then God must be wicked.

Now Job begins the attack on the position of his friends by showing them the absurdity of the premise that justice reigns on the earth. He first declares that he is guiltless. This, to Job, is a fact. But, though guiltless, he is being declared guilty if the friends' premise is correct. Job is facing the dilemma that either he, Job, is guilty, (and he knows he is not), or God is amoral at best, or immoral at worst (this is unthinkable). This is based on the premise that God is in control and justice reigns on the earth.

Next, Job observes that the guiltless and the wicked both experience tragedy. This statement parallels two other passages in the wisdom books:

Ecclesiastes 2:14 The wise man has eyes in his head,
while the fool walks in the darkness;
but I came to realize

Dialogues, Round 1

> that the same fate overtakes them both.
>
> **Ecclesiastes 9:11** I have seen something else under the sun:
> **The race is not to the swift**
>   **or the battle to the strong,**
> **nor does food come to the wise**
>   **or wealth to the brilliant**
>   **or favor to the learned;**
> **but time and chance happen to them all.**

Ecclesiastes and Job share a common theme in that they display the way things really are on the earth, while Proverbs and Psalms (with exceptions) show the way things ought to be.

Job declares that the earth is "given into the hand of the wicked"(NAS), and that if God and justice are in control, then God perverts justice. If God is not responsible, then who is? Job is approaching the right answer, but I don't think he will see it clearly until God speaks. The answer lies in the fact that we live in a world perverted by sin and rebellion. God is not responsible for tragedy. Man, to whom God gave dominion, is responsible, and tragedy strikes as a natural consequence of the rebellion of the human race.

Job's question in verse 24, "If it is not he, then who is it?" is an attempt to force his friends to face the fact that if their proposition is true, then they must classify God as wicked.

> **Job 9:25-31** "My days are swifter than a runner;
>   they fly away without a glimpse of joy.
> [26]**They skim past like boats of papyrus,**
>   **like eagles swooping down on their prey.**
> [27]**If I say, 'I will forget my complaint,**
>   **I will change my expression, and smile,'**
> [28]**I still dread all my sufferings,**
>   **for I know you will not hold me innocent.**
> [29]**Since I am already found guilty,**
>   **why should I struggle in vain?**
> [30]**Even if I washed myself with soap**
>   **and my hands with washing soda,**
> [31]**you would plunge me into a slime pit**
>   **so that even my clothes would detest me.**

JOB: Time is slipping away. Since I have evidently been found guilty, what's the use? Nothing I can do will make me appear clean.

Again, Job speaks from the premise that the friends are right and he, Job, is wicked. He still struggles with his dilemma, and since he cannot understand why he is accounted as wicked, he sees life as useless. The same emo-

The Absence of Justice

tions are again expressed in Ecclesiastes:

> **Ecclesiastes 7:15** In this meaningless life of mine I have seen both of these: a righteous man perishing in his righteousness, and a wicked man living long in his wickedness.

> **Ecclesiastes 8:14** There is something else meaningless that occurs on earth: righteous men who get what the wicked deserve, and wicked men who get what the righteous deserve. This too, I say, is meaningless.

The logical direction in which Job is headed is this: If the friends' premise is right, then either Job or God is wicked. Job knows he is innocent. This means that God must be wicked, but this position is untenable. Therefore, the friends' premise must be wrong.

> **Job 9:32-35** "He is not a man like me that I might answer him,
>   that we might confront each other in court.
> [33]If only there were someone to arbitrate between us,
>   to lay his hand upon us both,
> [34]someone to remove God's rod from me,
>   so that his terror would frighten me no more.
> [35]Then I would speak up without fear of him,
>   but as it now stands with me, I cannot.

JOB: If there were an arbitrator available, I would question God himself.

Job is beginning to think about suing God for an answer, but is not yet ready to take that step.

> **Job 10:1-7** "I loathe my very life;
>   therefore I will give free rein to my complaint
>   and speak out in the bitterness of my soul.
> [2]I will say to God: Do not condemn me,
>   but tell me what charges you have against me.
> [3]Does it please you to oppress me,
>   to spurn the work of your hands,
>   while you smile on the schemes of the wicked?
> [4]Do you have eyes of flesh?
>   Do you see as a mortal sees?
> [5]Are your days like those of a mortal
>   or your years like those of a man,
> [6]that you must search out my faults
>   and probe after my sin —

> 7though you know that I am not guilty
>   and that no one can rescue me from your hand?

JOB: I would ask God, "What do you have against me knowing that I am innocent and helpless?"

Job continues to think about his contemplated attempt to get an answer by suing God. In this passage he is already formulating the questions he will ask.

> Job 10:8-17 "Your hands shaped me and made me.
>   Will you now turn and destroy me?
> 9Remember that you molded me like clay.
>   Will you now turn me to dust again?
> 10Did you not pour me out like milk
>   and curdle me like cheese,
> 11clothe me with skin and flesh
>   and knit me together with bones and sinews?
> 12You gave me life and showed me kindness,
>   and in your providence watched over my spirit.
> 13"But this is what you concealed in your heart,
>   and I know that this was in your mind:
> 14If I sinned, you would be watching me
>   and would not let my offense go unpunished.
> 15If I am guilty — woe to me!
>   Even if I am innocent, I cannot lift my head,
> for I am full of shame
>   and drowned in my affliction.
> 16If I hold my head high, you stalk me like a lion
>   and again display your awesome power against me.
> 17You bring new witnesses against me
>   and increase your anger toward me;
>   your forces come against me wave upon wave.

JOB: You made me. But what for? Torture and destruction?

Having begun to formulate his questions in 10:2, Job continues to pour out the unanswered questions that fill his troubled heart. He is torn between the evident care God has taken in forming him and the present state of his being. He agrees with David in:

> Psalm 139:14 I praise you because I am fearfully and wonderfully made; your works are wonderful, I know that full well.

But he cannot relate these feelings to the suppurating sores full of maggots, the nightmares, the nausea, and the despair.

The Absence of Justice

> Job 10:18-22 "Why then did you bring me out of the womb?
> I wish I had died before any eye saw me.
> ¹⁹If only I had never come into being,
> or had been carried straight from the womb to the grave!
> ²⁰Are not my few days almost over?
> Turn away from me so I can have a moment's joy
> ²¹before I go to the place of no return,
> to the land of gloom and deep shadow,
> ²²to the land of deepest night,
> of deep shadow and disorder,
> where even the light is like darkness."

JOB: I wish I had never been born. Please, God, let me alone so I can have a moment's joy before this miserable life is over.

In this passage Job returns to his lament (Ch 3) and restates it.

> Job 11:1-6 Then Zophar the Naamathite replied:
> ²"Are all these words to go unanswered?
> Is this talker to be vindicated?
> ³Will your idle talk reduce men to silence?
> Will no one rebuke you when you mock?
> ⁴You say to God, 'My beliefs are flawless
> and I am pure in your sight.'
> ⁵Oh, how I wish that God would speak,
> that he would open his lips against you
> ⁶and disclose to you the secrets of wisdom,
> for true wisdom has two sides.
> Know this: God has even forgotten some of your sin.

ZOPHAR: Can no one answer this drivel? I wish God would really speak up because you would find out that you have got much less than you deserve!

It is interesting that while Zophar states in verse 6 that true wisdom has two sides, he and his friends can only see one side—their own.

> Job 11:7-12 "Can you fathom the mysteries of God?
> Can you probe the limits of the Almighty?
> ⁸They are higher than the heavens—what can you do?
> They are deeper than the depths of the grave—
> what can you know?
> ⁹Their measure is longer than the earth
> and wider than the sea.
> ¹⁰"If he comes along and confines you in prison

Dialogues, Round 1

    and convenes a court, who can oppose him?
[11]Surely he recognizes deceitful men;
    and when he sees evil, does he not take note?
[12]But a witless man can no more become wise
    than a wild donkey's colt can be born a man.

ZOPHAR: The mysteries of God are so far above you that you don't stand a chance. God sees right through you, you jackass.

Zophar voices his agitation. This is obvious in the intimation that Job, trying to penetrate the mysteries of his dilemma, is acting like a wild donkey.

Andersen believes that in verse 12, Zophar calls Job a donkey.[2] He also admits that this verse has many difficulties. Dhorme interprets this as a proverb that Zophar is quoting. It says, "A stupid man acquires wisdom just as a wild ass's colt becomes a master ass."[3] Dhorme points out that the same wording is used in this passage as is used in Genesis 16:12, where it is said of Ishmael that he will be "a wild ass of a man." So although the passage is difficult, the intimation is there. An insult was intended.

    Job 11:13-20 "Yet if you devote your heart to him
        and stretch out your hands to him,
    [14]if you put away the sin that is in your hand
        and allow no evil to dwell in your tent,
    [15]then you will lift up your face without shame;
        you will stand firm and without fear.
    [16]You will surely forget your trouble,
        recalling it only as waters gone by.
    [17]Life will be brighter than noonday,
        and darkness will become like morning.
    [18]You will be secure, because there is hope;
        you will look about you and take your rest in safety.
    [19]You will lie down, with no one to make you afraid,
        and many will court your favor.
    [20]But the eyes of the wicked will fail,
        and escape will elude them;
        their hope will become a dying gasp."

ZOPHAR: If you would repent, everything would turn out right. If you don't, you'll die.

Zophar sounds good here. His concepts of God's forgiveness and compassion are well developed. But he still holds to the conclusion that the three friends made when they first saw Job. He must have surely sinned to bring on this kind of calamity.

The Absence of Justice

Job 12:1-6 Then Job replied:
²"Doubtless you are the people,
  and wisdom will die with you!
³But I have a mind as well as you;
  I am not inferior to you.
  Who does not know all these things?
⁴"I have become a laughingstock to my friends,
  though I called upon God and he answered —
  a mere laughingstock, though righteous and blameless!
⁵Men at ease have contempt for misfortune
  as the fate of those whose feet are slipping.
⁶The tents of marauders are undisturbed,
  and those who provoke God are secure—
  those who carry their god in their hands.

JOB: You know it all!! But I know something too. It's easy for you to judge when you are at ease. God is just? I am just and I am a joke!

As the dialogues continue, Job becomes increasingly frustrated as evidenced by his sarcasm. But in all his depression, he does not lose his self-esteem. "I am not inferior to you."

On top of all his misery and loss, he laments that he has become nothing but a joke to his friends. Jeremiah experienced a similar difficulty:

Lamentations 3:14 I became the laughingstock of all my people; they mock me in song all day long.

Jesus, on the cross experienced the same abuse recorded in:

Luke 23:35-36 The people stood watching, and the rulers even sneered at him. They said, "He saved others; let him save himself if he is the Christ of God, the Chosen One."
³⁶The soldiers also came up and mocked him. They offered him wine vinegar.

It seems that the world cannot stand a righteous person because by comparison their sinfulness is quite obvious and their pride cannot endure the exposure.

Job has come to the conclusion that there is something dreadfully wrong with a world in which justice is supposed to reign when a just man is a joke.

Job 12:7-10 "But ask the animals, and they will teach you,
  or the birds of the air, and they will tell you;
⁸or speak to the earth, and it will teach you,
  or let the fish of the sea inform you.

Dialogues, Round 1

⁹Which of all these does not know
   that the hand of the LORD has done this?
¹⁰In his hand is the life of every creature
   and the breath of all mankind.

JOB: Ask the creatures of the earth if there is really justice on the earth.

Job sees that justice does not rule in nature. Beasts and birds that are innocent of any sin and incapable of sinning also suffer pain and tragedy.

———

**Job 12:11-25 Does not the ear test words
   as the tongue tastes food?
¹²Is not wisdom found among the aged?
   Does not long life bring understanding?
¹³"To God belong wisdom and power;
   counsel and understanding are his.
¹⁴What he tears down cannot be rebuilt;
   the man he imprisons cannot be released.
¹⁵If he holds back the waters, there is drought;
   if he lets them loose, they devastate the land.
¹⁶To him belong strength and victory;
   both deceived and deceiver are his.
¹⁷He leads counselors away stripped
   and makes fools of judges.
¹⁸He takes off the shackles put on by kings
   and ties a loincloth around their waist.
¹⁹He leads priests away stripped
   and overthrows men long established.
²⁰He silences the lips of trusted advisers
   and takes away the discernment of elders.
²¹He pours contempt on nobles
   and disarms the mighty.
²²He reveals the deep things of darkness
   and brings deep shadows into the light.
²³He makes nations great, and destroys them;
   he enlarges nations, and disperses them.
²⁴He deprives the leaders of the earth of their reason;
   he sends them wandering through a trackless waste.
²⁵They grope in darkness with no light;
   he makes them stagger like drunkards.**

JOB: You say justice rules on the earth. That is simplistic. It simply will not explain the realities of life.

How can a case for justice and order be made when:

The Absence of Justice

1. He withholds rain and the earth becomes a desert? (v 15)
2. He sends storms and floods the ground? (v 15)
3. Deceived and deceiver are both his slaves? (v 16)
4. He makes fools of counselors and judges? (v 17)
5. He reduces kings to slaves and frees their servants? (v 18)
6. Priests are led away as slaves? (v 19)
7. He overthrows the mighty? (v 19)
8. He takes away the insight of the elders? (v 20)
9. He pours contempt on princes and weakens the strong? (v 21)
10. He floods the darkness with light? (v 22)
11. He raises up a nation and then destroys it? (v 23)
12. He takes away the understanding of the chiefs? (v 24)
13. He makes them stagger like drunk men? (v 25)

Job 13:1-5 "My eyes have seen all this,
my ears have heard and understood it.
²What you know, I also know;
I am not inferior to you.
³But I desire to speak to the Almighty
and to argue my case with God.
⁴You, however, smear me with lies;
you are worthless physicians, all of you!
⁵If only you would be altogether silent!
For you, that would be wisdom.

JOB: I want to confront God himself with my dilemma. I wish you would just shut up.

Up to this point Job has been arguing his case with his friends. Now he openly expresses his intention to argue with God himself. This begins a shift in the direction of the statements that will culminate in a formal appeal to God.

His friends, he claims, would be wiser to keep quiet. Abe Lincoln is reported to have said, "It is better to keep quiet and let folks think you're a fool rather than to speak and remove all shadow of a doubt." In situations like this, silence indeed is golden.

Job 13:6-12 Hear now my argument;
listen to the plea of my lips.
⁷Will you speak wickedly on God's behalf?
Will you speak deceitfully for him?
⁸Will you show him partiality?
Will you argue the case for God?
⁹Would it turn out well if he examined you?
Could you deceive him as you might deceive men?

Dialogues, Round 1

>¹⁰He would surely rebuke you
>　if you secretly showed partiality.
>¹¹Would not his splendor terrify you?
>　Would not the dread of him fall on you?
>¹²Your maxims are proverbs of ashes;
>　your defenses are defenses of clay.

JOB: Don't feel so secure. How will it go when God examines you?

You are defending God with a false premise. How will that stand up to his scrutiny? Let's trade places. How would it go for you?

Job mentions his friends' maxims and proverbs. This is a familiar phenomenon in confronting tragedy. People compulsively come up with pat answers. Rabbi Harold Kushner lists a number of pat answers that are commonly used when people try to comfort the suffering.[4] They usually assume that God is the source of suffering. In reality, these pat answers help about as much as Job's friends' pat answers.

>**Job 13:13-19** "Keep silent and let me speak;
>　then let come to me what may.
>¹⁴Why do I put myself in jeopardy
>　and take my life in my hands?
>¹⁵Though he slay me, yet will I hope in him;
>　I will surely defend my ways to his face.
>¹⁶Indeed, this will turn out for my deliverance,
>　for no godless man would dare come before him!
>¹⁷Listen carefully to my words;
>　let your ears take in what I say.
>¹⁸Now that I have prepared my case,
>　I know I will be vindicated.
>¹⁹Can anyone bring charges against me?
>　If so, I will be silent and die.

JOB: I may die for this, but I intend to defend my case before God.

Job faced the definite possibility that his stand before God would result in death. (v 14) Verse 15 has been quoted as a statement of Job's faith in God. Yet a careful interpretation of the original language could result in an alternate meaning: "Though he slay me, yet will I pursue my case before him." His only hope is expressed in verse 16, where he states that no wicked person would dare such a thing. Verse 18 indicates that he had outlined his case and was confident he would be vindicated. Verse 19 brings a final challenge to anyone to prove him wicked.

>**Job 13:20-28** "Only grant me these two things, O God,

The Absence of Justice

>   and then I will not hide from you:
> ²¹Withdraw your hand far from me,
>   and stop frightening me with your terrors.
> ²²Then summon me and I will answer,
>   or let me speak, and you reply.
> ²³How many wrongs and sins have I committed?
>   Show me my offense and my sin.
> ²⁴Why do you hide your face
>   and consider me your enemy?
> ²⁵Will you torment a windblown leaf?
>   Will you chase after dry chaff?
> ²⁶For you write down bitter things against me
>   and make me inherit the sins of my youth.
> ²⁷You fasten my feet in shackles;
>   you keep close watch on all my paths
>   by putting marks on the soles of my feet.
> ²⁸"So man wastes away like something rotten,
>   like a garment eaten by moths.

JOB: God, here's my case. I want an answer.
1. How many wrongs and sins have I committed?
2. Why do you hide your face and consider me your enemy?
3. Why do you write down bitter things against me?

We are witnessing an ancient court procedure. It is a question and answer process. First one side asks questions and then the other. Here we see Job asking God "Why?" In Chapters 29 - 31 Job will state his case. Then in Chapters 38 to 41 God questions Job.

Note that in verse 26 Job mentions the sins of his youth. Job never claimed to be sinless. It is God who has declared him blameless.

Verse 28 is another reminder to God that he had better hurry up.

———

> **Job 14:1-6** "Man born of woman
>   is of few days and full of trouble.
> ²He springs up like a flower and withers away;
>   like a fleeting shadow, he does not endure.
> ³Do you fix your eye on such a one?
>   Will you bring him before you for judgment?
> ⁴Who can bring what is pure from the impure?
>   No one!
> ⁵Man's days are determined;
>   you have decreed the number of his months
>   and have set limits he cannot exceed.
> ⁶So look away from him and let him alone,
>   till he has put in his time like a hired man.

Dialogues, Round 1

JOB: The time I have left is short.

Job has mentioned repeatedly that he believes his time is running out. Actually, he will live another one hundred forty years, but he wouldn't have believed it at this point. Like James' description of the life of the rich man in James 1:10-11, he sees man like a flower with a brief existence. He believes that God determines his days and asks him to turn his eye from him so that he can rest for the few days left to him.

> Job 14:7-12 "At least there is hope for a tree:
>   If it is cut down, it will sprout again,
>   and its new shoots will not fail.
> ⁸Its roots may grow old in the ground
>   and its stump die in the soil,
> ⁹yet at the scent of water it will bud
>   and put forth shoots like a plant.
> ¹⁰But man dies and is laid low;
>   he breathes his last and is no more.
> ¹¹As water disappears from the sea
>   or a riverbed becomes parched and dry,
> ¹²so man lies down and does not rise;
>   till the heavens are no more, men will not awake
>   or be roused from their sleep.

JOB: If I die, it will be all over.

Job here again expresses his belief that death is final, and there is no life hereafter. Trees can be cut down and sprout again but when man dies, that's it.

> Job 14:13-22 "If only you would hide me in the grave
>   and conceal me till your anger has passed!
> If only you would set me a time
>   and then remember me!
> ¹⁴If a man dies, will he live again?
>   All the days of my hard service
>   I will wait for my renewal to come.
> ¹⁵You will call and I will answer you;
>   you will long for the creature your hands have made.
> ¹⁶Surely then you will count my steps
>   but not keep track of my sin.
> ¹⁷My offenses will be sealed up in a bag;
>   you will cover over my sin.
> ¹⁸"But as a mountain erodes and crumbles
>   and as a rock is moved from its place,

The Absence of Justice

>[19]as water wears away stones
>   and torrents wash away the soil,
>   so you destroy man's hope.
>[20]You overpower him once for all, and he is gone;
>   you change his countenance and send him away.
>[21]If his sons are honored, he does not know it;
>   if they are brought low, he does not see it.
>[22]He feels but the pain of his own body
>   and mourns only for himself."

JOB: I want to die, but I still want this issue settled. I fear that I will never know the outcome.

Job's affliction is wearing him down like a torrent that grinds up rocks. He observes that man doesn't know what will happen after he is gone. All he can know is sorrow and pain.

1. Koch, Kurt. *Between Christ and Satan.* Grand Rapids: Kregel, 1961. p. 125
2. Andersen, Francis I. *Job.* London: Inter-Varsity Press, 1976. p. 158
3. Dhorme, Edouard. *A Commentary on the Book of Job.* Translated by Harold Knight. Nashville: Thomas Nelson, 1984. p. 163
4. Kushner, Harold. *When Bad Things Happen to Good People.* New York: Schocken Books, 1981.

CHAPTER 5

DIALOGUES, ROUND 2

After all three friends speak and Job answers each in turn, they start in again. The three friends have not been convinced of Job's integrity. They camp on the same theological position they held during the first round. That is, God is just, God is sovereign on the earth; therefore, justice reigns on the earth. The righteous are blessed and the wicked suffer. Since Job is suffering, he is obviously wicked, although to this point they have not identified his sins. Their guessing game intensifies in this round, and unable to score any points against Job's profession of innocence, they simply get more hysterical in their arguments.

> **Job 15:1-6 Then Eliphaz the Temanite replied:**
> **²"Would a wise man answer with empty notions**
>   **or fill his belly with the hot east wind?**
> **³Would he argue with useless words,**
>   **with speeches that have no value?**
> **⁴But you even undermine piety**
>   **and hinder devotion to God.**
> **⁵Your sin prompts your mouth;**
>   **you adopt the tongue of the crafty.**
> **⁶Your own mouth condemns you, not mine;**
>   **your own lips testify against you.**

ELIPHAZ: Job, you're full of hot air. You're supposed to be wise, but you are condemning yourself.

Insults fly as the dialogues intensify. The friends hear only empty notions and useless words. Convinced that Job is still covering up his private sins, they hear his words as blasphemy.

> **Job 15:7-16 "Are you the first man ever born?**
>   **Were you brought forth before the hills?**
> **⁸Do you listen in on God's council?**
>   **Do you limit wisdom to yourself?**
> **⁹What do you know that we do not know?**
>   **What insights do you have that we do not have?**
> **¹⁰The gray-haired and the aged are on our side,**
>   **men even older than your father.**

The Absence of Justice

> [11] Are God's consolations not enough for you,
>   words spoken gently to you?
> [12] Why has your heart carried you away,
>   and why do your eyes flash,
> [13] so that you vent your rage against God
>   and pour out such words from your mouth?
> [14] "What is man, that he could be pure,
>   or one born of woman, that he could be righteous?
> [15] If God places no trust in his holy ones,
>   if even the heavens are not pure in his eyes,
> [16] how much less man, who is vile and corrupt,
>   who drinks up evil like water!

ELIPHAZ: You think you know more than we. We weren't born yesterday. What makes you think you have the right to get mad at God and speak such blasphemy? Even the angels and the heavens are not pure before God. How much less, you!

Eliphaz's frustration is evident as he proceeds to personally attack Job. It is commonly observed that when the point is weak the argument usually gets loud. Eliphaz does not try to counter any of Job's arguments except the one that claims Job's innocence. This seems to rankle Eliphaz's sensitivities to the point of exasperation.

> **Job 15:17-35** "Listen to me and I will explain to you;
>   let me tell you what I have seen,
> [18] what wise men have declared,
>   hiding nothing received from their fathers
> [19] (to whom alone the land was given
>   when no alien passed among them):
> [20] All his days the wicked man suffers torment,
>   the ruthless through all the years stored up for him.
> [21] Terrifying sounds fill his ears;
>   when all seems well, marauders attack him.
> [22] He despairs of escaping the darkness;
>   he is marked for the sword.
> [23] He wanders about—food for vultures;
>   he knows the day of darkness is at hand.
> [24] Distress and anguish fill him with terror;
>   they overwhelm him, like a king poised to attack,
> [25] because he shakes his fist at God
>   and vaunts himself against the Almighty,
> [26] defiantly charging against him
>   with a thick, strong shield.
> [27] "Though his face is covered with fat
>   and his waist bulges with flesh,
> [28] he will inhabit ruined towns

Dialogues, Round 2

    and houses where no one lives,
        houses crumbling to rubble.
[29]He will no longer be rich and his wealth will not endure,
        nor will his possessions spread over the land.
[30]He will not escape the darkness;
        a flame will wither his shoots,
        and the breath of God's mouth will carry him away.
[31]Let him not deceive himself by trusting what is worthless,
        for he will get nothing in return.
[32]Before his time he will be paid in full,
        and his branches will not flourish.
[33]He will be like a vine stripped of its unripe grapes,
        like an olive tree shedding its blossoms.
[34]For the company of the godless will be barren,
        and fire will consume the tents of those who love bribes.
[35]They conceive trouble and give birth to evil;
        their womb fashions deceit."

ELIPHAZ: I repeat: The wicked man (Job) suffers because he is arrogant and defies God. He is stubborn, but he will not prosper. There is justice on the earth!

Eliphaz continues to focus his attack on Job. Verses 20 and 24 refer to the agony Job is experiencing. Verse 21 refers to the raids of the Sabeans and Chaldeans which decimated Job's herds. Verses 28 and 29 refer to "The House of Job"; that is, Job & Company crumbling to rubble. Verses 30 and 32 refer to Job's bereaved children.

Eliphaz claims to have the wisdom of the ages on his side (vs 17-18). This wisdom states that the lot of the wicked is nothing but terror and destruction. His destiny is the sword...and all because he behaved arrogantly toward the Almighty. He will come to an early end.

    Job 16:1-5 Then Job replied:
[2]"I have heard many things like these;
        miserable comforters are you all!
[3]Will your long-winded speeches never end?
        What ails you that you keep on arguing?
[4]I also could speak like you,
        if you were in my place;
I could make fine speeches against you
        and shake my head at you.
[5]But my mouth would encourage you;
        comfort from my lips would bring you relief.

JOB: You are sorry comforters. Let's change places!

The Absence of Justice

Job's frustration mounts also as evidenced by his biting words: miserable comforters, long-winded speeches, and to cap it off, his sarcastic, "What ails you that you keep on arguing?" Job states that if their roles were reversed, he could also accuse the afflicted, but he wouldn't; he would try to comfort them. He is sincere in these words. His ministrations to the poor and afflicted are listed in Chapter 29 as the first part of his legal brief.

> Job 16:6-17 "Yet if I speak, my pain is not relieved;
>   and if I refrain, it does not go away.
> [7]Surely, O God, you have worn me out;
>   you have devastated my entire household.
> [8]You have bound me—and it has become a witness;
>   my gauntness rises up and testifies against me.
> [9]God assails me and tears me in his anger
>   and gnashes his teeth at me;
>   my opponent fastens on me his piercing eyes.
> [10]Men open their mouths to jeer at me;
>   they strike my cheek in scorn
>   and unite together against me.
> [11]God has turned me over to evil men
>   and thrown me into the clutches of the wicked.
> [12]All was well with me, but he shattered me;
>   he seized me by the neck and crushed me.
> He has made me his target;
>   [13]his archers surround me.
> Without pity, he pierces my kidneys
>   and spills my gall on the ground.
> [14]Again and again he bursts upon me;
>   he rushes at me like a warrior.
> [15]"I have sewed sackcloth over my skin
>   And buried my brow in the dust.
> [16]My face is red with weeping,
>   Deep shadows ring my eyes;
> [17]yet my hands have been free of violence
>   And my prayer is pure.

JOB: I still say that I am innocent, although God has abandoned me to evil and is destroying me.

In answer to Eliphaz's remarks in 15:1-6, Job states that his pain is no different whether he speaks or holds back. So he proceeds to make his bitter complaint against God. It makes an astonishing list:

1. God has worn Job out. (v 7)
2. He has devastated Job's entire household. (v 7)
3. He has bound him. (v 8)

Dialogues, Round 2

    4. God has turned him over to evil men. (vs 9-11)
    5. God shattered him. (v 12)
    6. God seized him by the neck and crushed him. (v 12)
    7. God used Job for target practice. (v 12)
    8. He pierced Job's kidneys. (v 13)
    9. He spills his gall on the ground. (v 13)
    10. He bursts upon him and rushes him like a warrior. (v 14)

This list is especially remarkable when we again read 42:7-8, where God declares that what Job said is right. Also in 2:10, "In all this Job did not sin in what he said." All this has happened, though he had humbled himself in sackcloth and dust with weeping. And he still contends that he is innocent and his prayer is pure.

Job still wrestles to make sense of these events. He sees that there is something dreadfully wrong with a world where justice is supposed to prevail, when such things happen to a just man whose hands have been free of violence, whose prayer is pure.

Job 16:18-22 "O earth, do not cover my blood;
    may my cry never be laid to rest!
¹⁹Even now my witness is in heaven;
    my advocate is on high.
²⁰My intercessor is my friend
    as my eyes pour out tears to God;
²¹on behalf of a man he pleads with God
    as a man pleads for his friend.
²²"Only a few years will pass
    before I go on the journey of no return.

JOB: May my case not die with me. There is someone in heaven who is pleading my cause before God.

The words in verse 18 are reminiscent of God's words in Genesis 4:10: "Your brother's blood cries to me from the ground." Job asks that his blood receive the same attention, and that this injustice not be hidden. In saying this it is evident that Job does not expect to recover from this affliction.

The "witness" of verse 19 and the "intercessor" of verse 20 are difficult to identify. Job is probably alluding to the same person as the "redeemer or defender" of 19:25. What Job knew about these matters is unclear (see 1 John 2:1, NAS), but I take it that these are tremendous statements of faith in the ultimate justice of God.

Job 17:1-5 My spirit is broken,
    my days are cut short,

The Absence of Justice

> the grave awaits me.
> ²Surely mockers surround me;
> my eyes must dwell on their hostility.
> ³"Give me, O God, the pledge you demand.
> Who else will put up security for me?
> ⁴You have closed their minds to understanding;
> therefore you will not let them triumph.
> ⁵If a man denounces his friends for reward,
> the eyes of his children will fail.

JOB: I am on my last legs. God, I have no one to turn to but you.

Job bitterly surveys his waning strength and his still-hostile friends and realizes that God is his only hope for comfort. Eliphaz, Bildad, and Zophar have closed minds.

> Job 17:6-16 "God has made me a byword to everyone,
> a man in whose face people spit.
> ⁷My eyes have grown dim with grief;
> my whole frame is but a shadow.
> ⁸Upright men are appalled at this;
> the innocent are aroused against the ungodly.
> ⁹Nevertheless, the righteous will hold to their ways,
> and those with clean hands will grow stronger.
> ¹⁰"But come on, all of you, try again!
> I will not find a wise man among you.
> ¹¹My days have passed, my plans are shattered,
> and so are the desires of my heart.
> ¹²These men turn night into day;
> in the face of darkness they say, 'Light is near.'
> ¹³If the only home I hope for is the grave,
> if I spread out my bed in darkness,
> ¹⁴if I say to corruption, 'You are my father,'
> and to the worm, 'My mother' or 'My sister,'
> ¹⁵where then is my hope?
> Who can see any hope for me?
> ¹⁶Will it go down to the gates of death?
> Will we descend together into the dust?"

JOB: I have been totally discredited, but I will hold fast to the integrity of my way of life. Come on, guys, you ought to know better. Not one of you is wise enough to solve this mystery. Nothing you say makes sense. My hope is all but gone.

Even from Job's depleted condition he has strength to ridicule the platitudes of his friends because they just do not apply here. Verse 12 is typical of people who adopt a set creed (usually set up by someone else) and then go

Dialogues, Round 2

through life adapting every experience they encounter to fit their creed, never daring to question their creed in the light of new evidence. Such were the friends. Their creed would not give way to the reality of a suffering, righteous man.

Job, in verses 13-16, questions whether the grave will be his only respite.

> **Job 18:1-4** Then Bildad the Shuhite replied:
> ²"When will you end these speeches?
>   Be sensible, and then we can talk.
> ³Why are we regarded as cattle
>   and considered stupid in your sight?
> ⁴You who tear yourself to pieces in your anger,
>   is the earth to be abandoned for your sake?
>   Or must the rocks be moved from their place?

BILDAD: Give up and wise up, Job. Why can't you see our point? Do you think God will change his system of justice just for you?

The dialogues become more and more hostile. As they do, the friends are less and less willing to try to see Job's side of the controversy. So Job and his friends hurl insults at each other. Bildad says here that Job is not being sensible. He thinks Job has, in effect, called him a "dumb ox," and Bildad is smarting from the epithet. He contends that Job's anger is not helping him physically. He states that Job defies the basic laws of the universe.

> **Job 18:5-21** "The lamp of the wicked is snuffed out;
>   the flame of his fire stops burning.
> ⁶The light in his tent becomes dark;
>   the lamp beside him goes out.
> ⁷The vigor of his step is weakened;
>   his own schemes throw him down.
> ⁸His feet thrust him into a net
>   and he wanders into its mesh.
> ⁹A trap seizes him by the heel;
>   a snare holds him fast.
> ¹⁰A noose is hidden for him on the ground;
>   a trap lies in his path.
> ¹¹Terrors startle him on every side
>   and dog his every step.
> ¹²Calamity is hungry for him;
>   disaster is ready for him when he falls.
> ¹³It eats away parts of his skin;
>   death's firstborn devours his limbs.
> ¹⁴He is torn from the security of his tent
>   and marched off to the king of terrors.

The Absence of Justice

> ¹⁵Fire resides in his tent;
>   burning sulfur is scattered over his dwelling.
> ¹⁶His roots dry up below
>   and his branches wither above.
> ¹⁷The memory of him perishes from the earth;
>   he has no name in the land.
> ¹⁸He is driven from light into darkness
>   and is banished from the world.
> ¹⁹He has no offspring or descendants among his people,
>   no survivor where once he lived.
> ²⁰Men of the west are appalled at his fate;
>   men of the east are seized with horror.
> ²¹Surely such is the dwelling of an evil man;
>   such is the place of one who knows not God."

BILDAD: Here, Job, look at your life! You are wicked!

Although Bildad in verse 5 identifies the subject of his tirade as "the wicked," the object is unquestionably Job. The implication is clear. Job has just witnessed (courtesy of Bildad) a flashback of his life. Is Job still going to insist that he has done no wrong to deserve this?

> **Job 19:1-6 Then Job replied:**
> ²"How long will you torment me
>   and crush me with words?
> ³Ten times now you have reproached me;
>   shamelessly you attack me.
> ⁴If it is true that I have gone astray,
>   my error remains my concern alone.
> ⁵If indeed you would exalt yourselves above me
>   and use my humiliation against me,
> ⁶then know that God has wronged me
>   and drawn his net around me.

JOB: How long will you attack and reproach me? Even if I have sinned— and I haven't—my sin is my own problem and none of your business.

Job asserts that if anyone has done wrong, it appears to be God. Bildad had referred to a net in 18:8 and now Job asserts that it is God who has wrongfully snared Job in his net.

> **Job 19:7-20** "Though I cry, 'I've been wronged!' I get no response;
>   though I call for help, there is no justice.
> ⁸He has blocked my way so I cannot pass;

> he has shrouded my paths in darkness.
> ⁹He has stripped me of my honor
> and removed the crown from my head.
> ¹⁰He tears me down on every side till I am gone;
> he uproots my hope like a tree.
> ¹¹His anger burns against me;
> he counts me among his enemies.
> ¹²His troops advance in force;
> they build a siege ramp against me
> and encamp around my tent.
> ¹³"He has alienated my brothers from me;
> my acquaintances are completely estranged from me.
> ¹⁴My kinsmen have gone away;
> my friends have forgotten me.
> ¹⁵My guests and my maidservants count me a stranger;
> they look upon me as an alien.
> ¹⁶I summon my servant, but he does not answer,
> though I beg him with my own mouth.
> ¹⁷My breath is offensive to my wife;
> I am loathsome to my own brothers.
> ¹⁸Even the little boys scorn me;
> when I appear, they ridicule me.
> ¹⁹All my intimate friends detest me;
> those I love have turned against me.
> ²⁰I am nothing but skin and bones;
> I have escaped with only the skin of my teeth.

JOB: I am coming to the conclusion that there is no justice on the earth! I've been wronged. Look what God has done to me.

This passage is laced with the loneliness, agony, and pathos that erupt from Job's heart. First and foremost is the pain that he feels because he perceives that he has been betrayed by God, who has not only abandoned him but now treats him as an enemy. Next he complains that God is also responsible for his social alienation. God has turned brothers, acquaintances, kinsmen, friends, guests, servants, and wife against him. Even children scorn him. While children have no inherited prejudices and can be very accepting, they can also be very cruel. We can imagine Job sitting in the city dump, the object of contempt of all passersby, exposed to every indignity that depraved humanity can think of, including spitting and ridiculing. Then the little children come along and mimic the actions of the adults. And to crown it off, these are probably people that Job has helped in the past. (See Ch 29). Physically, he is reduced to skin and bones. Emotionally, he is shattered, but spiritually, he is hanging on.

Job hits bottom in this passage. Job is innocent, and though he cries for help there is no answer.

The Absence of Justice

>Job 19:21-22 "Have pity on me, my friends, have pity,
>   for the hand of God has struck me.
>²²Why do you pursue me as God does?
>   Will you never get enough of my flesh?

JOB: Please, please have pity on me!

Some Bible students have scorned Job for being on a "pity party." This view is insensitive and ill-informed. This is the view of Eliphaz, Bildad, and Zophar, who criticize Job for his reaction to a situation which they have never experienced themselves. They are guilty of intolerance and judgment with no compassion.

This pathetic cry comes from the depths of Job's wretched being. That anyone in such a condition should have to beg for pity and compassion is pathetic. But instead of showing compassion, his friends choose to condemn him in the most despicable way.

>Job 19:23-29 "Oh, that my words were recorded,
>   that they were written on a scroll,
>²⁴that they were inscribed with an iron tool on lead,
>   or engraved in rock forever!
>²⁵I know that my Redeemer lives,
>   and that in the end he will stand upon the earth.
>²⁶And after my skin has been destroyed,
>   yet in my flesh I will see God;
>²⁷I myself will see him with my own eyes—I, and not another.
>   How my heart yearns within me!
>²⁸"If you say, 'How we will hound him,
>   since the root of the trouble lies in him,'
>²⁹you should fear the sword yourselves;
>   for wrath will bring punishment by the sword,
>   and then you will know that there is judgment."

JOB: I know that God will vindicate me.

From the depths of Job's despair comes this remarkable statement of faith, one of the best known in Scripture. Job believes that justice will reign on the earth and he knows that his redeemer lives. The NAS renders verse 25b, "And at the last he will take his stand on the earth." The "stand" he will take will include justice.

This statement is most remarkable because he utters it immediately after the expression of his lowest point of depression. This should be incontrovertible evidence that faith can triumph in the worst situations. Indeed, some of the greatest expressions of faith have come out of the most wretched situations. A devastated Jeremiah says:

> **Lamentations 3:19-26 I remember my affliction and my wandering,**
>   **the bitterness and the gall.**
> **[20]I well remember them,**
>   **and my soul is downcast within me.**
> **[21]Yet this I call to mind**
>   **and therefore I have hope:**
> **[22]Because of the LORD's great love we are not consumed,**
>   **for his compassions never fail.**
> **[23]They are new every morning;**
>   **great is your faithfulness.**
> **[24]I say to myself, "The LORD is my portion;**
>   **therefore I will wait for him."**
> **[25]The LORD is good to those whose hope is in him,**
>   **to the one who seeks him;**
> **[26]it is good to wait quietly**
>   **for the salvation of the LORD.**

Habakkuk, seeing his world collapsing around him, says:

> **Habakkuk 3:17-19 Though the fig tree does not bud**
>   **and there are no grapes on the vines,**
> **though the olive crop fails**
>   **and the fields produce no food,**
> **though there are no sheep in the pen**
>   **and no cattle in the stalls,**
> **[18]yet I will rejoice in the LORD,**
>   **I will be joyful in God my Savior.**
> **[19]The Sovereign LORD is my strength;**
>   **he makes my feet like the feet of a deer,**
>   **he enables me to go on the heights.**

There are many other examples in Scripture, such as Psalm 13. More modern examples of faith expressed in wretched situations are seen in the stories of Dietrich Bonhoffer and Corrie Ten Boom along with a host of others. It is said that the well-known gospel song "The Love of God" was found scrawled on the wall of an insane asylum cell. The author's faith reached above his circumstances and caught hold of a truth that transcended the terrible circumstance in which he found himself. In like manner, Job's faith reaches out to a God who will yet establish justice on the earth.

Whether this passage indicates that Job believed in an afterlife is doubtful given the previous indications from Job that death would be the end of things. (7:9-10 & 14:10-14) Rabbi Bemporad interprets 26b as, "Yet from my flesh I shall see God," and this indicates that Job still hoped to be vindicated before

The Absence of Justice

he died. But it would be deplorable to get caught up in these details and miss the grandeur of the tremendous statement of faith coming from this man in the ashes of despair.

Job ends the statement with another affirmation of his belief in the ultimate judgment of God. It comes as a warning to the friends who have unjustly accused him. If there is going to be justice (and Job still believes there will be) and if no one is just before God as his tormentors claim, then his friends are seriously in danger of God's judgment.

Job 20:1-29 Then Zophar the Naamathite replied:
²"My troubled thoughts prompt me to answer
   because I am greatly disturbed.
³I hear a rebuke that dishonors me,
   and my understanding inspires me to reply.
⁴"Surely you know how it has been from of old,
   ever since man was placed on the earth,
⁵that the mirth of the wicked is brief,
   the joy of the godless lasts but a moment.
⁶Though his pride reaches to the heavens
   and his head touches the clouds,
⁷he will perish forever, like his own dung;
   those who have seen him will say, 'Where is he?'
⁸Like a dream he flies away, no more to be found,
   banished like a vision of the night.
⁹The eye that saw him will not see him again;
   his place will look on him no more.
¹⁰His children must make amends to the poor;
   his own hands must give back his wealth.
¹¹The youthful vigor that fills his bones
   will lie with him in the dust.
¹²"Though evil is sweet in his mouth
   and he hides it under his tongue,
¹³though he cannot bear to let it go
   and keeps it in his mouth,
¹⁴yet his food will turn sour in his stomach;
   it will become the venom of serpents within him.
¹⁵He will spit out the riches he swallowed;
   God will make his stomach vomit them up.
¹⁶He will suck the poison of serpents;
   the fangs of an adder will kill him.
¹⁷He will not enjoy the streams,
   the rivers flowing with honey and cream.
¹⁸What he toiled for he must give back uneaten;
   he will not enjoy the profit from his trading.
¹⁹For he has oppressed the poor and left them destitute;
   he has seized houses he did not build.

²⁰"Surely he will have no respite from his craving;
   he cannot save himself by his treasure.
²¹Nothing is left for him to devour;
   his prosperity will not endure.
²²In the midst of his plenty, distress will overtake him;
   the full force of misery will come upon him.
²³When he has filled his belly,
   God will vent his burning anger against him
   and rain down his blows upon him.
²⁴Though he flees from an iron weapon,
   a bronze-tipped arrow pierces him.
²⁵He pulls it out of his back,
   the gleaming point out of his liver.
Terrors will come over him;
   ²⁶total darkness lies in wait for his treasures.
A fire unfanned will consume him
   and devour what is left in his tent.
²⁷The heavens will expose his guilt;
   the earth will rise up against him.
²⁸A flood will carry off his house,
   rushing waters on the day of God's wrath.
²⁹Such is the fate God allots the wicked,
   the heritage appointed for them by God."

ZOPHAR: You question whether there is justice. The wicked will get what is coming to them soon enough. Their prosperity is short on the earth.

Zophar complains that Job insults his intelligence (v 3). He still holds to the basic position he started with, but now modifies it slightly in the face of Job's arguments. Although he concedes that the wicked do sometimes prosper, he asserts that prosperity is short, their posterity will suffer, their joy is fleeting, and death will overtake them in their youth. All their pleasures will turn into suffering and misery.

Job 21:1-16 Then Job replied:
²"Listen carefully to my words;
   let this be the consolation you give me.
³Bear with me while I speak,
   and after I have spoken, mock on.
⁴"Is my complaint directed to man?
   Why should I not be impatient?
⁵Look at me and be astonished;
   clap your hand over your mouth.
⁶When I think about this, I am terrified;
   trembling seizes my body.
⁷Why do the wicked live on,

The Absence of Justice

> growing old and increasing in power?
> ⁸They see their children established around them,
> their offspring before their eyes.
> ⁹Their homes are safe and free from fear;
> the rod of God is not upon them.
> ¹⁰Their bulls never fail to breed;
> their cows calve and do not miscarry.
> ¹¹They send forth their children as a flock;
> their little ones dance about.
> ¹²They sing to the music of tambourine and harp;
> they make merry to the sound of the flute.
> ¹³They spend their years in prosperity
> and go down to the grave in peace.
> ¹⁴Yet they say to God, 'Leave us alone!
> We have no desire to know your ways.
> ¹⁵Who is the Almighty, that we should serve him?
> What would we gain by praying to him?'
> ¹⁶But their prosperity is not in their own hands,
> so I stand aloof from the counsel of the wicked.

JOB: Excuse me. Answer this and then you can continue mocking. If there is justice on the earth, why do the wicked prosper from the cradle to the grave?

Job interrupts Zophar's discourse with his disquieting observations. Job contends that the wicked do not die young, but live to a ripe old age, and even become more powerful. Their descendants do not suffer or fear suffering, but also prosper as their parents did. Even their cattle reproduce unfailingly. Their children are happy and carefree. They live long lives in ease and die suddenly with no pain or agony. What's more, they do this with an attitude of arrogance and independence toward God. They see no reason to serve God when they are doing so well by themselves.

There are similar passages in Psalms 10 and 73. In Psalm 73:3-20, David also complains about the prosperity of the wicked (v 5). "They are free from the burdens common to man; they are not plagued by human ills." David seems to come to almost the same conclusion that Zophar has been expounding. David, after pondering the problem in the sanctuary, was able to perceive the end of the wicked. God sets them in slippery places, casts them down to sudden destruction, and they are swept away by sudden terrors. The difference between David's and Zophar's position is that Zophar declares justice to be operational in a man's lifetime, while David looks forward to ultimate justice, not necessarily in this lifetime.

Jeremiah also questions God about this subject:

> **Jeremiah 12:1-2** You are always righteous, O LORD,
> when I bring a case before you.

Dialogues, Round 2

> Yet I would speak with you about your justice:
>> Why does the way of the wicked prosper?
>> Why do all the faithless live at ease?
> ²You have planted them, and they have taken root;
>> they grow and bear fruit.
> You are always on their lips
>> but far from their hearts.

Elie Wiesel, the noted Holocaust survivor, recalls that the Jews in the concentration camps also questioned the success of the Nazis as they proceeded to exterminate the Jews. He quotes one victim's conclusion: "I've got more faith in Hitler than in anyone else. He's the only one who's kept his promises, all his promises, to the Jewish people."[1] Many survivors of the Holocaust emerged from their experiences as agnostics or atheists.

> Job 21:17-26 "Yet how often is the lamp of the wicked snuffed out?
>> How often does calamity come upon them,
>> the fate God allots in his anger?
> ¹⁸How often are they like straw before the wind,
>> like chaff swept away by a gale?
> ¹⁹It is said, 'God stores up a man's punishment for his sons.'
>> Let him repay the man himself, so that he will know it!
> ²⁰Let his own eyes see his destruction;
>> let him drink of the wrath of the Almighty.
> ²¹For what does he care about the family he leaves behind
>> when his allotted months come to an end?
> ²²"Can anyone teach knowledge to God,
>> since he judges even the highest?
> ²³One man dies in full vigor,
>> completely secure and at ease,
> ²⁴his body well nourished,
>> his bones rich with marrow.
> ²⁵Another man dies in bitterness of soul,
>> never having enjoyed anything good.
> ²⁶Side by side they lie in the dust,
>> and worms cover them both.

JOB: There is no justice on the earth. Justice is all talk, not fact!

Job asks for statistics to support the thesis that justice reigns. "How often does it really happen the way you describe?" He then goes on to deal with a part of their doctrine that has only been hinted at so far (5:4 & 20:10). If the wicked do not suffer, then their children will. But Job asks, "What kind of justice is that? Let God repay him so that he may experience it. Let his own eyes see his decay, and let him drink of the wrath of the Almighty." (vs 19-20)

The Absence of Justice

Job then states the facts as he sees them. One man can live a life of luxury and ease while another never knows the meaning of the good life because of his adversity, yet the same ignominious end comes to both, and righteousness or wickedness have nothing to do with it.

> **Job 21:27-34** "I know full well what you are thinking,
>   the schemes by which you would wrong me.
> [28] You say, 'Where now is the great man's house,
>   the tents where wicked men lived?'
> [29] Have you never questioned those who travel?
>   Have you paid no regard to their accounts —
> [30] that the evil man is spared from the day of calamity,
>   that he is delivered from the day of wrath?
> [31] Who denounces his conduct to his face?
>   Who repays him for what he has done?
> [32] He is carried to the grave,
>   and watch is kept over his tomb.
> [33] The soil in the valley is sweet to him;
>   all men follow after him,
>   and a countless throng goes before him.
> [34] "So how can you console me with your nonsense?
>   Nothing is left of your answers but falsehood!"

JOB: So how can you comfort me with your false assumptions?

Job now answers in advance the challenge he expects from his friends to produce his own hard evidence. Job appeals to the witness of wayfaring men who have traveled and amassed experience from far places. Then he asks who will confront the wicked with his actions or who will repay the righteous after they are dead. And, he adds, there are countless like them who have gone before and there are countless more who will come after. Therefore, he sees no comfort in their words.

1. Wiesel, Elie. *Night.* New York: Hill & Wang, 1960. p. 77

CHAPTER 6

DIALOGUES, ROUND 3

Eliphaz, Bildad, and Zophar have not succeeded in convincing Job of some sin that is the cause of his suffering. They will try one more time. They have not moved from their original position, while Job has begun to think differently about his original philosophical position, which was similar to that of his friends.

The Scripture indicates that only Eliphaz and Bildad speak in this last round. This leaves a final response to Bildad that is not only long, but problematical since Job seems to change position in mid-speech to one of agreement with his friends. Dhorme[1] solves this problem by ascribing portions of Chapters 24 and 27 to Zophar. We will see that these sections fit Zophar's philosophy very well. With this adjustment, Job's consistency is not compromised and the geometric pattern of three sets of three discourses is maintained.

Since this is considered the oldest of the books of the Bible, it is reasonable to accept that the manuscripts could have become scrambled at some time or other. It is accepted that Jeremiah is not preserved in our Bible in consecutive order due to the tumultuous times in which the book was written and arranged.

I accept Dhorme's rearrangement of Job and present the dialogues in this form.

> **Job 22:1-3 Then Eliphaz the Temanite replied:**
> **²"Can a man be of benefit to God?**
> **Can even a wise man benefit him?**
> **³What pleasure would it give the Almighty if you were righteous?**
> **What would he gain if your ways were blameless?**

ELIPHAZ: Even if you are righteous, what difference does it make to God?

At this point, Eliphaz's anger gets the best of him. One can get a rather clear picture of Eliphaz's character from his concept of God. Eliphaz still sees Job as an exceedingly arrogant man. His concept of God leaves no room for God's compassion for man or his love for him. He is willing to attribute judgment, anger, and retribution to God, but not love, tenderness, or mercy.

The Absence of Justice

He asks Job what difference it could make to God if he is righteous. But we have seen in the prologue how God staked his reputation before the hosts of heaven on Job's righteousness. Indeed, it makes a great difference to God if Job and all the Jobs of history are righteous.

> **Job 22:4-11** "Is it for your piety that he rebukes you
>   and brings charges against you?
> ⁵Is not your wickedness great?
>   Are not your sins endless?
> ⁶You demanded security from your brothers for no reason;
>   you stripped men of their clothing, leaving them naked.
> ⁷You gave no water to the weary
>   and you withheld food from the hungry,
> ⁸though you were a powerful man, owning land—
>   an honored man, living on it.
> ⁹And you sent widows away empty-handed
>   and broke the strength of the fatherless.
> ¹⁰That is why snares are all around you,
>   why sudden peril terrifies you,
> ¹¹why it is so dark you cannot see,
>   and why a flood of water covers you.

ELIPHAZ: ...But it is obvious that you are very wicked. I think you are guilty of many sins.

He asks Job if he thinks God is punishing him for his reverence (Verse 4). "Admit it, Job, aren't you a very wicked person?" Eliphaz then goes on to fabricate a list of alleged sins he thinks Job may have committed:

1. You demanded security from your brothers for no reason. (v 6)
2. You stripped men of their clothing, leaving them naked. (v 6)
3. You gave no water to the weary. (v 7)
4. You withheld food from the hungry when you had plenty. (vs 7 & 8)
5. You sent widows away empty-handed. (v 9)
6. You broke the strength of the fatherless. (v 9)

"This is why you are suffering, Job."

This list stands in stark contrast to the list Job submits in his suit against God (Chs 29-31). In fact, just the opposite is true since God declared Job's statements to be true.

> **Job 22:12-20** "Is not God in the heights of heaven?
>   And see how lofty are the highest stars!
> ¹³Yet you say, 'What does God know?
>   Does he judge through such darkness?

Dialogues, Round 3

¹⁴Thick clouds veil him, so he does not see us
  as he goes about in the vaulted heavens.'
¹⁵Will you keep to the old path
  that evil men have trod?
¹⁶They were carried off before their time,
  their foundations washed away by a flood.
¹⁷They said to God, 'Leave us alone!
  What can the Almighty do to us?'
¹⁸Yet it was he who filled their houses with good things,
  so I stand aloof from the counsel of the wicked.
¹⁹"The righteous see their ruin and rejoice;
  the innocent mock them, saying,
²⁰'Surely our foes are destroyed,
  and fire devours their wealth.'

ELIPHAZ: I repeat, God is just and he is sovereign. The wicked will suffer and the innocent will prosper on the earth.

Eliphaz now tries another tack. By extolling the greatness of God and his sovereignty, he hopes to induce Job to confess his sins. Again he brings a trumped-up charge against Job. He alleges that Job had questioned God's ability to see his misery from heaven. In fact, Job had not questioned God's omniscience, but his justice on the earth.

Eliphaz then categorizes Job with the wicked generation before the flood and asks if he is going to persist in walking down those same ancient paths of defiance toward God. He wrongly assumes that Job's plea for God to let him alone is the same as the wicked man's attitude of independence from God. Then he reminds Job again that the righteous will rejoice while the wicked will be cut off.

Job 22:21-30 "Submit to God and be at peace with him;
  in this way prosperity will come to you.
²²Accept instruction from his mouth
  and lay up his words in your heart.
²³If you return to the Almighty, you will be restored:
  If you remove wickedness far from your tent
²⁴and assign your nuggets to the dust,
  your gold of Ophir to the rocks in the ravines,
²⁵then the Almighty will be your gold,
  the choicest silver for you.
²⁶Surely then you will find delight in the Almighty
  and will lift up your face to God.
²⁷You will pray to him, and he will hear you,
  and you will fulfill your vows.
²⁸What you decide on will be done,
  and light will shine on your ways.

The Absence of Justice

> [29]When men are brought low and you say, 'Lift them up!'
>   then he will save the downcast.
> [30]He will deliver even one who is not innocent,
>   who will be delivered through the cleanness of your hands."

ELIPHAZ: Let go and let God have his way. If you will repent, he will reward you with peace and prosperity.

Eliphaz makes one last appeal to Job with evangelistic fervor. But the righteousness he advocates is righteousness for reward, exactly the kind of righteousness that Satan accused Job of practicing. (Ch 1:1-11) The gospel he preaches is a prosperity gospel (v 21). He also subscribes to historicism or the cause-effect relationship. Note his list. He has his own four laws.

Cause	**Effect**
Submit, be at peace with him.	Prosperity will come to you. (v 21)
Return to the Almighty.	You will be restored. (v 23)
Remove wickedness far from you.	God will be your gold. (vs 23-25)
Give up your focus on the material. (v 24)	He will hear your prayer. (v 27)
	Light will shine on your ways. (v 28)
	You will have a ministry to others. (v 30)

Although his appeal was surely sincere, Eliphaz was sincerely wrong. He was appealing to the wrong man. It had already been proven that Job's motivation to righteousness was for righteousness' sake alone, not for gain or ease. So Eliphaz's carrot of reward in exchange for repentance would have no appeal to Job.

> **Job 23:1-7 Then Job replied:**
> [2]"Even today my complaint is bitter;
>   his hand is heavy in spite of my groaning.
> [3]If only I knew where to find him;
>   if only I could go to his dwelling!
> [4]I would state my case before him
>   and fill my mouth with arguments.
> [5]I would find out what he would answer me,
>   and consider what he would say.
> [6]Would he oppose me with great power?
>   No, he would not press charges against me.
> [7]There an upright man could present his case before him,
>   and I would be delivered forever from my judge.

JOB: If only I could find God to present my case to him.

Job complains that his friends are attributing rebellion against God to his complaint. Now Job is proceeding to the presentation of his case, first mentioned in 13:8, and actually presented in Chapters 29, 30, and 31. He yearns to approach God with the questions in his heart. His faith is secure that God will listen to him and deliver him.

Job 23:8-17 "But if I go to the east, he is not there;
if I go to the west, I do not find him.
⁹When he is at work in the north, I do not see him;
when he turns to the south, I catch no glimpse of him.
¹⁰But he knows the way that I take;
when he has tested me, I will come forth as gold.
¹¹My feet have closely followed his steps;
I have kept to his way without turning aside.
¹²I have not departed from the commands of his lips;
I have treasured the words of his mouth more than
my daily bread.
¹³"But he stands alone, and who can oppose him?
He does whatever he pleases.
¹⁴He carries out his decree against me,
and many such plans he still has in store.
¹⁵That is why I am terrified before him;
when I think of all this, I fear him.
¹⁶God has made my heart faint;
the Almighty has terrified me.
¹⁷Yet I am not silenced by the darkness,
by the thick darkness that covers my face.

JOB: Although I can't see him, I believe he sees me. I recognize this as a refining process.

Although Job recognizes that good can come from suffering (v 10), he obviously is not satisfied that the end results justify the means—even for God. Job expects God to play according to his own rules, which is reasonable since God's rules are an expression of his essence. While Job could clearly see the benefits derived through suffering (Rom. 5:3, KJV - "Tribulation worketh patience."), he could not accept the end result, though good, as explanation and justification for the evil he was experiencing. God does not do evil to achieve good. Yet, I believe Job recognizes here that God can enter a bad situation and turn it around, salvaging good from it. And it is true that while man was committing the most heinous crime since creation when crucifying the Son of God, God was busy turning it around, working out of it the plan of salvation for mankind.

David went through a similar experience, which he describes in the Psalms:

Psalm 13:1-2 How long, O LORD? Will you forget me forever?
How long will you hide your face from me?
²How long must I wrestle with my thoughts

The Absence of Justice

and every day have sorrow in my heart?
How long will my enemy triumph over me?

    I believe that Job's faith was growing through this experience. From the bottom of his misery came this wonderful testimony of faith. Hebrews 11:1 defines faith as "the assurance of things hoped for, the conviction of things not seen." Job could not find God no matter how he tried. But he had gained the assurance that God knew where he was and that when this was over, he would somehow "come forth as gold." James 2:20 says, "Faith without works is useless," so Job's faith had also produced works and a value system that put God's word above physical food (vs 11-12). Next, Job expressed his feeling of helplessness before God. His attitude in verse 14 almost sounds fatalistic, but if Job were a true fatalist, he would have been resigned to his situation. Verse 17 shows that Job was not resigned to the darkness that covered him, although he experienced dismay and terror at the thought of the very presence of God.

Job 24:1-17 "Why does the Almighty not set times for judgment?
    Why must those who know him look in vain for such days?
²Men move boundary stones;
    they pasture flocks they have stolen.
³They drive away the orphan's donkey
    and take the widow's ox in pledge.
⁴They thrust the needy from the path
    and force all the poor of the land into hiding.
⁵Like wild donkeys in the desert,
    the poor go about their labor of foraging food;
    the wasteland provides food for their children.
⁶They gather fodder in the fields
    and glean in the vineyards of the wicked.
⁷Lacking clothes, they spend the night naked;
    they have nothing to cover themselves in the cold.
⁸They are drenched by mountain rains
    and hug the rocks for lack of shelter.
⁹The fatherless child is snatched from the breast;
    the infant of the poor is seized for a debt.
¹⁰Lacking clothes, they go about naked;
    they carry the sheaves, but still go hungry.
¹¹They crush olives among the terraces;
    they tread the winepresses, yet suffer thirst.
¹²The groans of the dying rise from the city,
    and the souls of the wounded cry out for help.
    But God charges no one with wrongdoing.
¹³"There are those who rebel against the light,
    who do not know its ways
    or stay in its paths.
¹⁴When daylight is gone, the murderer rises up

Dialogues, Round 3

    and kills the poor and needy;
    in the night he steals forth like a thief.
¹⁵The eye of the adulterer watches for dusk;
    he thinks, 'No eye will see me,'
    and he keeps his face concealed.
¹⁶In the dark, men break into houses,
    but by day they shut themselves in;
    they want nothing to do with the light.
¹⁷For all of them, deep darkness is their morning;
    they make friends with the terrors of darkness.
(Verses 18 through 24 are a part of Zophar's last speech.)
    Job 24:25 "If this is not so, who can prove me false
    and reduce my words to nothing?"

JOB: If there is justice on the earth as you say, how do you account for all the injustice that we all can see everywhere we look? The righteous <u>do</u> suffer!

Job deals with the two prongs of the friends' position separately. He dealt with the thesis "the wicked suffer" in Chapter 21 and presented evidence to the contrary. Now he deals with the thesis "the innocent prosper" with evidence to the contrary. The chapter is filled with instances of victimization of the innocent by the wicked and their arrogance as they do it:

1. The wicked move boundary stones. (v 2)
2. They pasture flocks they have stolen. (v 2)
3. They drive away the orphan's donkey. (v 3)
4. They take the widow's ox as collateral. (v 3)
5. They thrust the needy from the path. (v 4)
6. They force the poor into hiding, foraging for food like wild animals. (vs 4-5)
7. They deprive the poor of clothing and shelter. (v 7-8)
8. They conscript babies and infants as payment for debts. (v 9)
9. They force the poor to work for insufficient pay to buy food. (vs 10-11)
10. The groans of the wounded and dying cry out to no avail. (v 12)
11. At night, the murderers, thieves, burglars, and adulterers go about their business unhindered. (vs 14-17)

Job ends the list with another challenge: "If this is not so, who can prove me false?"

Job would have vehemently disagreed with David when he said:

    Psalm 37:25 I was young and now I am old,
        yet I have never seen the righteous forsaken
        or their children begging bread.

As a child in elementary school, Alan Dershowitz recited this Psalm several times a day as a part of the prayer after meals. He recalls "raising questions in

The Absence of Justice

class about what these perplexing words could possibly mean. Surely they did not accurately describe reality. The remnants of the Holocaust were all around me—classmates with numbers tattooed on their arms, teachers who had lost entire families, friends who had experienced the displaced persons camps. Righteous people *had* been abandoned and their children left wanting." His yeshiva rabbis made heroic efforts to explain the passage, but all the explanations fell short as did those of Eliphaz, Bildad, and Zophar. Dershowitz finally concluded that "To my mind, the best and simplest explanation is that the passage is wrong. It is pretty poetry but ugly philosophy. There is in fact no relationship between righteousness and good fortune, or unrighteousness and bad fortune. If there was ever doubt about this sad reality, (it) was permanently erased by the Holocaust."[2] This psalm illustrates clearly that Psalms and Proverbs often describe the way things *ought to be* while Ecclesiastes and Job describe how things *are*.

> **Job 25:1-6 Then Bildad the Shuhite replied:**
> **[2]"Dominion and awe belong to God;**
> **he establishes order in the heights of heaven.**
> **[3]Can his forces be numbered?**
> **Upon whom does his light not rise?**
> **[4]How then can a man be righteous before God?**
> **How can one born of woman be pure?**
> **[5]If even the moon is not bright**
> **and the stars are not pure in his eyes,**
> **[6]how much less man, who is but a maggot—**
> **a son of man, who is only a worm!"**

BILDAD: Job, can't you see how arrogant you are? The moon and the stars are not pure, and men are worth less than they.

Bildad is preaching the error of piety through debasement. Some folks like Bildad think that there is virtue in running themselves down. (Although here he is busy trying to run Job down). They think to denigrate is to humble. While it may be true that man seems insignificant before the glory and majesty of God, we cannot ignore the fact that man is the crowning glory of God's creation. Bildad may have felt like David in:

> **Psalm 8:3-4 When I consider your heavens,**
> **the work of your fingers,**
> **the moon and the stars,**
> **which you have set in place,**
> **[4]what is man that you are mindful of him,**
> **the son of man that you care for him?**

But Bildad did not go far enough:

> **Psalm 8:5-6 You made him a little lower than the**

Dialogues, Round 3

>   heavenly beings
>   and crowned him with glory and honor.
> ⁶You made him ruler over the works of your hands;
>   you put everything under his feet:

In the light of this passage, Bildad has a very low opinion of man's humanity when he calls Job a maggot and a worm. In a sense, his attitude is an insult to God. **"God doesn't make junk!"**

>   **Job 26:1-4** Then Job replied:
> ²"How you have helped the powerless!
>   How you have saved the arm that is feeble!
> ³What advice you have offered to one without wisdom!
>   And what great insight you have displayed!
> ⁴Who has helped you utter these words?
>   And whose spirit spoke from your mouth?

JOB: (Sarcastically) Your speeches are really great! Where did you get this stuff?

Job shows his extreme frustration by replying with biting sarcasm. Verse 4 contains a very obvious insinuation: ". . . whose spirit spoke from your mouth?" Job implies that the spirit speaking through Bildad was certainly not God's spirit.

>   **Job 26:5-14** "The dead are in deep anguish,
>   those beneath the waters and all that live in them.
> ⁶Death is naked before God;
>   Destruction lies uncovered.
> ⁷He spreads out the northern skies over empty space;
>   he suspends the earth over nothing.
> ⁸He wraps up the waters in his clouds,
>   yet the clouds do not burst under their weight.
> ⁹He covers the face of the full moon,
>   spreading his clouds over it.
> ¹⁰He marks out the horizon on the face of the waters
>   for a boundary between light and darkness.
> ¹¹The pillars of the heavens quake,
>   aghast at his rebuke.
> ¹²By his power he churned up the sea;
>   by his wisdom he cut Rahab to pieces.
> ¹³By his breath the skies became fair;
>   his hand pierced the gliding serpent.
> ¹⁴And these are but the outer fringe of his works;
>   how faint the whisper we hear of him!
>   Who then can understand the thunder of his power?"

The Absence of Justice

JOB: Sure, I know how great God is, and I know that man knows only a fraction about him.

Bildad has tried to instruct Job on the majesty and splendor of God. But now Job has taken the floor and is instructing his friends on the same subject. He begins with the underworld, the grave, and the place of destruction. All tremble and are open to God. Verse 7 contains an amazingly accurate scientific observation for that day. The concept that the earth is a ball spinning in space is a relatively recent discovery (or rediscovery). There are those who (whether in jest or in seriousness) still hold to the flat earth theory in spite of our photographs from space. The flat earth concept was seriously held by many folks just several hundred years ago. That Job should know that the earth is not supported or suspended in any way is remarkable. His God was great enough to suspend the earth where it is. He created the weather, the moon, the sea, and the heavens. And, he concludes, these are but the "fringe of his works."

>**Job 27:1-6** And Job continued his discourse:
>²"As surely as God lives, who has denied me justice,
>   the Almighty, who has made me taste bitterness of soul,
>³as long as I have life within me,
>   the breath of God in my nostrils,
>⁴my lips will not speak wickedness,
>   and my tongue will utter no deceit.
>⁵I will never admit you are in the right;
>   till I die, I will not deny my integrity.
>⁶I will maintain my righteousness and never let go of it;
>   my conscience will not reproach me as long as I live.

JOB: My conscience is clear. I will not admit I am wrong when I know I am not.

Job's claim to innocence now comes in the form of a bitter oath. He swears by the God who has afflicted him that he has maintained his integrity. To the others, this must surely sound like blasphemy. To them it is unthinkable that a just God could take away the right of an innocent man or embitter the soul of a righteous man. Yet Job identifies the God by whom he is swearing to be the one who has done just that. He declares that to confess sin he has not committed and declare his friends right would be to speak unjustly and deceitfully. Moreover, he commits himself to maintain this integrity tenaciously until he dies.

>**Job 27:7-12** "May my enemies be like the wicked,
>   my adversaries like the unjust!
>⁸For what hope has the godless when he is cut off,

Dialogues, Round 3

> when God takes away his life?
> ⁹Does God listen to his cry
> when distress comes upon him?
> ¹⁰Will he find delight in the Almighty?
> Will he call upon God at all times?
> ¹¹"I will teach you about the power of God;
> the ways of the Almighty I will not conceal.
> ¹²You have all seen this yourselves.
> Why then this meaningless talk?

JOB: I know I am right and that makes you wrong, wicked, and godless.

Job now turns his friends' own arguments against them. He declares his friends to be his enemies. He asks what their hope will be when they are cut off. Will God hear their cries when calamities come to them?

> Job 27:13 "Here is the fate God allots to the wicked,
> the heritage a ruthless man receives from the Almighty:

ZOPHAR: I still maintain that the wicked receive judgment from a just God.

> Job 24:18-24 "Yet they are foam on the surface of the water;
> their portion of the land is cursed, so that no one goes
> to the vineyards.
> ¹⁹As heat and drought snatch away the melted snow,
> so the grave snatches away those who have sinned.
> ²⁰The womb forgets them,
> the worm feasts on them;
> evil men are no longer remembered
> but are broken like a tree.
> ²¹They prey on the barren and childless woman,
> and to the widow show no kindness.
> ²²But God drags away the mighty by his power;
> though they become established, they have no assurance of life.
> ²³He may let them rest in a feeling of security,
> but his eyes are on their ways.
> ²⁴For a little while they are exalted, and then they are gone;
> they are brought low and gathered up like all others;
> they are cut off like heads of grain.
>
> Job 27:14-23 However many his children,
> their fate is the sword;
> his offspring will never have enough to eat.
> ¹⁵The plague will bury those who survive him,

and their widows will not weep for them.
¹⁶Though he heaps up silver like dust
and clothes like piles of clay,
¹⁷what he lays up the righteous will wear,
and the innocent will divide his silver.
¹⁸The house he builds is like a moth's cocoon,
like a hut made by a watchman.
¹⁹He lies down wealthy, but will do so no more;
when he opens his eyes, all is gone.
²⁰Terrors overtake him like a flood;
a tempest snatches him away in the night.
²¹The east wind carries him off, and he is gone;
it sweeps him out of his place.
²²It hurls itself against him without mercy
as he flees headlong from its power.
²³It claps its hands in derision
and hisses him out of his place.

ZOPHAR: I still say that God's judgment comes quickly to the wicked.

Zophar will not move from the established position of the friends. He lists the calamities a wicked man should expect. Since Job has experienced many of these things, the conclusion is that Job is very wicked.

1. Their land is cursed. (24:18)
2. The grave snatches them away. (24:19)
3. They are forgotten. (24:20)
4. They are cruel to the childless and widows. (24:21)
5. They have no security. (24:22)
6. Though they prosper, they are cut off quickly. (24:23-24)
7. His children will starve and die violent deaths. (27:14)
8. They will not be mourned and their survivors will suffer. (27:15)
9. His treasure will be enjoyed by the righteous and innocent. (27:16-17)
10. He lies down wealthy and wakes up poor. (27:19)
11. He is plagued by terrors and calamities. (27:20-23)

In reality, the above list describes the experiences of the victims rather than the experiences of the wicked. The list is, in fact, a graphic description of what happened to the victims of the Holocaust.

At this point, all the participants are exhausted and angry, so the dialogues cease.

1. Dhorme, Edouard. *A Commentary on the Book of Job*. Translated by Harold Knight. Nashville: Thomas Nelson, 1984.
2. Dershowitz, Alan M. *Chutzpah*. Boston: Little, Brown & Co., 1991. p. 131-32

CHAPTER 7

THE WISDOM CHAPTER

The presence of Chapter 28 at this place in Job is puzzling to say the least. Some commentators think it is out of place since it is incompatible with what comes before and after. Some have suggested that it was added later. Andersen[1] considers it an interlude between the answers to the friends and Job's statement of his case before God.

To attribute this chapter to either Job or one of his friends does not really make sense. At this point, all the participants of the dialogues are far too hysterical. The tone of this poem is much too serene to come from any of them. If any of the debaters did give this speech, it would be Job, saying as a finale to the dialogues, "With all that man knows, he doesn't know where to find wisdom and understanding. It has a greater value than anything else. However, God has given this gift to man. The fear of the Lord is wisdom and to shun evil is understanding." After all the arguments we have just heard, perhaps this chapter is divinely placed here to cool the situation down and stimulate contemplation about what true wisdom is. Eliphaz, Bildad, and Zophar didn't have it as we have seen. And even Job, when confronted by God, will more fully understand how little he knows.

A study of the subject of wisdom would include the passages in Proverbs where wisdom is personified along with the references to logos in John 1.

**Job 28:1-28 "There is a mine for silver
and a place where gold is refined.
²Iron is taken from the earth,
and copper is smelted from ore.
³Man puts an end to the darkness;
he searches the farthest recesses
for ore in the blackest darkness.
⁴Far from where people dwell he cuts a shaft,
in places forgotten by the foot of man;
far from men he dangles and sways.
⁵The earth, from which food comes,
is transformed below as by fire;
⁶sapphires come from its rocks,
and its dust contains nuggets of gold.
⁷No bird of prey knows that hidden path,
no falcon's eye has seen it.**

The Absence of Justice

⁸Proud beasts do not set foot on it,
    and no lion prowls there.
⁹Man's hand assaults the flinty rock
    and lays bare the roots of the mountains.
¹⁰He tunnels through the rock;
    his eyes see all its treasures.
¹¹He searches the sources of the rivers
    and brings hidden things to light.
¹²"But where can wisdom be found?
    Where does understanding dwell?
¹³Man does not comprehend its worth;
    it cannot be found in the land of the living.
¹⁴The deep says, 'It is not in me';
    the sea says, 'It is not with me.'
¹⁵It cannot be bought with the finest gold,
    nor can its price be weighed in silver.
¹⁶It cannot be bought with the gold of Ophir,
    with precious onyx or sapphires.
¹⁷Neither gold nor crystal can compare with it,
    nor can it be had for jewels of gold.
¹⁸Coral and jasper are not worthy of mention;
    the price of wisdom is beyond rubies.
¹⁹The topaz of Cush cannot compare with it;
    it cannot be bought with pure gold.
²⁰"Where then does wisdom come from?
    Where does understanding dwell?
²¹It is hidden from the eyes of every living thing,
    concealed even from the birds of the air.
²²Destruction and Death say,
    'Only a rumor of it ached our ears.'
²³God understands the way to it
    and he alone knows where it dwells,
²⁴for he views the ends of the earth
    and sees everything under the heavens.
²⁵When he established the force of the wind
    and measured out the waters,
²⁶when he made a decree for the rain
    and a path for the thunderstorm,
²⁷then he looked at wisdom and appraised it;
    he confirmed it and tested it.
²⁸And he said to man,
    'The fear of the Lord — that is wisdom,
    and to shun evil is understanding.'"

Verses 1-14 describe the achievements that man has attained without finding wisdom. The science of mining and metallurgy probably represented the greatest engineering feats of that era. In fact, ancient mining skills were quite advanced, considering the equipment and instruments available. The impli-

The Wisdom Chapter

cation here is that the true source of wisdom cannot be found through technology.

Verses 15-19 state that wisdom cannot be bought. The most precious things on earth are not sufficient price to buy wisdom. Proverbs 8:11 says "...wisdom is more precious than rubies, and nothing you desire can compare with her." Wisdom cannot be acquired through materialism or wealth.

Verses 20-28 describe where wisdom can be found. God alone knows where it dwells (v 23). Verses 25-27 indicate that wisdom existed before creation. Proverbs 8:22-23 says, "The Lord possessed me at the beginning of his work, before his deeds of old; I was appointed from eternity, from the beginning, before the world began."

Verse 28 concludes the chapter, indicating that God had given to man the pathway to wisdom through fear of him, and that the key to understanding is to shun evil.

Certainly these principles apply to Job and the situation we have been observing. The ideas given in this chapter are not out of place, but they don't exactly fit the flow of the story either.

1. Andersen, Francis I. *Job.* London: Inter-Varsity Press, 1976. p. 222

CHAPTER 8

JOB PRESENTS HIS CASE TO GOD

At this point, Job gives up on his friends and turns his attention exclusively to God. In effect, he sues God for an answer. Job has already stated that he would not be surprised if he were to be killed for the impertinence of demanding an answer from God. Yet he also stated that his only hope was that he was innocent. His hope is the same as stated by Jeremiah in:

> **Lamentations 3:33-36 For he does not willingly bring affliction or grief to the children of men.**
> [34]**To crush underfoot all prisoners in the land,**
> [35]**to deny a man his rights before the Most High,**
> [36]**to deprive a man of justice— would not the Lord see such things?**

The NAS renders verse 36, "To defraud a man in his lawsuit—Of these things the Lord does not approve." This interpretation is significant in Job's situation.

JOB QUESTIONS GOD

Job follows an ancient court procedure, a question and answer process, first the prosecution, then the defense. Chapters 29, 30, and 31 are the case for the prosecution. God will present his case in the questions of Chapters 38 through 41. We will see that Job presents the way things *were* in Chapter 29. He presents the way things *are* in Chapter 30. In Chapter 31, Job lists all the iniquities he can think of that could possibly merit such suffering and declares himself innocent of each of them. Job's question addressed to God is: "I am innocent and should be receiving justice. But I am not. Why not?" It should be noted that Job lists many sins that we, in our culture, would consider insignificant or minor, or would even be justified as good business. Obviously, Job had a highly developed conscience.

The Book of Job gives us the most thorough picture of a righteous person in the whole Bible. Chapter 29 gives us a comprehensive list of the things a righteous person does. Chapter 31 gives us a list of the things a righteous person does not do.

Job Presents His Case to God

These three chapters demonstrate many characteristics that are typical for any suffering person. Whenever we hurt, it is natural for us to become very self-centered. This is evident in Job's presentation where we find that he uses the personal pronouns I, me, my, myself a total of one hundred seventy-two times. For some, this is evidence for convicting Job of evil self-righteousness. Pain normally prompts serious introspection and Job was no exception. The depth of his introspection and accompanying self-centeredness is proportional to the depth of his suffering but is no indicator of his guilt.

THE WAY THINGS WERE

Job 29:1-6 Job continued his discourse:
²"How I long for the months gone by,
  for the days when God watched over me,
³when his lamp shone upon my head
  and by his light I walked through darkness!
⁴Oh, for the days when I was in my prime,
  when God's intimate friendship blessed my house,
⁵when the Almighty was still with me
  and my children were around me,
⁶when my path was drenched with cream
  and the rock poured out for me streams of olive oil.

JOB: Oh, how I long for the good old days!

We may laugh at the thought of the good old days, but for Job this wasn't a joke. If anyone ever had a right to wish for the days gone by, it was Job. But note what it was that he missed most about the good old days. It was the close relationship with God that he had enjoyed, but now felt was absent. What he yearned for was God's intimate friendship expressed through:

1. God's watch-care over him. (v 2)
2. God's illumination on his life. (v 3)
3. God's intimate friendship. (v 4)
4. God's presence. (v 5)

Only after mentioning this fourfold blessing of God that he had enjoyed does Job mention his bereaved children, and then the opulent life he had enjoyed.

Job 29:7-17 "When I went to the gate of the city
  and took my seat in the public square,
⁸the young men saw me and stepped aside
  and the old men rose to their feet;
⁹the chief men refrained from speaking
  and covered their mouths with their hands;

The Absence of Justice

>¹⁰the voices of the nobles were hushed,
>   and their tongues stuck to the roof of their mouths.
>¹¹Whoever heard me spoke well of me,
>   and those who saw me commended me,
>¹²because I rescued the poor who cried for help,
>   and the fatherless who had none to assist him.
>¹³The man who was dying blessed me;
>   I made the widow's heart sing.
>¹⁴I put on righteousness as my clothing;
>   justice was my robe and my turban.
>¹⁵I was eyes to the blind
>   and feet to the lame.
>¹⁶I was a father to the needy;
>   I took up the case of the stranger.
>¹⁷I broke the fangs of the wicked
>   and snatched the victims from their teeth.

JOB: I was honored and respected by all men because I was a helper and protector of the suffering, the poor, and needy.

Job was indeed honored and respected. When he took his place in the gate of the city where all the notables gathered, he was treated with deference by all, both young and old. In a culture that honored age and its accompanying wisdom, even old men rose to their feet in his presence and the chief men deferred to Job by keeping silence. (Vs 8-10) This would mean that Job was treated as a king, which he probably was, as indicated in verse 25.

He goes on in verses 11 through 17 to state that he was commended and honored because of his humanitarianism. His benevolence extended to fighting for the rights of the poor and rescuing them from the power of the wicked.

>Job 29:18-20 "I thought, 'I will die in my own house,
>   my days as numerous as the grains of sand.
>¹⁹My roots will reach to the water,
>   and the dew will lie all night on my branches.
>²⁰My glory will remain fresh in me,
>   the bow ever new in my hand.'

JOB: I expected to live a peaceful, prosperous, vigorous, long life.

Job still believes that his righteousness and altruism entitle him to justice in this life. Although he has argued with his friends who propounded this doctrine and proved that justice is not evident on the earth, he still evidently believes that it ought to be. Therefore, his question to God is (by inference), "Why not?"

Job Presents His Case to God

> **Job 29:21-25** "Men listened to me expectantly,
>   waiting in silence for my counsel.
> ²²After I had spoken, they spoke no more;
>   my words fell gently on their ears.
> ²³They waited for me as for showers
>   and drank in my words as the spring rain.
> ²⁴When I smiled at them, they scarcely believed it;
>   the light of my face was precious to them.
> ²⁵I chose the way for them and sat as their chief;
>   I dwelt as a king among his troops;
>   I was like one who comforts mourners.

JOB: I was honored above all men.

Job continues his nostalgic mood by reminiscing again about how men had treated him with great respect and had followed his leading.

THE WAY THINGS ARE

> **Job 30:1-8** "But now they mock me,
>   men younger than I,
> whose fathers I would have disdained
>   to put with my sheep dogs.
> ²Of what use was the strength of their hands to me,
>   since their vigor had gone from them?
> ³Haggard from want and hunger,
>   they roamed the parched land
>   in desolate wastelands at night.
> ⁴In the brush they gathered salt herbs,
>   and their food was the root of the broom tree.
> ⁵They were banished from their fellow men,
>   shouted at as if they were thieves.
> ⁶They were forced to live in the dry stream beds,
>   among the rocks and in holes in the ground.
> ⁷They brayed among the bushes
>   and huddled in the undergrowth.
> ⁸A base and nameless brood,
>   they were driven out of the land.

JOB: Now look at me! The outcasts and dregs of society mock me without restraint.

In Chapter 30, Job moves from the nostalgia of the good old days (Ch 29) to the stark reality of the grim present. He complains that the "base and nameless brood" (v 8) now mock him with impunity. Verses 3 through 7 describe the worthless lot as hungry vagabonds, ostracized by society. They are the personification of depravity, living like animals. But now they consider Job

The Absence of Justice

lower than they and delight in tormenting this righteous, suffering, helpless man. Humiliation is always hard to bear, but such humiliation is unimaginably horrible to one who had known such honor and prestige. To top it all off, Job believes that God is responsible for this and the meaning behind it all is hidden to him.

> Job 30:9-15 "And now their sons mock me in song;
>   I have become a byword among them.
> [10]They detest me and keep their distance;
>   they do not hesitate to spit in my face.
> [11]Now that God has unstrung my bow and afflicted me,
>   they throw off restraint in my presence.
> [12]On my right the tribe attacks;
>   they lay snares for my feet,
>   they build their siege ramps against me.
> [13]They break up my road;
>   they succeed in destroying me—
>   without anyone's helping them.
> [14]They advance as through a gaping breach;
>   amid the ruins they come rolling in.
> [15]Terrors overwhelm me;
>   my dignity is driven away as by the wind,
>   my safety vanishes like a cloud.

JOB: The offspring of this wretched brood mock me and spit at me. They are terrorizing me and I have neither dignity nor safety.

One can hardly imagine the insults and indignities that this poor man suffers as these ragamuffins, children of the scum of society, singsong their mockery of him as they dodge in and out, seeing which ones are bold enough to get close enough to spit in his face. It is hard to imagine that a few short weeks before, these delinquents would not have dared to venture anywhere near Job. Instead, they would probably have been recipients of Job's largesse, since Job customarily helped the poor and needy. Now they mock him and take advantage of his misfortune. Who could refrain from becoming extremely bitter under such circumstances? But in all this we are told that Job did not sin.

> Job 30:16-23 "And now my life ebbs away;
>   days of suffering grip me.
> [17]Night pierces my bones;
>   my gnawing pains never rest.
> [18]In his great power God becomes like clothing to me;
>   he binds me like the neck of my garment.
> [19]He throws me into the mud,
>   and I am reduced to dust and ashes.
> [20]"I cry out to you, O God, but you do not answer;
>   I stand up, but you merely look at me.

Job Presents His Case to God

> ²¹You turn on me ruthlessly;
>   with the might of your hand you attack me.
> ²²You snatch me up and drive me before the wind;
>   you toss me about in the storm.
> ²³I know you will bring me down to death,
>   to the place appointed for all the living.

JOB: God is beating the life out of me! I cry out to God, but he ignores my pleas. With cruelty he attacks and tortures me to the point of death.

Job now turns from his social disgrace to his physical pain. Pain has a way of commanding one's attention. C. S. Lewis said, "God whispers to us in our pleasures, speaks in our conscience, but shouts in our pains: it is His megaphone to rouse a deaf world."[1] God certainly has Job's attention but Job is convinced that God is *not* paying attention. Job feels his life ebbing away as the days of suffering grind on and on. Nights are horribly long and pain pierces his bones. Along with the piercing pain, the gnawing pain continues unabated. The Septuagint renders verse 18 "God grasps my clothing." What Job feels is nothing less than abandonment and unmitigated cruelty as he charges God with the responsibility for his suffering in verse 21. Job's strong assertion that God is being cruel to him is difficult to accept in the light of 42:7-8, where God declares Job's statements right. Yet what else could Job's treatment be called? It was certainly no Sunday School picnic. Therefore God himself agrees that what Job is experiencing is cruel.

If God had not made this point clear in 42:7-8, we would surely condemn Job for making such statements. Despondency and depression can have many causes—physical, emotional, and spiritual. There are those who see depression as evidence of spiritual deficiency. But here we see a spiritual giant, declared so by God, so depressed that he is uttering shocking words against the God he loves. The cause for Job is not spiritual deficiency; the cause here is physical pain, emotional drain, grief, and behind it all, satanic oppression. The antidote for Job's problem is not that he should get right spiritually as his comforters insist. We will find the remedy when God replies.

> **Job 30:24-31** "Surely no one lays a hand on a broken man
>   when he cries for help in his distress.
> ²⁵Have I not wept for those in trouble?
>   Has not my soul grieved for the poor?
> ²⁶Yet when I hoped for good, evil came;
>   when I looked for light, then came darkness.
> ²⁷The churning inside me never stops;
>   days of suffering confront me.
> ²⁸I go about blackened, but not by the sun;
>   I stand up in the assembly and cry for help.
> ²⁹I have become a brother of jackals,

The Absence of Justice

> a companion of owls.
> ³⁰My skin grows black and peels;
>   my body burns with fever.
> ³¹My harp is tuned to mourning,
>   and my flute to the sound of wailing.

JOB: It is not right to kick a man when he's down. But I am getting the opposite from what I gave to others. My skin turns black and peels. I am burning up with fever. I am suffering from depression.

Job feels doubly afflicted. He is down and still being kicked. He has always shown compassion to the troubled and the poor. Now that it has come to him, there is no comforter. Even God is strangely silent. These circumstances are causing an emotional churning inside him that never stops (v 27).

He gives more symptoms of his illness: blackened skin that peels, burning fever, and a depressed state of mind that portends nothing but mourning and wailing for him in the future.

JOB (implied): God, in the light of how things were contrasted with how things are, here is my defense!

Many of Job's defenses in chapter 31 take the form of what is called a "negative confession."[2] It takes the form of "If I have committed such and such a sin, then let such and such a calamity overtake me." A more modern version would be the "cross my heart, I hope to die" that we used as children for proof that we were telling the truth. The idea was that if we did not die, that was proof that we were telling the truth.

Job now proceeds to list all the sins he can think of that warrant the treatment he has received. He declares himself innocent of all of them.

JOB'S PLEA

JOB: Here is a list of sins that should earn punishment.

> Job 31:1-4 "I made a covenant with my eyes
>   not to look lustfully at a girl.
> ²For what is man's lot from God above,
>   his heritage from the Almighty on high?
> ³Is it not ruin for the wicked,
>   disaster for those who do wrong?
> ⁴Does he not see my ways
>   and count my every step?

Job Presents His Case to God

LUST..........Not guilty!

Job had recognized that the sin of adultery begins with a lustful gaze. Therefore, to avoid such temptation from the start, he had exercised discipline by making a covenant with his eyes not to take that second look.

He injects an argument from the philosophy he and his friends had held which states that since God sees everything a man does, and sends disaster and calamity to the wicked, then it is unreasonable that a thinking man would so defy God.

> **Job 31:5-6** "If I have walked in falsehood
> or my foot has hurried after deceit—
> [6] let God weigh me in honest scales
> and he will know that I am blameless—

LYING OR DECEIT.........Not guilty!

Justice is portrayed by the artist as a blindfolded lady with a balance scale in her hand. Job understands this concept and is willing to be examined on honest scales.

> **Job 31:7-8** if my steps have turned from the path,
> if my heart has been led by my eyes,
> or if my hands have been defiled,
> [8] then may others eat what I have sown,
> and may my crops be uprooted.

DISHONESTY.........Not guilty!

Job denies the sins of dishonesty and carries them to the source, which is covetousness. He is not a thief. He has not desired, then taken. If so, let others consume his produce and destroy his crops.

> **Job 31:9-12** "If my heart has been enticed by a woman,
> or if I have lurked at my neighbor's door,
> [10] then may my wife grind another man's grain,
> and may other men sleep with her.
> [11] For that would have been shameful,
> a sin to be judged.
> [12] It is a fire that burns to Destruction;
> it would have uprooted my harvest.

ADULTERY..........Not guilty!

For a man who can make the statements made in verses 1 through 4, it is not surprising that he can also make this claim. He has neither succumbed to a strange woman's seduction, nor even coveted his neighbor's wife. If he had, he would be willing to see his wife go into slavery to another man, as a servant and a prostitute. Job goes on to declare that such behavior "is a fire that burns to Destruction" and it would have destroyed his wealth.

> Job 31:13-15 "If I have denied justice
> to my menservants and maidservants when
> they had a grievance against me,
> ¹⁴what will I do when God confronts me?
> What will I answer when called to account?
> ¹⁵Did not he who made me in the womb make them?
> Did not the same one form us both within our mothers?

INJUSTICE TOWARD MY SERVANTS..........Not guilty!

This incredible confession anticipates the prayer Jesus would teach his disciples in Matthew 6:12, "Forgive us our debts, as we also have forgiven our debtors." If Job had been unjust with his servants, he would have no right to answer when God speaks. His attitude toward his servants again shows him to be a remarkable man. He recognizes that, under God, "all men are created equal."

> Job 31:16-23 "If I have denied the desires of the poor
> or let the eyes of the widow grow weary,
> ¹⁷if I have kept my bread to myself,
> not sharing it with the fatherless—
> ¹⁸but from my youth I reared him as would a father,
> and from my birth I guided the widow—
> ¹⁹if I have seen anyone perishing for lack of clothing,
> or a needy man without a garment,
> ²⁰and his heart did not bless me
> for warming him with the fleece from my sheep,
> ²¹if I have raised my hand against the fatherless,
> knowing that I had influence in court,
> ²²then let my arm fall from the shoulder,
> let it be broken off at the joint.
> ²³For I dreaded destruction from God,
> and for fear of his splendor I could not do such things.

INDIFFERENCE TO THE LESS FORTUNATE ....Not guilty!

Job covers a lot of ground with this one. He covers the poor, the widowed, the fatherless, and the naked. He declares that he has never declined to help any of them in their distress. Who of us could say that? And if this statement is false, then let his arm fall off at the shoulder because the dread of God's destruction would have been upon him.

Job Presents His Case to God

> **Job 31:24-25** "If I have put my trust in gold
> or said to pure gold, 'You are my security,'
> ^{25}if I have rejoiced over my great wealth,
> the fortune my hands had gained,

GREED..........Not guilty!

Job certainly had been in a position to trust in his wealth. He was the greatest man in the east according to 1:3. But his trust was in God, and now God seems to have abandoned him.

> **Job 31:26-28** ...if I have regarded the sun in its radiance
> or the moon moving in splendor,
> ^{27}so that my heart was secretly enticed
> and my hand offered them a kiss of homage,
> ^{28}then these also would be sins to be judged,
> for I would have been unfaithful to God on high.

IDOLATRY..........Not guilty!

Sun and moon worship were common in the ancient world. These two heavenly bodies inspired whole cultures to idolatrous worship, but not Job. Even in the scientific ignorance of his day, Job knew better. He recognized that to join in such practices would be unfaithful to the Creator God he worshiped.

> **Job 31:29-31** "If I have rejoiced at my enemy's misfortune
> or gloated over the trouble that came to him—
> ^{30}I have not allowed my mouth to sin
> by invoking a curse against his life—
> ^{31}if the men of my household have never said,
> 'Who has not had his fill of Job's meat?'—

VINDICTIVENESS..........Not guilty!

The New Testament teachings anticipated in The Book of Job are remarkable. Jesus said in Matthew 5:43-44, "You have heard that it was said, 'You shall love your neighbors, and hate your enemy.' But I say to you, love your enemies, and pray for those who persecute you." In this oldest book of the Bible, the principle of loving one's enemies is clearly presented. Subsequently men have distorted the concept. Jesus brings us back to the first principles which Job observed. Incidently, Job will be found praying for those who persecuted him before the end of the book (42:10). Job declares that he has not prayed that his enemy die, but he has extended his hospitality to him.

The Absence of Justice

> **Job 31:32** ...but no stranger had to spend the night in the street,
> for my door was always open to the traveler—

INHOSPITALITY..........Not guilty!

For a man so wealthy to routinely welcome strangers into his home is unusual to say the least. Job claims that no stranger ever had to spend the night in the street because Job's door was always open. This certainly involved some risk, but evidently Job's commitment to generosity and hospitality were such that he was willing to be vulnerable.

> **Job 31:33-34** ...if I have concealed my sin as men do,
>   by hiding my guilt in my heart
> ³⁴because I so feared the crowd
>   and so dreaded the contempt of the clans
>   that I kept silent and would not go outside...

HYPOCRISY..........Not guilty! I have maintained my integrity.

Job has not concealed his sin as Adam had. Everything he has done has been open and aboveboard.

> **Job 31:35-37** ("Oh, that I had someone to hear me!
>   I sign now my defense—let the Almighty answer me;
>   let my accuser put his indictment in writing.
> ³⁶Surely I would wear it on my shoulder,
>   I would put it on like a crown.
> ³⁷I would give him an account of my every step;
>   like a prince I would approach him.)

Signed: JOB

Job is willing to put his signature on all this. The indictment of his adversary (God) would be carried proudly into court. He is unabashed and adamant about his innocence. He is willing to approach God confidently bearing his indictment and also his defense.

> **Job 31:38-40** "if my land cries out against me
>   and all its furrows are wet with tears,
> ³⁹if I have devoured its yield without payment
>   or broken the spirit of its tenants,
> ⁴⁰then let briers come up instead of wheat

Job Presents His Case to God

**and weeds instead of barley."
The words of Job are ended.**

P.S. EXPLOITATION..........Not guilty!

Job even declares his innocence of impropriety against the earth itself as an afterthought. If he has used the land or its fruits unworthily or has acted in any way to the disadvantage of his tenants, then "let briars grow instead of wheat and stinkweed instead of barley." (v 40, NAS)

With this, Job rests his case.

1. Lewis, C. S. *The Problem of Pain.* New York: Macmillan, 1962. Chapter 6
2. Andersen, Francis I. *Job.* London: Inter-Varsity Press, 1976. p. 238

CHAPTER 9

ELIHU, THE BRASH YOUNG MAN

This section of the book, Chapters 32 through 37, is the subject of much conjecture. Expositors have not agreed about the speeches of Elihu. Some argue that this section was added later by some scribe who was not satisfied with the answers given elsewhere in the book. On the other hand, some writers attribute to Elihu's monologue the real answers to the problems that Job's sufferings present. I believe this is an insult to God. If the answer to the problem is in Elihu's speech, then God's answer is superfluous. That Elihu could give a better answer than God is unthinkable.

Since he is identified as a Buzite, he is possibly a descendant of Nahor's son Buz, who was a nephew to Abraham (Gen 22:21).

> **Job 32:1-5 So these three men stopped answering Job, because he was righteous in his own eyes. ²But Elihu son of Barakel the Buzite, of the family of Ram, became very angry with Job for justifying himself rather than God. ³He was also angry with the three friends, because they had found no way to refute Job, and yet had condemned him. ⁴Now Elihu had waited before speaking to Job because they were older than he. ⁵But when he saw that the three men had nothing more to say, his anger was aroused.**

Elihu introduces himself as an angry young man. In the first five verses of Chapter 32 his anger is mentioned three times. He was angry with Job because Job claimed to be just before God, and he was angry with the three friends because they had not been able to answer Job and yet condemned him.

He has observed the oriental custom of deferring to age. But while this young man waited, he didn't wait patiently. His anger was building up. Verse 5 says "his anger was aroused." The NAS says "his anger burned."

> **Job 32:6-10 So Elihu son of Barakel the Buzite said:**
> **"I am young in years,**
> **   and you are old;**
> **that is why I was fearful,**
> **   not daring to tell you what I know.**

Elihu, the Brash Young Man

> ⁷I thought, 'Age should speak;
>   advanced years should teach wisdom.'
> ⁸But it is the spirit in a man,
>   the breath of the Almighty, that gives him understanding.
> ⁹It is not only the old who are wise,
>   not only the aged who understand what is right.
> ¹⁰"Therefore I say: Listen to me;
>   I too will tell you what I know.

ELIHU: I thought age brought wisdom, but I see that is not necessarily true. Listen to me. I have the answer!

Elihu claims shyness as his reason for keeping quiet, but these chapters show him to be more arrogant than shy. He implies strongly that, although he is young, God has given him understanding. He states that age does not guarantee wisdom nor an understanding of justice. He shows his impertinence by declaring he will tell us what he thinks (v 10) and his opinion (v 17).

———

> Job 32:11-22 I waited while you spoke,
>   I listened to your reasoning;
>   while you were searching for words,
>   ¹²I gave you my full attention.
> But not one of you has proved Job wrong;
>   none of you has answered his arguments.
> ¹³Do not say, 'We have found wisdom;
>   let God refute him, not man.'
> ¹⁴But Job has not marshaled his words against me,
>   and I will not answer him with your arguments.
> ¹⁵"They are dismayed and have no more to say;
>   words have failed them.
> ¹⁶Must I wait, now that they are silent,
>   now that they stand there with no reply?
> ¹⁷I too will have my say;
>   I too will tell what I know.
> ¹⁸For I am full of words,
>   and the spirit within me compels me;
> ¹⁹inside I am like bottled-up wine,
>   like new wineskins ready to burst.
> ²⁰I must speak and find relief;
>   I must open my lips and reply.
> ²¹I will show partiality to no one,
>   nor will I flatter any man;
> ²²for if I were skilled in flattery,
>   my Maker would soon take me away.

ELIHU: I listened very closely to you and none of you has the answer. I have a better idea. You can't think of anything else to say, but I'm

The Absence of Justice

about to burst because I've got the answer!

Elihu gives himself away in verse 18, ("for I am full of words"). He makes no more true statement in his whole discourse. He asks permission to speak that he may get relief. In verse 22 he states that he doesn't know how to flatter. True enough. Neither he nor the three friends know how to use tact, although Eliphaz seemed to try. Elihu excuses himself from the obligation to be tactful because he feels flattery is wrong. This is a common misconception: Because there is virtue in telling the truth, then the more naked and blunt the telling, the more virtuous the teller. Elihu and the three friends are among those who glory in telling the whole naked truth (as they see it) no matter who gets hurt.

> **Job 33:1-7 "But now, Job, listen to my words;**
>   **pay attention to everything I say.**
> ²**I am about to open my mouth;**
>   **my words are on the tip of my tongue.**
> ³**My words come from an upright heart;**
>   **my lips sincerely speak what I know.**
> ⁴**The Spirit of God has made me;**
>   **the breath of the Almighty gives me life.**
> ⁵**Answer me then, if you can;**
>   **prepare yourself and confront me.**
> ⁶**I am just like you before God;**
>   **I too have been taken from clay.**
> ⁷**No fear of me should alarm you,**
>   **nor should my hand be heavy upon you.**

ELIHU: Job, from the bottom of my righteous heart, I want to help you. Don't be afraid of me.

Elihu now directs his attention to Job (although one can be sure that he spoke loud enough for all to hear). He tries to establish a common ground by stating that they are equal before God (but does he protest too much?).

Verse 7 sounds like wishful thinking. Why, after Job has stood up to Eliphaz, Bildad, and Zophar, should he be terrified of Elihu?

> **Job 33:8-12 "But you have said in my hearing—**
>   **I heard the very words—**
> ⁹**'I am pure and without sin;**
>   **I am clean and free from guilt.**
> ¹⁰**Yet God has found fault with me;**
>   **he considers me his enemy.**
> ¹¹**He fastens my feet in shackles;**
>   **he keeps close watch on all my paths.'**

Elihu, the Brash Young Man

> ^{12}"But I tell you, in this you are not right,
> for God is greater than man.

ELIHU: I've heard all that you have said, and you are wrong!

Elihu quotes Job, but he uses snatches of Job's discourses out of context, which puts Job in a bad light.

He quotes Job as saying, "I am pure and without sin," when in truth, the friends accused Job of making this statement. (Eliphaz in 4:17 & 15:14, Bildad in 8:6 & 25:4, and Zophar in 11:4) The nearest Job came to using these words was in 16:17 where he stated "...my prayer is pure." Yet Elihu asserts in verse 8 that he had "...heard the very words—"

He quotes Job as saying: "I am innocent...no guilt." (9:21, 10:7)
"He invents pretexts against me." (13:23-26)
"He counts me as his enemy." (13:24, 19:11)
"He puts my feet in the stocks and watches all my paths."(13:27)

Elihu is shocked and dismayed that Job would allegedly so elevate himself and so demean God. Had we been in the audience at this occasion, Elihu's remark in verse 12 would undoubtedly have elicited strong agreement.

However, God agrees with Job's assessment and his statements (in context); therefore, Elihu is the one who is wrong, as are the three friends. (42:7) So at the outset of Elihu's discourse, his position is established as being at variance with God's position—a fact that should give little comfort to those who claim that the answer to the problems in the book are found in Elihu's discourse.

> **Job 33:13-18 Why do you complain to him
> that he answers none of man's words?
> ^{14}For God does speak—now one way, now another—
> though man may not perceive it.
> ^{15}In a dream, in a vision of the night,
> when deep sleep falls on men
> as they slumber in their beds,
> ^{16}he may speak in their ears
> and terrify them with warnings,
> ^{17}to turn man from wrongdoing
> and keep him from pride,
> ^{18}to preserve his soul from the pit,
> his life from perishing by the sword.

ELIHU: You say God doesn't answer. He does, but no one listens. He speaks in dreams.

The Absence of Justice

Elihu states that man has no right to question God, and Job is wrong to ask God for the reasons for his suffering. He implies that God has indeed spoken to Job through horrible dreams (7:14), but Job has not listened as God tried to correct him and turn him back from the prideful course that will drive him to the grave. But as we have seen before, pride couldn't have been Job's problem. So Elihu is again, by implication, stating that Job is wrong and needs to repent.

> **Job 33:19-22 Or a man may be chastened on a bed of pain**
> **with constant distress in his bones,**
> **²⁰so that his very being finds food repulsive**
> **and his soul loathes the choicest meal.**
> **²¹His flesh wastes away to nothing,**
> **and his bones, once hidden, now stick out.**
> **²²His soul draws near to the pit,**
> **and his life to the messengers of death.**

ELIHU: God also speaks through pain.

Elihu speaks in generalities, but we can be sure he was specifically aiming at Job. So when he speaks of "pain," "constant distress in his bones," "loss of appetite," etc., we can imagine him looking keenly at Job and directly describing him. "In all this pain, Job, God is speaking to you," Elihu says.

David in Psalm 119:71 says, "It was good for me to be afflicted, so that I might learn your decrees." And in verse 75 he says, "...in faithfulness you have afflicted me." So, yes, God does speak through pain, but there is no evidence that God was chastening Job or trying to get his attention. It seems Job's attention was focused on God quite well. Besides, it was Satan who afflicted Job, not God. So while Elihu may have made a true statement, it was still wrong when applied to Job.

> **Job 33:23-28 "Yet if there is an angel on his side**
> **as a mediator, one out of a thousand,**
> **to tell a man what is right for him,**
> **²⁴to be gracious to him and say,**
> **'Spare him from going down to the pit;**
> **I have found a ransom for him'—**
> **²⁵then his flesh is renewed like a child's;**
> **it is restored as in the days of his youth.**
> **²⁶He prays to God and finds favor with him,**
> **he sees God's face and shouts for joy;**
> **he is restored by God to his righteous state.**
> **²⁷Then he comes to men and says,**
> **'I sinned, and perverted what was right,**

> but I did not get what I deserved.
> ²⁸He redeemed my soul from going down to the pit,
>   and I will live to enjoy the light.'

ELIHU: If you are fortunate enough to have an angel who will intercede for you, God might redeem you.

Elihu seems to say here that there is an outside chance—one out of a thousand—that Job might gain favor with God, provided, of course, that his attitude is properly repentant. (v 27) Again Elihu's barbs miss Job completely, for Job in his integrity could not say, "I have sinned and perverted what is right." (27:5)

> **Job 33:29-33** "God does all these things to a man—
>   twice, even three times—
> ³⁰to turn back his soul from the pit,
>   that the light of life may shine on him.
> ³¹Pay attention, Job, and listen to me;
>   be silent, and I will speak.
> ³²If you have anything to say, answer me;
>   speak up, for I want you to be cleared.
> ³³But if not, then listen to me;
>   be silent, and I will teach you wisdom."

ELIHU: This is how God often works to turn man from evil. Don't you have anything to say, Job? If not, I've only started.

It almost seems that Elihu is disappointed that Job doesn't bother to argue with him. But Job's silence just goads Elihu into further discourse. Perhaps Elihu wonders if he is really getting through to Job.

> **Job 34:1-9** Then Elihu said:
> ²"Hear my words, you wise men;
>   listen to me, you men of learning.
> ³For the ear tests words
>   as the tongue tastes food.
> ⁴Let us discern for ourselves what is right;
>   let us learn together what is good.
> ⁵"Job says, 'I am innocent,
>   but God denies me justice.
> ⁶Although I am right,
>   I am considered a liar;
> although I am guiltless,
>   his arrow inflicts an incurable wound.'
> ⁷What man is like Job,
>   who drinks scorn like water?

The Absence of Justice

> ⁸He keeps company with evildoers;
>   he associates with wicked men.
> ⁹For he says, 'It profits a man nothing
>   when he tries to please God.'

ELIHU: It is obvious to anyone with the least discernment that Job is wrong.

Elihu addresses the three silenced friends as "wise men" and appeals to their judgment. He explains that discernment of Job's wrong is as easy as tasting food.

Elihu's proposal in verse 4 could well be the life-text for a hedonist. "Let us discern for ourselves what is right. Let us learn together what is good." This attitude is in direct contrast with the proposition implied by God in the prologue that righteousness stands by itself; that there is such a thing as right apart from human judgment or feelings.

It is one thing to apply one's personal standard of right and wrong to oneself. It is quite another to try to impose it on another. The friends were guilty of violating the principle recorded in Matthew 7:1: "Do not judge, or you too will be judged." Incidently, it is interesting that, after wrongly judging Job, the three friends will themselves be judged by God as the Matthew passage promises (42:7).

Elihu again quotes Job in verse 9, implying that the statements Job has made are ridiculous according to Job's own standard of right and wrong. Not only are Job's statements ridiculous, but Job is worthy of scorn (v 7), and Elihu associates Job with the workers of iniquity because of his attitude.

Again Elihu takes Job's statements out of context (v 5). According to Elihu's account, Job had made an implication that he was righteous, while God in taking away Job's wealth and health was therefore unrighteous. Job, in making his statements, was always seeking an answer, not making judgments about God. I believe that while Job made some strong statements, he made them not to judge God, but to demonstrate how ludicrous his situation was if his friends' position were true. They were statements that said, "Something is really haywire here!"

While Job may have made implications that resembled verse 9, Elihu seems to be a bit confused, as he here quotes Eliphaz in 22:1-3, not Job.

> Job 34:10-15 "So listen to me, you men of understanding.
>   Far be it from God to do evil,
>   from the Almighty to do wrong.
> ¹¹He repays a man for what he has done;
>   he brings upon him what his conduct deserves.

Elihu, the Brash Young Man

> [12]It is unthinkable that God would do wrong,
>   that the Almighty would pervert justice.
> [13]Who appointed him over the earth?
>   Who put him in charge of the whole world?
> [14]If it were his intention
>   and he withdrew his spirit and breath,
> [15]all mankind would perish together
>   and man would return to the dust.

ELIHU: Listen! God is sovereign. God is just. God is in control!

Elihu appeals to his whole audience, calling them "men of understanding." In this, he was wrong again since God later declares that the three friends are wrong. (42:7-9)

Given the basic premise that the righteous prosper and the wicked suffer, suffering Job, in declaring himself righteous, declares God wicked. Elihu strongly defends God's integrity. "Far be it from God to do evil." Verse 12: "It is unthinkable that God would do wrong, that the Almighty would pervert justice." Elihu strongly believes that a just God is in complete control on the earth. He asks in verse 13, "Who appointed him over the earth? Who put him in charge of the whole world?" This implies that since the obvious answer is "no one," that God himself is the sovereign over the earth. He answers to no one. All flesh is dependent on him.

Elihu's intent is to expose Job's outrageous arrogance in questioning a sovereign God.

> **Job 34:16-20** "If you have understanding, hear this;
>   listen to what I say.
> [17]Can he who hates justice govern?
>   Will you condemn the just and mighty One?
> [18]Is he not the One who says to kings, 'You are worthless,'
>   and to nobles, 'You are wicked,'
> [19]who shows no partiality to princes
>   and does not favor the rich over the poor,
>   for they are all the work of his hands?
> [20]They die in an instant, in the middle of the night;
>   the people are shaken and they pass away;
>   the mighty are removed without human hand.

ELIHU: You are talking like this to God? You don't even talk back to kings or princes or nobles—or even the rich!

Elihu points out that even on a human scale, respect is given to those of higher station. How much more awe and respect should be given to God, considering that man is mortal?

The Absence of Justice

> Job 34:21-30 "His eyes are on the ways of men;
>   he sees their every step.
> ²²There is no dark place, no deep shadow,
>   where evildoers can hide.
> ²³God has no need to examine men further,
>   that they should come before him for judgment.
> ²⁴Without inquiry he shatters the mighty
>   and sets up others in their place.
> ²⁵Because he takes note of their deeds,
>   he overthrows them in the night and they are crushed.
> ²⁶He punishes them for their wickedness
>   where everyone can see them,
> ²⁷because they turned from following him
>   and had no regard for any of his ways.
> ²⁸They caused the cry of the poor to come before him,
>   so that he heard the cry of the needy.
> ²⁹But if he remains silent, who can condemn him?
>   If he hides his face, who can see him?
> Yet he is over man and nation alike,
> ³⁰to keep a godless man from ruling,
>   from laying snares for the people.

ELIHU: God is omniscient. He is in control of all the affairs of men.

No one can hide his wickedness from God's all-seeing eye. (By implication, "Job, you didn't get by with your sin. God saw it and is making recompense.") Elihu indicates in verse 23 that Job's appeal to be judged by God is futile. God is already judging Job.

The rest of this passage declares that God is just and that his justice rules the affairs of the poor and also the rich.

> Job 34:31-37 "Suppose a man says to God,
>   'I am guilty but will offend no more.
> ³²Teach me what I cannot see;
>   if I have done wrong, I will not do so again.'
> ³³Should God then reward you on your terms,
>   when you refuse to repent?
> You must decide, not I;
>   so tell me what you know.
> ³⁴"Men of understanding declare,
>   wise men who hear me say to me,
> ³⁵'Job speaks without knowledge;
>   his words lack insight.'
> ³⁶Oh, that Job might be tested to the utmost

> for answering like a wicked man!
> ³⁷To his sin he adds rebellion;
> scornfully he claps his hands among us
> and multiplies his words against God."

ELIHU: Can you imagine the impudence of this man who challenges a sovereign God? He not only has obviously sinned grievously, but he continues by rebelling against God.

In the light of God's sovereignty, omniscience, and justice, Elihu attempts to display Job's audacity and sin. His tone is full of ridicule. "Job ought to be tried to the limit." (v 36, NAS). Elihu sees evidence of repeated sin: the sin that resulted in Job's suffering, to which he has now added the sin of rebellion. "...scornfully he claps his hands among us." pictures his opinion that Job was insolent and impertinent. This statement by Elihu puts him in direct opposition to God's position stated in 42:7-8. Perhaps a lesson to be learned here is that not everyone who speaks grand and glowing things about God is necessarily right.

> Job 35:1-3 Then Elihu said:
> ²"Do you think this is just?
> You say, 'I will be cleared by God.'
> ³Yet you ask him, 'What profit is it to me,
> and what do I gain by not sinning?'

ELIHU: Do you really think you are justified in questioning the profit in serving God?

Elihu is challenging Job's conscience about his position. He is building on inferences and deductions from Job's speeches that may or may not be warranted, but Job is nevertheless charged with making himself more righteous than God. God's final response, however, indicates that this was not Job's attitude at all. Perhaps Elihu is referring to 21:15, but Job is citing the attitudes of the wicked, and disclaims any such position for himself.

> Job 35:4-8 "I would like to reply to you
> and to your friends with you.
> ⁵Look up at the heavens and see;
> gaze at the clouds so high above you.
> ⁶If you sin, how does that affect him?
> If your sins are many, what does that do to him?
> ⁷If you are righteous, what do you give to him,
> or what does he receive from your hand?
> ⁸Your wickedness affects only a man like yourself,
> and your righteousness only the sons of men.

The Absence of Justice

ELIHU: Just look up into the heavens created by Almighty God. Do you really think your righteousness or sin will add or detract from him?

Elihu claims that God is so infinitely greater than man, that what we do, good or evil, really does not affect him. Furthermore, Elihu points out that our wickedness may harm other men and our righteousness may benefit other men (v 8), but God is not obligated to us in any sense because we are righteous. However, if Elihu is right, and if God is unaffected by man's response, why does God speak to Satan of Job with confidence and pride? (1:8) Why does he get angry because of our sin? (Deut 29:24-28) Why is he pleased with our righteousness? (Luke 19:17) While it is true that we can neither add to nor subtract from God, he does not remain unaffected by our actions.

>Job 35:9-16 "Men cry out under a load of oppression;
>   they plead for relief from the arm of the powerful.
>¹⁰But no one says, 'Where is God my Maker,
>   who gives songs in the night,
>¹¹who teaches more to us than to the beasts of the earth
>   and makes us wiser than the birds of the air?'
>¹²He does not answer when men cry out
>   because of the arrogance of the wicked.
>¹³Indeed, God does not listen to their empty plea;
>   the Almighty pays no attention to it.
>¹⁴How much less, then, will he listen
>   when you say that you do not see him,
>that your case is before him
>   and you must wait for him,
>¹⁵and further, that his anger never punishes
>   and he does not take the least notice of wickedness.
>¹⁶So Job opens his mouth with empty talk;
>   without knowledge he multiplies words."

ELIHU: Multitudes suffer, but they do not seek God; therefore, they get what they deserve, and God will not respond to them.

Elihu tries to answer Job's question about God's silence. His answer repeats an old excuse, that the oppressed deserve it because they did not respond to God properly (v 10). This explanation can be applied to any unanswered prayer. It is hardly helpful to Job in explaining his dilemma. He uses this explanation to infer that Job's prayers were worthless and arrogant (v 16).

>Job 36:1-15 Elihu continued:
>²"Bear with me a little longer and I will show you
>   that there is more to be said in God's behalf.
>³I get my knowledge from afar;

Elihu, the Brash Young Man

> I will ascribe justice to my Maker.
> ⁴Be assured that my words are not false;
>   one perfect in knowledge is with you.
> ⁵"God is mighty, but does not despise men;
>   he is mighty, and firm in his purpose.
> ⁶He does not keep the wicked alive
>   but gives the afflicted their rights.
> ⁷He does not take his eyes off the righteous;
>   he enthrones them with kings
>   and exalts them forever.
> ⁸But if men are bound in chains,
>   held fast by cords of affliction,
> ⁹he tells them what they have done —
>   that they have sinned arrogantly.
> ¹⁰He makes them listen to correction
>   and commands them to repent of their evil.
> ¹¹If they obey and serve him,
>   they will spend the rest of their days in prosperity
>   and their years in contentment.
> ¹²But if they do not listen,
>   they will perish by the sword
>   and die without knowledge.
> ¹³"The godless in heart harbor resentment;
>   even when he fetters them, they do not cry for help.
> ¹⁴They die in their youth,
>   among male prostitutes of the shrines.
> ¹⁵But those who suffer he delivers in their suffering;
>   he speaks to them in their affliction.

ELIHU: Listen, Job, I've got more to say in defense of God's righteousness. Listen, because my knowledge is perfect. God *does* dispense justice on the earth!

This passage ranks about first in arrogance in the book. That a young man should claim perfect knowledge and undertake to defend God on that basis displays the ultimate in gall.

He goes on to explain the basis for claiming there is justice on the earth. He starts in verse 5 with a declaration of God's sovereignty, tempered by his compassion and understanding. He states his case again in verse 6: "He does not keep the wicked alive but gives the afflicted their rights." He ascribes to God the establishment of kings (v 7). If tragedy befalls anyone, it is because they have sinned and need correction (vs 8-10). If they will repent, God will prosper them (v 11). If not, they will perish (v 12). He goes on to describe the fate (in this life) of the godless and the wicked.

Job 36:17-21 But now you are laden with

The Absence of Justice

> the judgment due the wicked;
> judgment and justice have taken hold of you.
> ¹⁸Be careful that no one entices you by riches;
> do not let a large bribe turn you aside.
> ¹⁹Would your wealth
> or even all your mighty efforts
> sustain you so you would not be in distress?
> ²⁰Do not long for the night,
> to drag people away from their homes.
> ²¹Beware of turning to evil,
> which you seem to prefer to affliction.

ELIHU: Job, you're walking on very thin ice!

Andersen[1] states that this passage is a difficult one. Whether Elihu is warning Job, accusing him, or encouraging him is not clear. However, in the light of all the previous accusations, it would be out of character for Elihu to suddenly insert an encouragement. Verse 19 seems sarcastic since Job no longer has any riches. Verse 20 betrays a total inability to empathize with Job in his despair.

> **Job 36:22-33** "God is exalted in his power.
> Who is a teacher like him?
> ²³Who has prescribed his ways for him,
> or said to him, 'You have done wrong'?
> ²⁴Remember to extol his work,
> which men have praised in song.
> ²⁵All mankind has seen it;
> men gaze on it from afar.
> ²⁶How great is God—beyond our understanding!
> The number of his years is past finding out.
> ²⁷"He draws up the drops of water,
> which distill as rain to the streams;
> ²⁸the clouds pour down their moisture
> and abundant showers fall on mankind.
> ²⁹Who can understand how he spreads out the clouds,
> how he thunders from his pavilion?
> ³⁰See how he scatters his lightning about him,
> bathing the depths of the sea.
> ³¹This is the way he governs the nations
> and provides food in abundance.
> ³²He fills his hands with lightning
> and commands it to strike its mark.
> ³³His thunder announces the coming storm;
> even the cattle make known its approach.

ELIHU: Remember WHO it is you are accusing, Job. Beware!

Elihu, the Brash Young Man

Elihu's defense of God covers much ground in this passage. He describes God's magnificent power and knowledge (v 22). Man is incapable of comprehending an eternal God (v 26) who controls the rain, thunder, lightning, the depths of the sea, and even the provision of our food.

Elihu's philosophy seems to be that "God does everything that happens." However, it has been pointed out that "If God is good, and if God does everything that happens, then everything that happens is good, and the category of evil disappears altogether."

Elihu seems to be moving away from the subject of God's justice to the subject of God's inscrutable wisdom. Andersen[2] points out that this trend "might be no more than to hide God away in a cloud of mystification."

Job 37:1-13 "At this my heart pounds
and leaps from its place.
²Listen! Listen to the roar of his voice,
to the rumbling that comes from his mouth.
³He unleashes his lightning beneath the whole heaven
and sends it to the ends of the earth.
⁴After that comes the sound of his roar;
he thunders with his majestic voice.
When his voice resounds,
he holds nothing back.
⁵God's voice thunders in marvelous ways;
he does great things beyond our understanding.
⁶He says to the snow, 'Fall on the earth,'
and to the rain shower, 'Be a mighty downpour.'
⁷So that all men he has made may know his work,
he stops every man from his labor.
⁸The animals take cover;
they remain in their dens.
⁹The tempest comes out from its chamber,
the cold from the driving winds.
¹⁰The breath of God produces ice,
and the broad waters become frozen.
¹¹He loads the clouds with moisture;
he scatters his lightning through them.
¹²At his direction they swirl around
over the face of the whole earth
to do whatever he commands them.
¹³He brings the clouds to punish men,
or to water his earth and show his love.

ELIHU: God makes and controls the mighty thunderstorm with all its power. He is the master of meteorological phenomena.

The Absence of Justice

Elihu is being carried away with the majesty of God as expressed in the manifestations of the weather. His poem describing the thunderstorm is magnificent, and it is conjectured by some commentators that the storm he is describing is actually the approaching storm out of which God speaks in Chapter 38. But throughout the text we see that Elihu portrays God to be in complete and immediate control, using these phenomena for his various purposes.

> Job 37:14-20 "Listen to this, Job;
> stop and consider God's wonders.
> ¹⁵Do you know how God controls the clouds
> and makes his lightning flash?
> ¹⁶Do you know how the clouds hang poised,
> those wonders of him who is perfect in knowledge?
> ¹⁷You who swelter in your clothes
> when the land lies hushed under the south wind,
> ¹⁸can you join him in spreading out the skies,
> hard as a mirror of cast bronze?
> ¹⁹"Tell us what we should say to him;
> we cannot draw up our case because of our darkness.
> ²⁰Should he be told that I want to speak?
> Would any man ask to be swallowed up?

ELIHU: Listen, Job, how can we as mortal men presume to challenge such a God?

Elihu now includes himself in this section. By thinking on the majesty of God, he has even humbled himself (the one who is perfect in knowledge — 36:4) to the point of speaking of the relationship to God using "us" instead of "you," thereby including himself with Job. The questions he asks are almost a prelude to the questions God asks when he answers Job, but Elihu's point is quite different from God's answer, as we will see. Elihu was attempting to describe to Job the awe that would bury Job's nagging questions about justice on the earth. God's point was quite different.

> Job 37:21-24 Now no one can look at the sun,
> bright as it is in the skies
> after the wind has swept them clean.
> ²²Out of the north he comes in golden splendor;
> God comes in awesome majesty.
> ²³The Almighty is beyond our reach and exalted in power;
> in his justice and great righteousness, he does not oppress.
> ²⁴Therefore, men revere him,
> for does he not have regard for all the wise in heart?"

Elihu, the Brash Young Man

ELIHU: This majestic, all-powerful God will not violate the principle of justice, and if you are wise, Job, you will fear him.

The picture here is still one of majestic splendor, but the splendor of the sun breaking through the abating storm. Elihu concludes (either willingly, or simply because he got cut off by God's answer) by stating that "God comes in awesome majesty" (v 22), and because of God's majesty, he states that God will not violate the principles of justice on the earth or elsewhere.

Whether Elihu was finished or not is unclear. It seems that he possessed the ability to ramble on indefinitely. Whether or not he was finished, he was undoubtedly startled by God's appearance. He probably thought he had provided the last word in the matter, especially since the other friends had already been silenced, and Job had shown no inclination to respond.

Elihu's philosophy, in a nutshell, is **"God is great, God is good, don't ask questions!"** That he is ignored is great comfort to those of us with questioning minds.

Elihu simply does not fit well into the narrative. He is not mentioned in the prologue with Job's other friends, and he is not included in the epilogue when Job prays for his friends. The only possible recognition Elihu gets may be in God's opening statement where he asks, "Who is this that darkens my counsel with words without knowledge?" However, Job, in 40:1-5 seems to accept this statement as pertaining to him. Elihu's arguments therefore elicit no response. He is virtually ignored. It is not justifiable to allow Elihu more credibility than God or even Job gave him. His views differ somewhat from the views of the three friends, but we find no answer to Job's problem in Elihu's words.

If God did address his first statement in Chapter 38 to Elihu as Morgan[3] asserts, this would explain why no further mention is made of Elihu in the book. Anyway, one can imagine him, thoroughly discredited by God's opening statement, slinking off in humiliation. The other characters in the book remain for the conclusion, but Elihu evidently did not. While everyone else fixed their attention on God, he unobtrusively slipped away into oblivion.

1. Andersen, Francis I. *Job*. London: Inter-Varsity Press, 1976. p. 262
2. Ibid, p. 262
3. Morgan, G. Campbell. *The Answers of Jesus to Job*. Grand Rapids: Baker Books, 1973. p. 208

CHAPTER 10

GOD'S ANSWER, PART 1

After all man's ideas have been exhausted, after all the pat answers have been explored and found wanting, after finding no solutions, there is God. After all of man's ideas had failed, God had not yet begun to speak. Now he speaks, and I am sure that Job, Eliphaz, Bildad, and Zophar listen with bated breath.

There are two difficult problems that must be confronted as we study the Book of Job:
The first is the problem described in the book.

1. Why do the innocent and righteous suffer?

The second is the problem we now face.

2. What did God say?

If we could figure out the answer to the second question, it would shed light on the answer to the first.

There are those who hold that Elihu's discourse holds the answers to Job's problem. But as we have stated before, this would be an insult to God and make his response totally unnecessary. There are those who say that there is no answer to the question posed by the Book of Job. Yet Chapter 38, verse 1 puts it very clearly:

Job 38:1 Then the LORD answered Job out of the storm.

If there is no answer, or if the answer is to be found elsewhere, what is the sense of God speaking at all? But verse 1 very pointedly states that the Lord answered. So, clearly, the answer must be found in God's discourse, whether we are intelligent enough to comprehend it or not. Because it is so important that we not miss any part of God's answer, I will not attempt to condense the meaning of the text as I did with the discourses.

It would be well to remind ourselves at this point just what Job's question was for which he demanded an answer. In Chapter 29 Job describes the good life he had enjoyed before the calamities that destroyed him. Chapter 30 describes the pitiable lot of Job after tragedy had struck. Chapter 31 explores all the possible reasons Job can think of that would explain why one should be

God's Answer, Part 1

thus afflicted. Job declares himself innocent on all counts. In a nutshell, Job says, "I was blessed, now I am cursed for no apparent reason. Why?" To put his question in the context of the arguments with his friends, "There ought to be justice on the earth, but I'm not receiving it. Why not?"

God answers Job in a very unusual and exciting way. As we look over God's answer, we are at first perplexed about the relationship of God's speech to Job's suffering. Think about it. Down here is a dying man, depressed, abandoned by all friends and family, stripped down to his naked faith, and God now wants to talk about meteorology, geology, oceanography, astronomy, physics, and zoology. What's the connection?

Of course, to Job in his dejection, the fact that God is now really speaking to him after a protracted silence would bring unbounded relief, no matter what God talks about (as Andersen[1] suggests). But there *must* be more content to God's discourse than mere chitchat among friends. Most commentators see God's answer as rhetorical. Some say that *what* God said is not important. *That* he said anything at all is more important, and **most** important is the effect God's appearance has on Job.

This position is unacceptable to me. True, what God says to man may be quite incomprehensible at the time. However, I find it hard to believe that God would say anything to man that is unimportant or totally and forever obscure. God's communication with man is always relevant, meaningful, and ultimately comprehensible. If this is so, then God's answer to Job must be a meaningful response to Job's question and not an attempt to humble Job using rhetoric.

It is obvious from our perspective in history that God was not yet ready to establish justice on the earth. To establish justice on the earth in Job's day would have required that God destroy civilization since no man has been totally righteous since the Garden of Eden. Because God loved us, he planned to provide a redeemer who would take the punishment for man's sin on himself and therefore save us from the penalty of our unrighteousness. And so we see that Job's demand for justice was premature. God was not yet ready to establish justice on the earth.

There were issues of education and maturity for mankind as well because God almost always acts in relation *to* mankind by acting *through* mankind. Scripture makes it clear that the saints will assist God in the tasks of bringing justice to the earth, and ruling the earth.

> **2 Timothy 2:12** ...if we endure, we will also reign with him.
>
> **Revelation 5:10** ...you have made them to be a kingdom and priests to serve our God, and they will reign on the earth."
>
> **Revelation 22:5** There will be no more night. They will not need

The Absence of Justice

the light of a lamp or the light of the sun, for the Lord God will give them light. And they will reign for ever and ever.

These passages make it clear that God will work through us in establishing justice on the earth. Since the evil we observe on earth is to be abolished, there will be a lot of work to do, and we will have an active part in the process. God did not make us puppets and I do not believe we will be puppets serving in the kingdom. Certainly he will use us in our areas of expertise, and there will be a place for every one of us in his service. This is not to say that God could not accomplish this all by himself. However, God's pattern is to work through man. Therefore, we will need to know a lot about this planet on which we live if we are to be effective in serving our Lord in his kingdom. If the evil effects of storms and weather are to be corrected, we will need to know about meteorology. If the oceans will be cleaned up and utilized, we will need to know about oceanography. If animal life is to be protected and enjoyed, we will need to know about zoology. In fact, we will need to know all the hows and whys of the functions of this planet. God's questions cover many of these subjects, but I'm sure his list is not exhaustive. And so God is saying to Job (and mankind) "Are you ready for this job? Do you know what you will need to know when we set up the kingdom and establish justice on the earth?"

Take for example a thirteen-year-old girl who insists that she be allowed to marry or a thirteen-year-old boy who demands the privilege of driving the family vehicle. The parent, knowing that a thirteen-year-old lacks the maturity and education for adult responsibilities, could well ask the child a series of questions. The girl might be asked, "Do you know how to manage a household (in the light of how you organize your room)? Can you manage a household budget? Are you emotionally mature enough to handle the give-and-take of marriage? Are you mature enough to raise the inevitable children?"

The boy similarly might be asked, "Can you pass a driving test? Has your judgment matured to the point where you would be able to safely handle an automobile on the freeway? Have your emotions matured so that you could control them in hostile situations? (This question could be asked of many adults driving today.) Are you prepared to pay for the gasoline and the insurance (if you could even obtain it)? Do you know enough about the operation of an automobile to maintain and service it properly?"

God, therefore, is questioning Job about his knowledge and preparedness in relation to the task of establishing justice on the earth. I do not believe he is trying to show Job how stupid and ignorant he is or to humble him. I also find it hard to accept that Scripture can become obsolete. What God had to say to Job must have relevance to modern man as well. God asks questions about subjects which will be vital and relevant to the task of judging and ruling the earth with justice. Obviously, Job does not pass the test. Modern man, however, will score rather high on this test. This suggests that the time may be near when God will finally establish justice on the earth!

God's Answer, Part 1

The significance of the storm or whirlwind in verse 1 is unclear. Some commentators suggest that the whirlwind was part of the storm described by Elihu (36:27 through 37:20). However, 37:21-22 describes the abating of the storm so it is doubtful that there would still be a whirlwind.

Whatever the significance, one can rest assured that it captured everyone's attention, and that the total scene was terrifying and awe-inspiring.

GOD QUESTIONS JOB

**Job 38:2 "Who is this that darkens my counsel
with words without knowledge?**

There is disagreement among the commentators whether God addressed Job or Elihu in verse 2. Which one is inconsequential since God could appropriately say this to any man.

**Job 38:3 Brace yourself like a man;
I will question you,
and you shall answer me.**

Job now faces "God's turn" in this ancient court ritual.

Perhaps God's sense of humor shows through just a bit in the way he addresses Job. "Brace yourself like a man," I can picture God with a slight grin on his face saying, "Job, get ready. You asked for it. Here it comes!"

ORIGINS AND GEOLOGY

**Job 38:4 "Where were you when I laid the earth's foundation?
Tell me, if you understand...."**

The answer from Job would surely have been "I don't know," or "nowhere." In a sense, modern man would also have to answer negatively. None of us can remember even our own birth, much less what happened before our birth. In fact, if Job lived during the patriarchal age, he did not even have the Book of Genesis to consult regarding origins since it was written by Moses. However, God has given us information in the Old and New Testaments that would help us answer this question. Calling the prophet Jeremiah, God said:

**Jeremiah 1:5 "Before I formed you in the womb I knew you,
before you were born I set you apart; I appointed you as a
prophet to the nations."**

While Genesis states that God created the universe, and Psalms has many references to our origins, the New Testament, in Ephesians 1:4, says that he chose us before the creation of the world... So we existed in God's mind long before we were born.

The knowledge covered by this category will be a crucial basis for our understanding of the functioning of this planet as we work in the kingdom to reverse the effects of the curse imposed after the Garden of Eden debacle. Any course of study in any discipline starts with the history and basis for the principles derived in that field. While the exact reasons for each question may not be clear today, they will emerge as we cooperate with God in the task of establishing justice.

Job 38:5 Who marked off its dimensions? Surely you know! Who stretched a measuring line across it?

Of course Job had no revelation of the details of creation. However, we have been told who created the earth:

Genesis 1:1 In the beginning God created the heavens and the earth.

Therefore, the answer for which Job only had oral traditions, we know through written records, is again, God the creator.

Job 38:6a On what were its footings set,

I take this to be a reference to the core of the earth. Certainly Job had no idea about the composition of the core of the earth. However, modern man has determined quite accurately the composition and even the state of the core of the earth, to the extent that, using the tools of mathematics and physics, knowing the mass (composition and weight) of the earth, he can accurately determine the gravitational pull on a man-made satellite circling the globe, or on a space vehicle passing through the orbits of our sister planets into outer space. The material that makes up the core of the earth is molten nickel and iron according to the *Cambridge Encyclopedia of Astronomy*.[2] This is determined by analyzing seismic waves and the magnetic properties compared to the mass of the earth. Some might object that no one has actually gotten a sample of the innermost material of the earth for analysis. While this is true, we have analyzed thousands of meteorites that have fallen to earth and have found them to be of two basic compositions. There are the stony meteorites and the nickel-iron meteorites.[3] The nickel-iron composition fits the calculations we make about the earth's core, while the stony meteorites correspond to the earth's mantle and crust as confirmed by the analysis of the material constantly spewed from volcanoes..

Those who anticipated discovering new elements or new compounds on the moon or on Mars were disappointed. While there were many features to be studied for years to come, no startling new materials were found. So it seems that the stuff that makes up the earth and the stuff we have found falling from the sky are quite similar. This leads us to the conclusion that the composition of the bodies in our section of the galaxy is homogenous.

No, Job didn't know about these things, but we have learned a great deal about them and no doubt will learn even more, given enough time.

> **Job 38:6b-7** ...or who laid its cornerstone—
> ⁷while the morning stars sang together
> and all the angels shouted for joy?

The answer to this question is the same as the answer to verse 5, which we have by revelation. It is interesting that verse 7 mentions the morning stars singing. Obviously, the stars emit light radiation. We have also measured radio waves from outer space and we are studying the cosmic radiation from space. But it has also been noted that the planets emit sound waves. Observers have noted that the earth seems to hum a deep bass note, detected at various places on the planet on very quiet nights. So, in a sense we can tune in to the song of the stars mentioned in verse 7a.

THE SEA

> **Job 38:8-9** "Who shut up the sea behind doors
> when it burst forth from the womb,
> ⁹when I made the clouds its garment
> and wrapped it in thick darkness,

The short and simple answer is again, God. There are some interesting texts in the Old Testament that also speak of this creation period:

> **Psalm 74:12-17** But you, O God, are my king from of old;
> you bring salvation upon the earth.
> ¹³It was you who split open the sea by your power;
> you broke the heads of the monster in the waters.
> ¹⁴It was you who crushed the heads of Leviathan
> and gave him as food to the creatures of the desert.
> ¹⁵It was you who opened up springs and streams;
> you dried up the ever flowing rivers.
> ¹⁶The day is yours, and yours also the night;
> you established the sun and moon.
> ¹⁷It was you who set all the boundaries of the earth;
> you made both summer and winter.

> **Isaiah 51:9-11** Awake, awake! Clothe yourself with strength,
> O arm of the LORD;

The Absence of Justice

> **awake, as in days gone by,**
> **as in generations of old.**
> **Was it not you who cut Rahab to pieces,**
> **who pierced that monster through?**
> **[10]Was it not you who dried up the sea,**
> **the waters of the great deep,**
> **who made a road in the depths of the sea**
> **so that the redeemed might cross over?**
> **[11]The ransomed of the LORD will return.**
> **They will enter Zion with singing;**
> **everlasting joy will crown their heads.**
> **Gladness and joy will overtake them,**
> **and sorrow and sighing will flee away.**

Levenson[4] makes a connection between the Sea, the Sea Monster, Rahab, and Leviathan mentioned in these texts and believes they describe a participant in a great primordial battle at or before the Creation. Furthermore, these entities are equated with evil and God mastered them in the acts of creation. These creatures and the sea are mentioned in ancient Near East myths.

> **Job 38:10-11 ...when I fixed limits for it**
> **and set its doors and bars in place,**
> **[11]when I said, 'This far you may come and no farther;**
> **here is where your proud waves halt'?**

These verses are a continuation of the previous passage, with God identifying himself as the one who fixed the limits on the sea and mastered it. That the sea is more than just the oceans as we know them is obvious, since the shores of the oceans are constantly changing catastrophically with earthquakes, volcanoes, and tidal waves. Genesis 10:25 mentions that in the days of Peleg the earth was divided. Believing geologists speculate that this refers to the splitting up of the continents, which would certainly violate the "fixed limits" if the oceans were what God was really referring to. There is probably more here than we can readily understand, but the obvious answer to the question is God.

Since the oceans cover three-fourths of the surface of the earth, it is easy to understand why we will need to know, in detail, about many aspects of the seas. Mankind has been polluting the oceans, especially since the age of industrialization began. This process is fast approaching a critical line where we are all threatened by the poisons and toxic wastes polluting our oceans and therefore the fish and the sea animals. Part of our job in establishing justice on the earth will be to clean up the oceans. We will need to know a lot about this subject to get the job done.

God's Answer, Part 1

THE DAWN

**Job 38:12-15 "Have you ever given orders to the morning,
or shown the dawn its place,
¹³that it might take the earth by the edges
and shake the wicked out of it?
¹⁴The earth takes shape like clay under a seal;
its features stand out like those of a garment.
¹⁵The wicked are denied their light,
and their upraised arm is broken.**

Job's (and our) answer, on first thought, is a resounding "no" since we do not make the world go 'round and cause dawn and dusk. However, there is a specific aspect of day versus night described here which the parallelism of Hebrew poetry helps us understand. Night is the time when the wicked man lurks and accomplishes his evil purposes. Surely the coming of day puts an end to his evil deeds. Modern man recognizes this propensity of evil for darkness. We have used our invention of artificial light to deter wickedness by placing floodlights in parking lots, lining our residential streets with street lights, etc. And it works! We are safer in well-lit areas.

Lest someone ridicule the correlation, imagine a man like Job transported through time to a busy metroplex at night. He would be awe-struck at how modern man can "give orders to the morning" by pushing a little button. So, in that sense, at least, modern man can indeed "give orders to the morning" and deter the wicked in their purposes.

A world where crime exists at all is not a just world. This subject will need to be addressed at length in the kingdom. Looking at our current global problems with crime and evil, it is easy to understand why Scripture would state that Messiah will rule with a "rod of iron." (Rev 19:15)

OCEANOGRAPHY

**Job 38:16 "Have you journeyed to the springs of the sea
or walked in the recesses of the deep?**

Of course Job had not, but modern man, while he would admit that there is much to be discovered in the ocean depths, has made great strides in the fields of oceanography. We have mapped the floors of the oceans. We have found rich deposits of minerals there and plan to recover them. We drill for oil there.

Jacques Costeau is perhaps the most famous oceanographic explorer. It was Costeau who pioneered the use of scuba gear so that men could indeed enter "the springs of the sea" and walk in the "recesses of the deep." For example, he documented the exploration of miles of underwater caves under the floor of the Caribbean Sea. Of course, scuba gear has limitations. Therefore, deep-diving submarines have been designed to withstand the awesome pressures of the deep oceans. Exploration is going on there now, discovering new life forms and modes of existence in the totally dark world of the depths of the sea.

DEATH

**Job 38:17 Have the gates of death been shown to you?
Have you seen the gates of the shadow of death?**

Recent years have seen the emergence of phenomena that shed light on this passage. Modern medical technology has made it possible to resuscitate people who, only a few years ago, would have surely died. The stories these people are telling after their near-death experiences have been strange to say the least. Because modern science did not admit to an afterlife, it was only after the evidence, subjective though it was, had grown to such a volume it could no longer be ignored, that science began to take note. Elisabeth Kubler-Ross, M.D., and Dr. Raymond Moody have both published their compilations of patients' stories. They began to notice, as the evidence mounted, that there were striking similarities in the accounts. Some of these were:

> Finding oneself outside his body, watching the efforts of resuscitation, but unable to communicate.
> A journey through a long gray or dark tunnel toward an intense light.
> Finding departed friends and loved ones at the end of the tunnel to welcome them.
> An atmosphere of indescribable love.
> A line or barrier to be crossed.
> A review of life supervised by a "being of light."
> A change in values upon resuscitation.

Others have returned in a state of extreme panic and agitation, claiming to have seen indescribable horrors. These patients usually forget their experiences very quickly, perhaps because things too painful to remember are blanked out by the mind to retain sanity.

In the light of these recent compilations of near-death experiences, I would suggest that perhaps modern man has indeed seen the "gates of death" and the "gates of the shadow of death." Phenomena and data of this type must be taken with a grain of salt, however. They should not be accepted without reservation, and should not be considered at all except where they confirm Scriptural principles.

Of course, it is doubtful that Job knew anything of these matters.

God's Answer, Part 1

Isaiah 65:20 in describing the kingdom declares that a child will die at one hundred years of age. Therefore we conclude that death, if it occurs at all, will be a rarity in a just world.

GEOLOGY

Job 38:18 Have you comprehended the vast expanses of the earth?
Tell me, if you know all this.

During the Middle Ages and until the fifteenth century man generally believed the earth to be flat. However, there is evidence that earlier cultures had figured out that the earth was round. There is one passage in the Old Testament that could indicate the shape of the earth:

Isaiah 40:22 He sits enthroned above the circle of the earth,
and its people are like grasshoppers.
He stretches out the heavens like a canopy,
and spreads them out like a tent to live in.

Whether Job was aware of the earth's shape is unknown. That he did not know its dimensions is certain. However, by our day, man has determined the expanse of the earth. In round numbers, it is eight thousand miles in diameter. Satellite pictures have corrected many an error on maps and very precise measurements can be made from space. It would also be difficult, short of the antarctic regions, to find a place where man has not set foot. That we know the precise distances on the earth was dramatically demonstrated during the Gulf War when we were able to put missiles down air-conditioner vents on target buildings from hundreds of miles away.

LIGHT & DARKNESS

Job 38:19-21 "What is the way to the abode of light?
And where does darkness reside?
[20]Can you take them to their places?
Do you know the paths to their dwellings?
[21]Surely you know, for you were already born!
You have lived so many years!

The language used in these verses is obviously poetic. Light and darkness are personified as if they had dwelling places or homes. Of course, Job's knowledge of light probably consisted of a meager understanding of the sun, moon, and stars without knowing at all why they each shone in the sky. Undoubtedly they used oil lamps and candles for lights in their homes. And perhaps people in those times puzzled about the ability of fireflies to emit light.

The Absence of Justice

From the technical point of view, today we know a great deal about not only light, but the electromagnetic spectrum of which visible light occupies just a tiny part. We know that white light is made up of all the colors of the visible spectrum. We know of ways to generate light, such as electric arcs, fluorescence, incandescence, and lasers. We have measured light's speed and this has made possible studies in the fields of astronomy and astrophysics. We have harnessed light and we communicate by means of light waves traveling through tiny light conductors called fiber optics. With lasers we can perform delicate surgery, make accurate scientific measurements, drill holes with speed and accuracy in various materials, to mention only a few of light's uses.

Physicists have analyzed the dynamic forces at work in our sun and have determined that our major light and heat source is fueled by a continuous nuclear reaction. Someone has rewritten an old nursery rhyme to keep up with our modern times:

> Twinkle, twinkle giant star
> We know exactly what you are.
> An incandescent ball of gas
> Condensing to a solid mass.
>
> Twinkle, twinkle giant star
> We need not wonder what you are
> For seen through spectroscopic ken
> You're helium and hydrogen.
> Author unknown

What about darkness? Is it a separate entity from light or is it the absence of light? The passage here seems to infer that light and darkness are separate entities. Science would insist that darkness is simply the absence of light. Perhaps there are philosophical inferences here?

Another use for the word "light" is spiritual. In this sense, light and darkness are separate entities. We have more "light" on this subject than Job did because of revelation. There are many references to light and darkness throughout the Old Testament that contain a spiritual connotation with God as the source of light, and darkness conveying the idea of evil. In the New Testament, Jesus said "I am the light of the world. Whoever follows me will never walk in darkness, but will have the light of life." We are admonished in Ephesians 5:8 to walk as "children of light." Therefore, by revelation we can say that the source of spiritual light is God. The "home" of spiritual darkness is described by the New Testament as a place of weeping and gnashing of teeth (Matthew 8:12) and a place of separation from God.

In this passage in Job, is God speaking of physical or spiritual light and darkness? I don't know, but scientifically we know a great deal about physical light, and by revelation, we have been told a great deal about spiritual light and darkness.

Verse 21 sounds sarcastic in the extreme in most translations. It is difficult to understand why God would find it necessary to make such a sarcastic remark about how old he was to a man who had testified about the brevity of life (9:25-26, 14:1-6, 16:22). The Masoretic and Lamsa texts do not sound quite as sarcastic as the others, but the meaning is still obscure. Perhaps God is referring to Job's need to take in the full picture of what God is accomplishing on the earth since Job is a finite human being. We will have more to say about whether God uses sarcasm in speaking to Job in the next chapter.

The subject of light and darkness, and indeed the subject of the total electromagnetic spectrum, is very important to an understanding of many subjects in our modern world. It involves an understanding of the gravitational forces, heat, light, radio waves, x-rays, cosmic rays, and more. To govern this world will require an understanding of how these forces and energy sources function and how they can be utilized for the benefit of mankind.

METEOROLOGY

Job 38:22-23 "Have you entered the storehouses of the snow or seen the storehouses of the hail,
²³which I reserve for times of trouble, for days of war and battle?

If I imagine myself living in Job's time, it is easy to conceive that snow and hail would present a tremendous puzzle to me. From where does it come? What makes it fall sometimes and not at other times? It is easy to understand that snow and hail would be regarded as the direct acts of God (or the gods) by primitive humans and that they were stored somewhere in vast storage bins or warehouses. God asks Job, "Have you seen them?" and Job's answer would be "no."

But we know that there are no storehouses for snow and hail on earth (unless you want to consider the arctic and antarctic continents). Snow and hail are formed in the atmosphere by conditions incomprehensible to Job, but they are predicted and understood as an everyday task of our meteorologists. We have even made snow machines to cover our ski slopes when nature does not comply with our recreational desires. Snow machines are also used in testing laboratories to simulate harsh weather conditions for testing various types of equipment.

The reference to the day of battle is obscure in the light of modern warfare, but God has used the phenomenon of hail several times in the context of battle as recorded in the Old Testament. Exodus 9 describes the plague of hail which God sent on the Egyptians. Joshua 10:11 tells of a great victory God gave Israel against the Amorites by means of a great hail storm. Isaiah 30:30 mentions hail as a weapon of God, and Revelation 16:21 predicts God's

The Absence of Justice

use of hail in judgment on the earth.

The results of these forces on the earth covered by this category are often called "acts of God." In establishing justice on the earth, it will be necessary to harness the earthquakes, volcanoes, tornadoes, hurricanes, hailstorms, floods, lightning, winds, etc. that cause so much suffering. We have learned a lot about these subjects, and our knowledge is only rudimentary. Under God's leadership in the kingdom, we will be able to utilize our knowledge and control these forces for the benefit of mankind.

> **Job 38:24 What is the way to the place where the lightning is dispersed,**
> **or the place where the east winds are scattered over the earth?**

Depending on the translation or commentator, lightning has been translated as lightning (NIV), light (KJV & NAS), or mist (Dhorme).[5] Since the subject of light has already been addressed in verse 19, and since lightning will be addressed in verse 35, Dhorme's choice of mist makes the most sense. He points out that the following passage describes the east wind, rain storms, and thunder, which are not normally associated with light. However, the fog or mist is followed by the dry east wind.

In Job's day, this mist and east wind were unpredictable. But in our days of advanced meteorology, we have learned much about predicting such phenomena by mapping the jet streams and locating high and low pressure areas. Just a few years ago our fathers would watch the sky and listen to radio stations upwind from our homes to try to predict the weather. Now we can see the cloud patterns for hundreds of miles around every morning and night by watching the satellite photos on the weather channel. So modern man would again claim understanding.

Our abilities were dramatically demonstrated during the Gulf War. The U.S. had every advantage of modern meteorology in planning their military maneuvers.

> **Job 38:25-27 Who cuts a channel for the torrents of rain,**
> **and a path for the thunderstorm,**
> **[26]to water a land where no man lives,**
> **a desert with no one in it,**
> **[27]to satisfy a desolate wasteland**
> **And make it sprout with grass?**

Exactly what God is asking Job in verse 25 is not immediately clear. The most obvious answer would be God. Perhaps God is implying "I have, but have you, Job?" Again Job's answer would probably have been "no." But we

God's Answer, Part 1

have "cut many a channel" for the purposes of irrigation, which may be the thrust here. We have built dams to restrain flooding and hydroelectric plants to convert the torrents to useable power; to "produce the dawn" as it were.

Verses 26 and 27 would suggest the vast irrigation projects man has undertaken such as tunnels carved through mountains to irrigate deserts, or dams constructed to conserve water for agricultural purposes. One of the great modern-day miracles is the abundance of food being produced through land management and irrigation in Israel. In Job's day, such projects would have been unthinkable, but today man can do almost anything of this kind if enough money is available. Ability and technology are no hindrance to this type of project.

Yet another interpretation of these verses is given by Tsevat.[6] He points out that God here declares nature to be amoral. Rain falls on a desert land while inhabited land may desperately need it. God is therefore agreeing with Job (12:7-25) that there is no justice in nature.

Job 38:28 Does the rain have a father?
Who fathers the drops of dew?

Ancient man was probably quite ignorant of the processes we commonly know today as evaporation and condensation, although Elihu shows remarkable insight in 36:27-28. Here we see a common phenomenon that must have puzzled ancient men: How can tons of water be floating around in the sky? Where does it come from? How does it get there? What makes it fall? When it doesn't, why not? One is reminded of the Amerindian cultures who thought that beating a drum and dancing would make it rain.

Actually, the phenomena that make rain happen are easily demonstrated in the school laboratory and are taught in elementary science textbooks.

PHYSICS

Job 38:29-30 From whose womb comes the ice?
Who gives birth to the frost from the heavens
[30] when the waters become hard as stone,
when the surface of the deep is frozen?

Elihu's answer to this question is found in 37:10. "The breath of God produces ice." His contemporaries probably had many such ideas to explain how water could evaporate in the presence of heat and then become hard like rocks in the presence of cold.

These verses are probably an extension of the question in verse 28. The answer is the same. Modern man is well aware of the laws that control these processes, and makes use of them in many ways. Refrigerators, freezers, and air conditioners are but a few of the uses of these principles.

The laws of physics are fundamental to the operation of this planet, and indeed the universe. These basic laws form the foundation of all our technical know-how. A knowledge about this field will be quite crucial in establishing justice in the technical areas of our task.

ASTRONOMY & MYTHOLOGY

**Job 38:31-32 "Can you bind the beautiful Pleiades?
Can you loose the cords of Orion?
³²Can you bring forth the constellations in their seasons
or lead out the Bear with its cubs?**

Of all God's questions, this is perhaps the most difficult to comprehend for modern man. We do know that the stars and the constellations were imbued with deep and mysterious secrets of ancient mythology. Dhorme[7] suggests a connection between Nimrod and Orion, but concludes his excellent discussion of this passage with, "It is difficult to see what astro-mythological legend would be alluded to by the idea of consolation offered to the Bear for the loss of its little ones." And so Dhorme also seems to conclude that the meanings of this question are lost in ancient mythology.

While many ancient legendary meanings have been lost, the astronomical facts concerning these constellations have become much more clear, especially since we have engaged in space travel. Views of the stars from outside our atmosphere reveal much more than we could ever have seen from earth. Since the launching of the Hubbell telescope and its repair, astronomers have been swamped with new observations and discoveries as the information comes in. We now have a much more accurate understanding of the bodies and clusters with their relative positions that make up these constellations.

Nikola Tesla has been described as the greatest inventor of all time. He made many startling predictions and described phenomena that other scientists of his day thought ridiculous. Some of them still sound incredible and would be dismissed out of hand if so many of his inventions had not worked and if so many of his predictions had not come true. They are still coming true as science has finally learned to take the writings and observations of this visionary man seriously. Tesla has many followers today who are still exploring his ideas. Frederic Jueneman, "Innovative Notebook" columnist for *Industrial Research* magazines says: "If Tesla's resonance effects, as shown by the Stanford team, can control enormous energies by minuscule triggering signals, then by an extension of this principle we should be able to affect the environment of the very stars in the sky....With godlike arrogance, we someday may yet direct the stars in their courses."[8]

God's Answer, Part 1

If Tesla's ideas have merit (and most of them do), and such powerful instruments are indeed possible, we can rest assured that these secrets are held fast within the highly classified archives of the government's defense research agencies along with many of the rest of Tesla's papers known to be there.

It is at least incredible that, since Job's time, man has advanced technologically to the point where serious scientists would even conjecture about such things.

This category expands from the laws of physics to include the whole universe. I suspect we will literally explore the universe during the millennium and we will need to know a lot about this subject to establish justice wherever we go.

**Job 38:33 Do you know the laws of the heavens?
Can you set up God's dominion over the earth?**

God continues his questions about the field of astronomy with this interesting question. The ancients dealt with the stars and constellations in terms of myth and legend. Although they had a remarkable knowledge based on observation of the relative positions and appearances of the stars, their knowledge pales beside ours, which is based on science and technology.

That we now know a great deal about the ordinances of the heavens is demonstrated in the successes of our space exploration programs. With the help of computers, we can calculate the infinitesimal gravitational influences of the heavenly bodies and propel our probes into space, guiding them with amazing accuracy to targets invisible to the naked eye.

The NIV renders 33b "Can you set up God's dominion over the earth?" But the footnotes point out that "God's" could be translated "his or their." "Set up" is rendered "establish" in the Masoretic text, and Dhorme[9] translates this portion "Do you fulfill on earth what is written there?" It seems to me that the thrust of the question is more in the area of man's understanding and utilization of these ordinances rather than comparing man's creative power (which is zero) to that of God's. I would suggest that the question could be presented as "Have you established what the influences of the heavens are over the earth?" The question then more nearly parallels the meaning of the first part of the verse and our answers would coincide.

METEOROLOGY

**Job 38:34 Can you raise your voice to the clouds
and cover yourself with a flood of water?**

Ancient man tried many things to induce clouds to give up their rain. The

The Absence of Justice

early and latter rains were crucial to farmers in the Near East (Amos 4:7-8, Jer.5:24, 14:2-4) as in any arid country. The American Indians tried rain dances, drum beating, and huge bonfires, but with little predictable success. (Actually, if one beats a drum or dances long enough, it will eventually rain, but not as a result of our exertions). With the advent of the airplane man began to learn the dynamics of the earth's atmosphere and the interrelations of the different forces that control the rains. The results are that man *has* learned how to induce clouds to yield their moisture. Cloud seeding with silver iodide crystals and dry ice has brought success, but at an unjustifiable expense. Attempts to control the rains in this manner have proved to be a "rob Peter to pay Paul" matter. Forcing the clouds to yield their moisture at one location deprives another location of its rain, so while studies go on that now include satellite surveillance, cloud seeding is not yet a common practice.

Tesla also speculated about weather control. Dr. Robert Helliwell and John Katsufrakis of Stanford University's Radio Science Laboratory experimented in the Antarctic with some of Tesla's ideas. Jueneman points out that "The theoretical implication suggested by their work is that global weather control can be attained by the injection of relatively small 'signals' into the Van Allen belts—something like a super-transistor effect."[10]

An article titled "Weather Warfare" in the April 21, 1997 *Insight* magazine stated "...as early as 1966 the United States successfully conducted weather modification in Vietnam. The experiment, known as "Project Popeye," extended the monsoon season and thereby increased the mud on the Ho Chi Minh trail—the main enemy supply route into South Vietnam. To produce the rain, U.S. aircraft dispensed a rain-making agent nicknamed "Olive Oil." The article cites a study in which "...scientists claim that within three decades U.S. aerospace forces will be able to control the weather on the battlefield." The Monday, September 9, 2002 issue of the *Wall Street Journal* reported "A Russian ministry claims it used an ionization machine to make rain that for a time eased smoke engulfing Moscow from wildfires."

It is also true on the other hand that modern man has learned to farm without the rains using dry land farming techniques and irrigation. Irrigation is, after all, bringing rain that rained somewhere else to land where the moisture is needed. So in that sense, even with irrigation we can make it "rain" where we want.

Job 38:35 Do you send the lightning bolts on their way?
Do they report to you, 'Here we are'?

Elihu implied that lightning was a direct act of God in 36:30, and so it must have seemed to ancient man. An electrical storm is still an awe-inspiring phenomenon. But we have learned that lightning is produced by the interaction of natural forces following the laws of physics. The phenomenon is reproducible in the laboratory on a smaller scale, so that modern man can generate lightning, and predict its occurrence and effects, if only on a small scale. Job and his contemporaries called lightning "the fire of God" (1:16), and Job, therefore, would plead ignorance about this subject. Modern man cannot yet control thunderstorms (although Tesla claimed to know how). However, he understands the forces that cause them and has learned how to avoid their consequences. That is, don't stand under a tree in a thunderstorm. Use lightning rods and lightning arresters, etc.

WISDOM

**Job 38:36 Who endowed the heart with wisdom
or gave understanding to the mind?**

If we take this question at face value, Job's answer would probably be as good as ours. The answer is obviously "God" as revealed in Scripture:

**Proverbs 2:6 For the LORD gives wisdom,
and from his mouth come knowledge and understanding.**

**Proverbs 3:19 By wisdom the LORD laid the earth's foundations,
by understanding he set the heavens in place;**

James 1:5 If any of you lacks wisdom, he should ask God, who gives generously to all without finding fault, and it will be given to him.

Many passages throughout Scripture speak of wisdom and understanding, declaring God as their source. Job did not have the Scriptures as we do, so we know the answer through revelation. However, Job might have made a very good try at guessing the answer.

If, however, the answer required an understanding of how the thought processes work and the procedures of making judgment, modern man surely would have a greater understanding. Research in this field continues with the end in mind of building greater and better computers. Some of the latest research in computer science focuses on making a machine that has the ability to use logic in making decisions.

While knowledge is useful, it can be catastrophic without wisdom. If we consider God as the ruler on this earth, it is certain that the earth will be governed with wisdom from the top down.

METEOROLOGY

**Job 38:37-38 Who has the wisdom to count the clouds?
Who can tip over the water jars of the heavens**

The Absence of Justice

> ³⁸when the dust becomes hard
> and the clods of earth stick together?

This question is similar to the question in verses 38:26-28. In both cases, the question is not "can you?" but "Who?" Job's answer would be, "Only God." But does modern man have any more to add to Job's answer? Possibly so. Matthew 10:30 states that even the hairs on our heads are numbered (by God). That must be a far greater number than the clouds.

The second part of God's question pictures a desert or drought-stricken area. Modern man may not find it economically feasible to seed the clouds in order to "tip the water jars of the heavens," but we have turned many desert places like Israel into gardens by means of irrigation.

ZOOLOGY

> **Job 38:39-40 "Do you hunt the prey for the lioness**
> **and satisfy the hunger of the lions**
> **⁴⁰when they crouch in their dens**
> **or lie in wait in a thicket?**

As we pass into the realm of the animal kingdom, it is appropriate that we start with the king of the beasts. It is interesting that the text is quite accurate because it is the lioness that does most of the hunting while the male lions watch from a distance. When the males hear that a kill has been made, they make their appearance for the "lion's share."

The answer is also given in the Psalms:

> **Psalm 104:21 The lions roar for their prey**
> **and seek their food from God.**

In Job's day, the lions were considered ferocious beasts and were feared and avoided. However, we have placed all kinds of wild beasts in zoos and we indeed satisfy the appetites of the young lions. We also keep them healthy, something that would likely have been impossible for Job since a thorough knowledge of veterinary medicine is required to maintain a zoo.

> **Job 38:41 Who provides food for the raven**
> **when its young cry out to God**
> **and wander about for lack of food?**

God continues with the animal kingdom by now referring to the ravens. Again the question is "Who?" And again we can find the answer in Psalms:

> **Psalm 147:9 He provides food for the cattle**

God's Answer, Part 1

> and for the young ravens when they call.

In the same sense as verses 39-40, ornithologists have determined the diets of ravens and do keep them successfully in zoos. Again, Job would plead ignorance while modern man could not.

> **Job 39:1-4** "Do you know when the mountain goats give birth?
> Do you watch when the doe bears her fawn?
> ²Do you count the months till they bear?
> Do you know the time they give birth?
> ³They crouch down and bring forth their young;
> their labor pains are ended.
> ⁴Their young thrive and grow strong in the wilds;
> they leave and do not return.

The first words of this chapter and other subsequent phrases seem to set the sense of the questions. "Do you know?" God points out a number of animals and then describes some peculiarities about them. It would make sense that God is primarily asking Job, "Do you know about the habits and habitats of these animals?"

The animal described in verse 1 is an extremely timid animal, inhabiting areas quite inaccessible to most men. It is no surprise then that zoologists have only recently unlocked the secrets of this secluded animal. Job would certainly have pleaded ignorance about such details about this animal and her gestation period.

> **Job 39:5-8** "Who let the wild donkey go free?
> Who untied his ropes?
> ⁶I gave him the wasteland as his home,
> the salt flats as his habitat.
> ⁷He laughs at the commotion in the town;
> he does not hear a driver's shout.
> ⁸He ranges the hills for his pasture
> and searches for any green thing.

In this passage, God asks again "Who?" and the obvious answer is God, who goes on in verse 6 to describe what he did. He describes some of the donkey's mannerisms that indicate that this is also a timid animal, avoiding humans. Therefore it is likely that Job and his contemporaries knew little of the habits of this creature in the wild although he had owned five hundred of the domesticated variety (1:3).

> **Job 39:9-12** "Will the wild ox consent to serve you?
> Will he stay by your manger at night?

The Absence of Justice

> ¹⁰Can you hold him to the furrow with a harness?
> Will he till the valleys behind you?
> ¹¹Will you rely on him for his great strength?
> Will you leave your heavy work to him?
> ¹²Can you trust him to bring in your grain
> and gather it to your threshing floor?

Since Job had owned five hundred yoke of oxen (1:3), he probably knew very well that the answers to God's questions here were "no." Most wild animals are impossible to domesticate, and even those who succeed in doing so to a degree find that there are severe limits to how much trust can be placed in them.

A modern farmer would probably answer God in terms of the absurdity of using oxen to till his fields, do his heavy work, or thresh his wheat since we have invented machinery that makes the use of beasts of burden obsolete (although not in Third World countries.)

> **Job 39:13-18** "The wings of the ostrich flap joyfully,
> but they cannot compare with the pinions and
> feathers of the stork.
> ¹⁴She lays her eggs on the ground
> and lets them warm in the sand,
> ¹⁵unmindful that a foot may crush them,
> that some wild animal may trample them.
> ¹⁶She treats her young harshly, as if they were not hers;
> she cares not that her labor was in vain,
> ¹⁷for God did not endow her with wisdom
> or give her a share of good sense.
> ¹⁸Yet when she spreads her feathers to run,
> she laughs at horse and rider.

No question is asked in this section on the ostrich. It is as if the strange ways of this huge bird generate their own questions. Yet, since Job's day, we have studied and learned much about them. There are even ostrich farms scattered around the United States. It is reportedly a very profitable business. Yet to Job, the strange ways of the ostrich must have been a mystery.

Our world has seen much cruelty and injustice imposed on animals. Since the Scriptures on the kingdom mention animals, it is obvious that animals will also enjoy the change to a just society. We have gained much knowledge in this field and I am sure we will use it to bring a halt to the cruelty and injustice animals suffer.

God's Answer, Part 1

WAR HORSES & THE ART OF WAR

> **Job 39:19-25** "Do you give the horse his strength
> or clothe his neck with a flowing mane?
> [20]Do you make him leap like a locust,
> striking terror with his proud snorting?
> [21]He paws fiercely, rejoicing in his strength,
> and charges into the fray.
> [22]He laughs at fear, afraid of nothing;
> he does not shy away from the sword.
> [23]The quiver rattles against his side,
> along with the flashing spear and lance.
> [24]In frenzied excitement he eats up the ground;
> he cannot stand still when the trumpet sounds.
> [25]At the blast of the trumpet he snorts, 'Aha!'
> He catches the scent of battle from afar,
> the shout of commanders and the battle cry.

In verses 19 and 20a Job is again asked rhetorical questions. The answer from Job and also from modern man is "no." But then certain aspects and uses of this majestic creature are described. The war-horse seems to be the center of the focus of this passage. War-horses, though now obsolete except for traditional ceremonies, presented a terrifying sight to ancient foot soldiers. The Incan Empire in Peru was conquered in part because the Spaniards had horses. The Indians had never seen horses before and were terrified. Thousands of fierce Inca soldiers were conquered by one hundred fifty-three Spaniards with a few horses. The picture presented here is of battle and the accompanying excitement and terror. Yet this terror is mild to a modern soldier who has seen the terrible slaughter of the war machines that have replaced horses.

AERODYNAMICS & OPTICS

> **Job 39:26-30** "Does the hawk take flight by your wisdom
> and spread his wings toward the south?
> [27]Does the eagle soar at your command
> and build his nest on high?
> [28]He dwells on a cliff and stays there at night;
> a rocky crag is his stronghold.
> [29]From there he seeks out his food;
> his eyes detect it from afar.
> [30]His young ones feast on blood,
> and where the slain are, there is he."

If the meaning of these questions involves an understanding of aerodynamics, then modern man in this age of air and space travel could answer "yes." Men of all ages have admired birds and their ability to fly. Neverthe-

The Absence of Justice

less, it was not until the twentieth century that man learned how birds fly, and how to do it himself. Job would plead ignorance, but modern man understands how birds can fly.

Another aspect of these beautiful birds of prey is covered in verse 29. Job and his contemporaries must have marveled at the ability of these birds to see from great heights with such astounding clarity. It has taken many years to develop the technology of optics. Modern man understands how these birds can see telescopically from great heights. In fact, we now surpass the birds in this regard. It is reported that a satellite camera can zoom in on your backyard picnic, identify the people who are there, and even identify what you are eating! However, the true extent of the abilities of these devices is still cloaked in secrecy.

These disciplines are an extension of the laws of physics and may indicate that these sciences will be utilized as we travel more efficiently and explore the universe more extensively.

So God ends his first speech. The questions have covered many subjects and the answers from Job have all been negative, while our answers to the same questions would be largely in the affirmative. The three friends have failed to answer Job's dilemma. Elihu has spoken at great length and his ideas have been totally disregarded by God and the others. There are those who would say there is no answer as to why the innocents suffer. But surely such a great literary work inspired by God himself would not leave such an important question unanswered. The logical place to find the answer, and indeed the *only* place it could be, is in God's response to Job which we have just covered. But what is the answer? This question has puzzled students of the Bible for centuries. Certainly, the answer is not immediately obvious.

It is interesting that two questions predominate in God's response to Job. The question "Who?" and the question "How?" The scientific world has found the answers to most of God's questions of "How?" Curiously, they refuse to accept the "Who?" part of the response that theology supplies.

SUMMARY

What did God say?

For interpreting God's answer, what are our options? Some would say that God is asserting to Job that he is in control and is all-powerful since he created these phenomena that Job doesn't understand. Job should simply trust and not ask questions. However, this view is too much like Elihu's view and is unacceptable. Another option is that God is humbling or humiliating a sinfully self-righteous and proud Job. But God had declared Job blameless and upright, so how could he also be self-righteous and proud? God does not treat his choice servants this way. We will have to look for another option.

God's Answer, Part 1

38:1 said "...the Lord answered Job..." So at this point, let us review again what Job's question was. Job said: "I should be getting justice. I am not. Why not?"

Now God has just completed a treatise on different disciplines of science that most surely baffled poor Job. He first hoped for pity from his friends and got none. Now his friend God speaks and surely God will have some words of comfort. But it doesn't seem so, at least not at first. Try reading these chapters to someone suffering in the hospital and note the comfort they bring. But Job was comforted and satisfied with God's answer. That Job now has a deeper insight and understanding from God's answer is made clear in 42:6.

While Job was surely baffled regarding the specific answers to God's questions, a modern Job might answer, "Sure, we know that stuff. It's all written down in books at the library. What does this have to do with my pain and suffering, or Job's for that matter?" For the Bible to be relevant and timeless, the answer we find must satisfy Job and also have meaning for us.

The fact that God asked questions that we now can answer *must* have significance. God could just as easily have asked questions no one but God himself could have ever answered, but he didn't.

If we interpret God's questions (as others have done) as unanswerable or as a means to humble Job, then the answer God gives Job has no meaning to modern man because we could now, boastfully, take pride in our knowledge. I do not believe the Bible is subject to obsolescence. There *must* be a deeper meaning behind God's questions.

There is a clue that could shed some light on this problem tucked away in the Book of Daniel:

Daniel 12:4 But you, Daniel, close up and seal the words of the scroll until the time of the end. Many will go here and there to increase knowledge."

The thrust of this verse is that knowledge will be increased by the time of the end. It is significant that most of the questions God asked relate to scientific discoveries of the past hundred years. On the basis of this verse and since we know most if not all the answers to the questions of God, I suggest that God's answer could be:

"Job, I agree you are not getting justice now. But I will establish justice on the earth. It will happen when mankind knows the answers to these questions."

This is a declaration of God's ultimate sovereignty even when he does not appear to be sovereign in an immediate sense.

The Absence of Justice

The knowledge that the establishment of justice is a future certainty will be scarce comfort for Job in his present dilemma, but Job's faith in God's ultimate triumph and justice will have been restored. He didn't get the pity he was looking for (19:21-22), but he got the satisfaction of understanding that justice will someday be established. I believe that Job, somehow, during God's discourse, got at least a glimpse of God's grand plan for the ages. His confidence in God's goodness and ultimate justice had been restored. And while he *had* believed in God's immediate sovereignty, this was replaced by a belief in God's *ultimate* sovereignty.

God's answer is also scarce comfort to us if we insist on believing, as Job and his friends believed, that justice now rules on the earth. But our comfort and satisfaction will be the same as Job's if we realize that God has a plan for the ages and he will ultimately triumph over evil and establish a just rule over the earth through the Messiah. More than being comforted, we will enjoy the thrill of anticipation as we realize that, since we know the answers to God's questions, we are now living in or very near the days when God promised Job that justice will come. In the New Testament we are told:

> **Luke 21:28 When these things begin to take place, stand up and lift up your heads, because your redemption is drawing near."**

Job's confidence had been in a God from whom he expected justice now, on this earth. As Tsevat[11] points out, "No less than three times God refers to the "foundation," "the basis," and "the cornerstone" of the inhabited world, the earth (38:4,6). "What then makes you assume that it is justice which is its foundation?" Job now sees that he and his friends had been wrong in their assumption that justice should be expected on the earth. I believe he somehow gets a glimpse of God's great panorama of the ages, with justice ultimately being established in the last days. Also, since God had finally spoken, Job's sense of communion with him was restored.

Certainly this is not the *only* possible interpretation of God's answer. Scriptures may have many levels of meaning, especially where eschatology is concerned, and it is safe to assume that there is much more here than meets the eye. Perhaps we have only just begun to scratch the surface of the meaning of God's answer. However, I cannot compare God's answer to the "Yellow Pages," or call it a "non-answer" as some have done. Nor can I accept that *what* God said was irrelevant and *that* he spoke to Job was the important fact. I also believe that what God said was more than just a "science quiz." To arrive at our interpretation requires that a number of blank spaces be filled in, hopefully not without a rational basis.

Someone may ask, "Why did God create such a world in which he does not dispense justice?" There is a very important, fundamental reason why this would have been impossible. We will explain that reason in the thirteenth chapter of this book.

1. Andersen, Francis I. *Job*. London: Inter-Varsity Press, 1976. p. 269
2. Mitton, Simon, ed. *The Cambridge Encyclopedia of Astronomy*. New York: Crown Publishers, 1977. p. 174
3. LeMaire, T. R. *Stones from the Stars*. New York: Prentice Hall, 1980.
4. Levenson, Jon D. *Creation and the Persistence of Evil*. HarperSanFrancisco, 1988.
5. Dhorme, Edouard. *A Commentary on the Book of Job*. Translated by Harold Knight. Nashville: Thomas Nelson, 1984. p. 585
6. Tsevat, Matitiahu. *The Meaning of the Book of Job and Other Biblical Studies*. New York: Ktav, 1980.
7. Dhorme, Edouard. *A Commentary on the Book of Job*. Translated by Harold Knight. Nashville: Thomas Nelson, 1984. p. 589-90
8. Jueneman, Frederic. "Innovative Notebook," *Industrial Research*. February 1974.
9. Dhorme, Edouard. *A Commentary on the Book of Job*. Translated by Harold Knight. Nashville: Thomas Nelson, 1984. p. 590-91
10. Jueneman, Frederic. "Innovative Notebook," *Industrial Research*. February 1974.
11. Tsevat, Matitiahu. *The Meaning of the Book of Job and Other Biblical Studies*. New York: Ktav, 1980. p. 29

CHAPTER 11

JOB'S RESPONSES & GOD'S ANSWER, PART 2

God has completed his discourse on science and nature. He now turns his whole attention to Job with a penetrating question.

GOD CONFRONTS JOB

Job 40:1-2 The LORD said to Job:
²"Will the one who contends with the Almighty correct him?
Let him who accuses God answer him!"

We have almost shuddered as Job vehemently defended his claim of innocence, stating that it appeared to him that God must be wicked. We are told that Job never stepped over the "line" by committing a sin (1:22). One characteristic of the wicked mentioned repeatedly throughout the book is that they have no perceived need of God (15:25, 21:14, 22:17). In all of Job's suffering, he challenged God freely, but never crossed the "line" to the position where he gave up on God, or became angry *with* God or shook his fist at God. It seems that the "sin line" is the act of turning our backs on God, not that we challenge him or contend with him. Job had indeed been contending with the Almighty, and he was not censured for it.

We do not know the tone of voice God used in asking Job the questions in this chapter. Most who read it assume that God is angry and the tone he uses is accusatory and intimidating to say the least. I am not so sure that we can make such assumptions. Remember the scene in heaven when God opened the subject of Job before Satan. We noted the words he used were similar to the words a proud father would use in bragging about his children. Job was a man God loved. God had doted on him, showering him with blessing after blessing until he was challenged by Satan to remove the protective hedge. I believe it is inconsistent that God would now suddenly start castigating Job, especially since he had admitted that Job had been afflicted without cause (2:3).

Yet Job had certainly contended with God and even accused him of cruelty (30:21, NAS) among other things. Nevertheless, God certainly knew where Job was coming from. Therefore it is doubtful that God is "putting Job down" in this passage. While God uses circumstances to humble his children, he does not humiliate them. Job had started as a very humble man (Chapters 29 & 31) so it is unreasonable that he needed humbling. Humility would certainly have been one of the virtues exhibited by a "blameless and upright" man.

Job's Responses & God's Answer, Part 2

**Psalm 103:14 ...for he knows how we are formed,
he remembers that we are dust.**

But since Job had made many insinuations and speculations as he wrestled with his dilemma, it is appropriate that God confronts him now in the light of what Job has just learned from God's discourse. That is, Job and his friends were all wrong in assuming that the earth is governed by justice. I can believe that God asks this question in a very gentle way. And Job replies appropriately:

JOB'S MEEK REPLY

**Job 40:3-5 Then Job answered the LORD:
⁴"I am unworthy—how can I reply to you?
I put my hand over my mouth.
⁵I spoke once, but I have no answer—
twice, but I will say no more."**

There are at least two explanations why Job, whose approach to God had been confrontational, now answers meekly.

> 1. William Safire says, "In the prosaic epilogue, the browbeaten and awestruck Job caves in."[1] In the presence of his God, he summarily gives up.

> 2. Job now sees things differently because of God's answer.

I think the second option is more credible. Essentially, Job says, "I have nothing more to say." His response is typical of those incidents recorded in Scripture where men have come face to face with even an angel. Isaiah (Isa 6:5), Ezekiel (Eze 3:23), Daniel (Dan 10:7-9), and John (Rev 1:17) all record being overwhelmed by the splendor they witnessed. Job is no different. Although he spoke bravely enough when God seemed to be absent (Ch 23), God's presence has silenced him. He will no longer contend with God because he is seeing things differently now that God has revealed to him his plan to ultimately establish justice.

GOD CHALLENGES JOB

**Job 40:6-14 Then the LORD spoke to Job out of the storm:
⁷"Brace yourself like a man;
I will question you,
and you shall answer me.
⁸"Would you discredit my justice?
Would you condemn me to justify yourself?**

The Absence of Justice

⁹Do you have an arm like God's,
    and can your voice thunder like his?
¹⁰Then adorn yourself with glory and splendor,
    and clothe yourself in honor and majesty.
¹¹Unleash the fury of your wrath,
    look at every proud man and bring him low,
¹²look at every proud man and humble him,
    crush the wicked where they stand.
¹³Bury them all in the dust together;
    shroud their faces in the grave.
¹⁴Then I myself will admit to you
    that your own right hand can save you.

This is admittedly a very difficult passage. Most commentators interpret God's words here as angry, condescending, and very sarcastic, "putting Job in his place." As I have just mentioned, this is inconsistent with God's attitude in the prologue and the epilogue. God does not zap his children when they ask "Why?" But he doesn't always give us the kind of answer we want either. All people of conscience still ask "Why?" about the Holocaust. Even Jesus, on the cross asked "Why?" and there is no record that God responded to his question. The text here certainly sounds angry and sarcastic enough, but we cannot discern the tone of voice God used. In the light of all the rest of God's statements to and about Job, there seems to be little justification for interpreting this passage as censorious.

It is important that we note that God's answer is interrogative in verses seven through nine. In verse ten, he changes to the imperative.

WAS GOD SARCASTIC?

Someone has said that sarcasm is the most cruel use of a language. God uses sarcasm often in the Old Testament when dealing with his stubborn and rebellious people. The prophets often used sarcasm in speaking to the people for God.

> **Amos 4:1** Hear this word, you cows of Bashan on Mount Samaria,
> you women who oppress the poor and crush the needy
> and say to your husbands, "Bring us some drinks!"

This passage from Amos is saturated with sarcasm. God was both grieved over his people's sin and angry with their perfidious ways. However, does God ever use sarcasm, the most cruel use of the language, to speak to his children, especially one like Job whom God had declared perfect and upright in all his ways? I think that we are justified in doubting a sarcastic interpretation of God's answer to Job.

The Bible is its own best commentator, and so we will support our position against sarcasm in this passage by citing several similar imperatives from

Job's Responses & God's Answer, Part 2

Scripture where God obviously was not sarcastic.

> **Deuteronomy 16:20 Follow justice and justice alone, so that you may live and possess the land the LORD your God is giving you.**

God here gives Israel a directive that is not sarcastic. It is a legitimate command that is achievable. (See Deut 30:11)

> **Proverbs 31:8-9 "Speak up for those who cannot speak for themselves, for the rights of all who are destitute.**
> **9Speak up and judge fairly;**
> **defend the rights of the poor and needy."**

The Job passage focuses on the defeat of the wicked while this passage focuses on the defense of the innocent. The ideas are parallel and there is no sarcasm here.

> **Isaiah 2:11-12 The eyes of the arrogant man will be humbled**
> **and the pride of men brought low;**
> **the LORD alone will be exalted in that day.**
> **12The LORD Almighty has a day in store**
> **for all the proud and lofty,**
> **for all that is exalted**
> **(and they will be humbled),**

In this passage, Isaiah is looking forward to the Day of the Lord. The wording and thrust of the passage are similar to the Job passage, and there is no sarcasm here.

> **Jeremiah 22:3 This is what the LORD says: Do what is just and right. Rescue from the hand of his oppressor the one who has been robbed. Do no wrong or violence to the alien, the fatherless or the widow, and do not shed innocent blood in this place.**

In this passage and also in Jeremiah 21:12 and Zechariah 7:9, God's commands are similar to Job 40, without sarcasm.

> **Amos 5:14-15 Seek good, not evil,**
> **that you may live.**
> **Then the LORD God Almighty will be with you,**
> **just as you say he is.**
> **15Hate evil, love good;**
> **maintain justice in the courts.**
> **Perhaps the LORD God Almighty will have mercy**
> **on the remnant of Joseph.**

The Absence of Justice

The attitude expressed in this passage from Amos is similar to the attitude described in Job 40:11-13, and there is no sarcasm here. This is a legitimate command.

> **Malachi 4:3 Then you will trample down the wicked; they will be ashes under the soles of your feet on the day when I do these things," says the LORD Almighty.**

This passage predicts the Day of the Lord when justice will indeed be established throughout the earth. The wording is similar to Job 40:12-13. There is no sarcasm here.

So there are no Scriptural parallels to support the sarcastic interpretation of this passage. Job's perceptions about justice had been wrong and he will confess this and retract his statements. But at the same time, we are told that he did not sin nor did he speak wrongly of God.

IF GOD IS NOT BEING SARCASTIC HERE, WHAT IS HE SAYING?

First, he asks a question (40:8) to which Job would surely answer "no." Job had been arguing from his (and his friends') position that justice is supposed to rule on the earth. He had said that if this is so, knowing that he did not deserve such treatment, then the logical conclusion would be that God is not just. But this is all based on the premise that justice rules, and Job (but not his friends) had come to the position where he had strong suspicions about that premise.

Next, God asks Job another question in verse 9. "Do you have an arm like God's and can your voice thunder like his?" At first inclination, Job's (and our) answer would be "absolutely no!" But let's think this through. Man was created in God's image.

> **Genesis 1:26 Then God said, "Let us make man in our image, in our likeness, and let them rule over the fish of the sea and the birds of the air, over the livestock, over all the earth, and over all the creatures that move along the ground."**

Although man is not God, he has an "arm like God" because he was made in God's image. "...can your voice thunder like his?" speaks of authority. Man has been given authority as seen in:

> **Psalm 8:6 You made him ruler over the works of your hands;**
> **you put everything under his feet:**

> **Psalm 115:16 The highest heavens belong to the LORD,**
> **but the earth he has given to man.**

Job's Responses & God's Answer, Part 2

The New Testament writer quotes Psalm 8 and includes a commentary on the passage:

> **Hebrews 2:7-8 You made him a little lower than the angels; you crowned him with glory and honor** [8]**and put everything under his feet." In putting everything under him, God left nothing that is not subject to him. Yet at present we do not see everything subject to him.**

So, in the sense of the above verses, Job and we could answer God's question "yes."

Then, in verses 10 through 13, God issues a directive. It could be called the Great Commission of the Old Testament for mankind. What I suggest that God is saying in these verses is:

Stand up and be the noble creature I created you to be. Establish justice in every area of your influence. Crush and put down injustice in every form.

It is difficult to make verse 14 appear anything but sarcastic. However Dhorme,[2] while he interprets this verse as being ironic, reads, "...and even I myself...will praise you." It is possible to live such lives that even God would praise us. Job is a prime example of this fact.

Bemporad[3] interprets this passage as a positive command: "...God has placed upon *man* the task of "treading the wicked." *Man* must do the work on earth. *He* must realize that it is his own hand that will give him victory. It is not up to God to do man's work."

In substance I would suggest that God's complete answer to Job thus far could be:

"Job, I agree you are not getting justice now. But I will establish justice on the earth. It will happen when mankind knows the answers to these questions.
In the meantime, be the noble creature I created you to be. Establish justice in every area of your influence. Crush and put down injustice in every form."

God now moves on to the very interesting conclusion to his great commission for mankind.

The Absence of Justice

THE CHOICES

BEHEMOTH

> Job 40:15-24 "Look at the behemoth,
>   which I made along with you
>   and which feeds on grass like an ox.
> [16]What strength he has in his loins,
>   what power in the muscles of his belly!
> [17]His tail sways like a cedar;
>   the sinews of his thighs are close-knit.
> [18]His bones are tubes of bronze,
>   his limbs like rods of iron.
> [19]He ranks first among the works of God,
>   yet his Maker can approach him with his sword.
> [20]The hills bring him their produce,
>   and all the wild animals play nearby.
> [21]Under the lotus plants he lies,
>   hidden among the reeds in the marsh.
> [22]The lotuses conceal him in their shadow;
>   the poplars by the stream surround him.
> [23]When the river rages, he is not alarmed;
>   he is secure, though the Jordan should surge against his mouth.
> [24]Can anyone capture him by the eyes,
>   or trap him and pierce his nose?

Commentators have pondered and puzzled over the identity of this animal and also leviathan in the next section. They have come up with all sorts of possibilities for behemoth, from the hippopotamus to the brontosaurus. For leviathan, they guess anything from a crocodile to a whale to a sea monster of some kind.

The theology of Job's day was probably rather simple. Many of the belief systems of ancient man were expressed in mythology. The creation myths of the different cultures often included a sea monster which opposed God. This monster had to be subdued in order for the creation of the earth to proceed. Jon Levenson in his book *Creation and the Persistence of Evil* compares the monsters described in Scripture with the mythical monsters, and notes that they are usually opposed to God. He asks the question, "Why, in the act of creation, did God only subdue evil and not totally destroy it?" The question that comes to mind is, "Is there a connection between the 'opposing monsters' and the fallen Lucifer?"

The Scriptures have numerous examples of government systems described as animals. The more ferocious the government, the more ferocious the beast used to describe it. Daniel 7 describes four world empires using the symbolism of beasts:

Job's Responses & God's Answer, Part 2

Babylonian	Lion with eagle's wings
Medo-Persian	Vicious bear
Greek	Leopard with four wings and four heads
Roman	Terrible, unusual beast with iron teeth and ten horns

The final world empire opposed to God is described in Revelation 9 and 10 as a "beast out of the sea having seven heads and ten horns." He derives his power from the dragon which is identified in 12:9 as Satan. This connection will be developed further when we deal with Leviathan later in this chapter. Ellul,[4] in discussing the beasts of the Book of Revelation, says: "This is Political Power in its *abstraction*—the absolute power of the political." The point we are making is that there are systems of government that are found in Scripture that are described as beasts and are opposed to God.

Not all beasts described in the Bible are opposed to God, however. Four unusual beasts are described in Revelation 4:6-9 and have a function in heaven including the worship of God. Jesus himself is described as both a lamb and the lion of the tribe of Judah. So there is in Scripture a precedent for a benevolent system of government symbolized by a beast.

Historically, Leviathan has been identified with human government. Thomas Hobbes' classic book on civil government is titled *Leviathan*.

To interpret Behemoth and Leviathan in this section of God's answer as forms of government is consistent with other uses of animal symbolism in the Scripture. Otherwise, it is difficult to understand just why God would mention a hippopotamus and a crocodile. We have already determined that God was not trying to humble or humiliate or overwhelm Job with his questions in the first part of his answer. Why would God mention two other animals almost as an afterthought? That God would describe mankind's options in establishing government systems by utilizing the symbolism of beasts is consistent with the descriptions of world governments in Daniel and Revelation.

I believe that this section is a natural follow-up to what God has just said. God implies:

"If you do what I have commissioned you to do, then..."

I believe God now paints a very graphic *word picture* that describes the beneficial consequences to both individuals and to society for obeying his commission. The picture here is similar to the situation at Mount Gerizim and Mount Ebal where God sets before Israel the options of blessing or cursing (Deut 27:9-26). God first illustrates the "blessing" option in the graphic word picture of behemoth. So let's back away from the details of the text and try to discern the content of the picture God is painting. If mankind obeys God's commission, here are the characteristics of the society he will enjoy.

CHARACTERISTICS OF BEHEMOTH

In verse 16a, we find the characteristic of *strength.* A society that crushes evil and promotes justice will be a strong society. Its efforts will be toward positive, virtuous goals.

In verses 16b through 19, we find the characteristic of *power.* A society that obeys God's rules will be powerful. It will be unified around the ideas of justice and righteousness.

In verse 20, we see the characteristic of *productivity.* A society that focuses on justice and righteousness will be productive. The text here implies that there will be plenty.

In verses 21 and 22, we see the characteristic of *peace.* Such a society will enjoy rest and peace.

In verse 23a we see the characteristic of *composure.* Such a society will be free from apprehension, worry, and trepidation.

In verse 23b we see the characteristic of *security.* Though outside forces threaten, there is no fear in this society.

In verse 24 we see the characteristic of *invincibility.* Evil, antagonistic forces will not be able to penetrate this society's defenses.

Such will be the characteristics of a society that pursues justice and righteousness. We have seen a partial outworking of this commission in the history of the United States. Our founding fathers established this country on the principles of liberty and justice, which were in turn based on the principles of Scripture. Tight totalitarian controls were not needed because the citizens saw themselves primarily accountable to God and they disciplined themselves accordingly. There has been (until recent times) a full recognition of our dependence on Almighty God and a willingness to follow his precepts. Many of our presidents were praying men who gave God the honor and respect due him.

As a result, in the United States we have enjoyed an unprecedented era of strength, power, productivity, peace, composure, security, and invincibility in the history of the world, rivaled only by the state of the kingdom of Israel when David relinquished the throne to his son Solomon.

Peoples all over the world have envied the United States. They have wanted our prosperity. They envied our economic stability. They envied our freedoms. They wanted our medical expertise. They have wanted our scientific excellence. But they haven't sought after God's righteousness and justice that have made all these things possible.

Job's Responses & God's Answer, Part 2

Frighteningly, in recent decades we are seeing the erosion of our passion for justice and righteousness in the United States. No longer can we boast of the wonderful characteristics listed above, at least in full measure. Our strength, security, reputation, and productivity plus the other characteristics are in decline. We would do well to heed the warning that God described to Job and mankind in the form of Leviathan, the terrible beast.

LEVIATHAN

Job 41:1-34 "Can you pull in the leviathan with a fishhook
   or tie down his tongue with a rope?
²Can you put a cord through his nose
   or pierce his jaw with a hook?
³Will he keep begging you for mercy?
   Will he speak to you with gentle words?
⁴Will he make an agreement with you
   for you to take him as your slave for life?
⁵Can you make a pet of him like a bird
   or put him on a leash for your girls?
⁶Will traders barter for him?
   Will they divide him up among the merchants?
⁷Can you fill his hide with harpoons
   or his head with fishing spears?
⁸If you lay a hand on him,
   you will remember the struggle and never do it again!
⁹Any hope of subduing him is false;
   the mere sight of him is overpowering.
¹⁰No one is fierce enough to rouse him.
   Who then is able to stand against me?
¹¹Who has a claim against me that I must pay?
   Everything under heaven belongs to me.
¹²"I will not fail to speak of his limbs,
   his strength and his graceful form.
¹³Who can strip off his outer coat?
   Who would approach him with a bridle?
¹⁴Who dares open the doors of his mouth,
   ringed about with his fearsome teeth?
¹⁵His back has rows of shields
   tightly sealed together;
¹⁶each is so close to the next
   that no air can pass between.
¹⁷They are joined fast to one another;
   they cling together and cannot be parted.
¹⁸His snorting throws out flashes of light;
   his eyes are like the rays of dawn.
¹⁹Firebrands stream from his mouth;

The Absence of Justice

    sparks of fire shoot out.
[20]Smoke pours from his nostrils
    as from a boiling pot over a fire of reeds.
[21]His breath sets coals ablaze,
    and flames dart from his mouth.
[22]Strength resides in his neck;
    dismay goes before him.
[23]The folds of his flesh are tightly joined;
    they are firm and immovable.
[24]His chest is hard as rock,
    hard as a lower millstone.
[25]When he rises up, the mighty are terrified;
    they retreat before his thrashing.
[26]The sword that reaches him has no effect,
    nor does the spear or the dart or the javelin.
[27]Iron he treats like straw
    and bronze like rotten wood.
[28]Arrows do not make him flee;
    slingstones are like chaff to him.
[29]A club seems to him but a piece of straw;
    he laughs at the rattling of the lance.
[30]His undersides are jagged potsherds,
    leaving a trail in the mud like a threshing sledge.
[31]He makes the depths churn like a boiling caldron
    and stirs up the sea like a pot of ointment.
[32]Behind him he leaves a glistening wake;
    one would think the deep had white hair.
[33]Nothing on earth is his equal—
    a creature without fear.
[34]He looks down on all that are haughty;
    he is king over all that are proud."

    The other option God paints into this graphic illustration is an entirely different picture. Whereas behemoth is only mentioned in this one place in the Bible, Leviathan is mentioned several times, each passage giving us more clues to the identity of this beast. (See Job 3:8, Job 41:1, Psalm 74:14, Psalm 104:26, Isaiah 27:1) Leviathan is always associated with chaos. By far, this passage in Job 41 is the longest in the Bible concerning this creature. While most commentators identify this creature to be a crocodile, I believe the implications in Scripture suggest far more than just an animal. Follow some clues through the Scripture:

Isaiah 27:1 In that day,
the LORD will punish with his sword,
    his fierce, great and powerful sword,
Leviathan the gliding serpent,
    Leviathan the coiling serpent;
he will slay the monster of the sea.

Job's Responses & God's Answer, Part 2

Note that Leviathan is here equated with the "serpent" and with the "sea monster." If we cross to other Scriptures that mention "serpent," we learn even more. The trail of clues leads us into the New Testament. For example:

Revelation 20:2 He seized the dragon, that ancient serpent, who is the devil, or Satan, and bound him for a thousand years.

This passage equates the "serpent" (Leviathan) with the devil, Satan, and interestingly enough, the "dragon." Interesting because our passage in Job 41 describes Leviathan as having scales (vs 15-17), and breathing fire (vs 18-20). In addition, if we cross "sea monster" from Isaiah 27:1, we find:

Isaiah 51:9 Awake, awake! Clothe yourself with strength,
   O arm of the LORD;
awake, as in days gone by,
   as in generations of old.
Was it not you who cut Rahab to pieces,
   who pierced that monster through?

So now we find connections for Leviathan with Rahab (that monster) mentioned in Job 9:13 and 26:12. Putting it together, we have:

Leviathan - serpent - dragon - devil - Satan - sea monster - Rahab

It is evident that all these entities are at least related. I believe they are different names for the same being or different aspects of the rebellion against God.

However, leviathan in Job 41 is spelled with a small "l." This could mean that leviathan represents the world system generated by Leviathan. In Revelation there is another reference that makes an additional connection that bears on this subject.

Revelation 13:2 The beast I saw resembled a leopard, but had feet like those of a bear and a mouth like that of a lion. The dragon gave the beast his power and his throne and great authority.

So the dragon imparts his power to the beast which is worshiped by men in rebellion against God. Again, we see a connection with a rebellious society or world system whose agenda is contrary to God's but in accord with Satan's. Now as we proceed to analyze the word picture God gives as an alternative to behemoth, it becomes plain that this picture is the opposite of the picture of behemoth.

In terms of the commission by God, here are the characteristics that will result if an individual on a small scale or a society on a larger scale does not pursue justice and righteousness:

The Absence of Justice
CHARACTERISTICS OF LEVIATHAN

In verses 1 through 7 we see a picture of *wildness*. There is an untamed aspect to the society that does not pursue justice and righteousness.

In verse 8 we see a picture of a *struggle* if any attempt is made to restrain a society bent on rebellion against justice.

In verse 9 we see a picture of *overpowering strength*. This is the strength of mob violence and certainly not in the same category as the strength of behemoth.

Verses 10 and 11 pose a problem since the pronoun "me" is mentioned three times. This does not fit in the text with the preceding and following verses. Dhorme[5] translates this section as follows:

1. See now, his expectation is disappointed:
   He is knocked down by the mere sight of him!
2. Is *he not* cruel as soon as awakened?
   And who can stand and face *him?*
3. Who has confronted *him* and *has* remained safe?
   No one under the whole heavens!

So the picture we see here is one of *cruelty*. A society marked by disregard for justice and righteousness is vicious.

Verses 12 to 14 show a picture of *unbridled strength*. A society with no justice and righteousness is strong with a power that will not be accountable to any. It will lack the tempering of compassion and mercy. Its judgments are indisputable.

Verses 15 to 17 describe a system that is *impenetrable* by good. It will have no "Achilles' heel" accessible by man.

Verses 18 through 21 describe the results of this system as *destruction*. We see several references to firebrands, smoke, and sparks which kindle destructive fires and inspire fear.

Verse 22 pictures the *fear* and dismay this godless system promotes.

Verses 23 and 24 add to the "impenetrability" picture of verses 15-17.

Verse 25 is a picture of *violence and terror* that subdues the mightiest of foes.

Verses 26 through 29 give a picture of *supernatural power* that is unfazed by normal methods of dealing with wickedness.

Verses 30 through 32 speak of the *chaos* generated by godless disregard for justice and righteousness.

Job's Responses & God's Answer, Part 2

Verses 33 and 34 describe the source of the power of such a system as *satanic*. The wording here reminds us of Ezekiel 28:12-17 and Isaiah 14:12-15, which describe Satan's beginning and fall.

We need not look far to find many examples of wild, cruel, destructive regimes characterized by unbridled, overpowering strength inspired by supernatural Satanic power, regimes that produce violence, fear, and terror resulting in political and social chaos. In Biblical times we see this in the reigns of Manasseh and Ahab. In modern times, we have seen this in the godless communistic regimes of the former Soviet Union (correctly called the "Evil Empire" by President Reagan, who was criticized for his harshness), and especially the regimes of Albania, Bulgaria, and Romania, which were exposed as the Iron Curtain collapsed. President G. W. Bush has followed suit by identifying the "Evil Axis" operating in our current times. This includes the regimes of Saddam Hussein in Iraq and Kim Jong-Il in North Korea, which fit the picture.

However, we have the prime example in The Third Reich under Adolph Hitler, who spread fear, terror, and destruction across all of western civilization, murdering six million Jews and more than nine million others. Civilized peoples still shudder at the horror caused by that Satanic, oppressive regime. Memorials have been erected to insure that mankind will never forget that twelve-year reign of terror. And yet, we *have* already forgotten, it seems, for since those relatively recent days, we have endured communism, the killing fields of Cambodia, the ethnic cleansing of the former Yugoslavia, starvation and death in Somalia and Rwanda to list only a few of the worst examples. And the list goes on—and on—and on!

The human race cannot say it has not been warned. God predicted the results of injustice and unrighteousness in this, the oldest book of the Bible. In modern jargon, God said, "You'll have a dragon by the tail, and you won't know what to do with it."

The language of verses 33 and 34 reminds us of Ezekiel 28:12-17 where, according to many commentators, Satan and his fall are described. Mankind's choice is therefore between God, who brings justice and righteousness and all their benefits, and Satan, whose agenda is to instigate rebellion against God with the ensuing evil, suffering, and chaos.

SUMMARY

WHAT DID GOD SAY?

We are now ready to pull all the sections of God's answer together. We will see that he does indeed answer Job's nagging questions about the absence of justice on the earth.

The Absence of Justice

God said: "Job (and mankind), I agree you are not getting justice now. But I *will* establish justice on the earth. It will happen when mankind knows the answers to these questions. In the meantime, be the noble creature I created you to be. Establish justice in every area of your influence. Crush and put down injustice in every form. If you do this, you will enjoy a peaceful, prosperous, secure, and happy existence. If you do not, you will have a dragon by the tail that brings violence and destruction, and you won't know what to do with it."

Job now makes his final response to God:

JOB'S CONCLUSION

Job 42:1-6 Then Job replied to the LORD:
²"I know that you can do all things;
   no plan of yours can be thwarted.
³You *asked*, 'Who is this that obscures my counsel without knowledge?'
   Surely I spoke of things I did not understand,
   things too wonderful for me to know.
⁴"You *said*, 'Listen now, and I will speak;
   I will question you,
   and you shall answer me.'
⁵My ears had heard of you
   but now my eyes have seen you.
⁶Therefore I despise myself
   and repent in dust and ashes."

Job has somehow caught a glimpse of God's plan for the ages and he begins his response by acquiescing and bowing to it. In verse 2 he confesses to the ultimate sovereignty of God. In verse 3, he agrees that he spoke from ignorance. He acknowledges God's questions and responses according to the ancient court procedure referred to in verse 4.

In verse 5, Job confesses that he now has new insight that he has not had before. Bemporad[6] asks, "What does Job now understand? What is God's answer? First, that man is not the center of the world. Second, that the order of the world is amoral. Third, that God has placed upon *man* the task of 'treading the wicked.' *Man* must do the work on earth. *He* must realize that it is his 'own hand that will give him victory.' It is not up to God to do man's work. Fourth, that the world is unfinished, and that man must strive to *become* for he is not yet its center." While Job's love and respect for God have been great before, they have now grown by several magnitudes.

Painful as it was, Job grew through this experience. As we all look back over our lives, we will confess that we have grown most during the tough

Job's Responses & God's Answer, Part 2

times. Some, such as Job, grow better. Others, sadly, grow bitter. Dobson, in his book *When God Doesn't Make Sense,* quotes R.T. Kendall: "In his opinion, one hundred percent of believers eventually go through a period when God seems to let them down." He goes on to say that more than ninety percent of us fail to break through this betrayal barrier after feeling abandoned by God. "Our faith is then hindered by a bitter experience that we can't forget." Where do we get the idea that righteous people should not experience suffering? I would suggest that we get it from the same source that gave it to Job, Eliphaz, Bildad, and Zophar. We hear clichés all the time like "God is just," or "God is in control," or "God is good," or "God loves us." These statements may be true, but like Job and his friends, we draw the wrong conclusions from them. We will deal at length with these when we deal with the problem of evil in the thirteenth chapter of this book.

But here we see that Job has broken through the "betrayal barrier."

Now Job makes his final statement in verse 6. He expresses his final position before God by stating, "I despise myself." His next statement is puzzling since he had not sinned and God had declared him blameless, having said what is right. Of what does Job repent in dust and ashes? Repentance means "to turn" and does not absolutely presume sin. Certainly, Job had held an erroneous view about the rule of justice on the earth, so he could have repented of (turned from) his ignorance. Also he had been afflicted with tunnel vision, unable to see the panorama of God's plan for the ages. So he could have repented of (turned from) that. Also he had come perilously close to condemning God. He now repents of his words, although God did not count them against him. I believe that Job's "repentance" is simply an expression of his profound embarrassment in the presence of God.

The Job we see as this chapter ends is a vastly different man than the one we saw as the story began. He has grown in faith and insight. I believe he also has grown in his love for God and his devotion to him.

1. Safire, William. *The First Dissident.* New York: Random House, 1992. p. 17
2. Dhorme, Edouard. *A Commentary on the Book of Job.* Translated by Harold Knight. Nashville: Thomas Nelson, 1984. p. 618
3. Bemporad, Jack, ed. *Essays in Honor of Rabbi Levi A. Olan.* New York: Ktav Publishing, 1977. p. 47
4. Ellul, Jacques. *Apocalypse: The Book of Revelation.* New York: The Seabury Press, 1977. p. 93
5. Dhorme, Edouard. *A Commentary on the Book of Job.* Translated by Harold Knight. Nashville: Thomas Nelson, 1984. p. 630-31
6. Bemporad, Jack, ed. *Essays in Honor of Rabbi Levi A. Olan.* New York: Ktav Publishing, 1977. p. 47

CHAPTER 12

THE HAPPY ENDING

The story is finished. God has answered Job's dilemma, although Job still doesn't know what was behind this whole episode. Job has learned a great deal and now no longer has a wrong view of justice on the earth. However, there is still some unfinished business.

JOB IS EXONERATED

Job 42:7-9 After the LORD had said these things to Job, he said to Eliphaz the Temanite, "I am angry with you and your two friends, because you have not spoken of me what is right, as my servant Job has. ⁸So now take seven bulls and seven rams and go to my servant Job and sacrifice a burnt offering for yourselves. My servant Job will pray for you, and I will accept his prayer and not deal with you according to your folly. You have not spoken of me what is right, as my servant Job has." ⁹So Eliphaz the Temanite, Bildad the Shuhite and Zophar the Naamathite did what the LORD told them; and the LORD accepted Job's prayer.

God now deals with the sin of Job's three friends. They were told in no uncertain terms that what they had said was wrong and this had made God angry. In contrast, Job's statements were declared right. One of the meanings of "folly" as used in verse eight has the connotation of sin, wickedness, or a lack of morality. What, specifically was the "sin" that Eliphaz, Bildad, and Zophar had committed?

The third of the ten commandments is:

Exodus 20:7 You shall not misuse the name of the LORD your God, for the LORD will not hold anyone guiltless who misuses his name.

Eliphaz, Bildad, and Zophar had spoken for God..."in his name." God here states that they were wrong, and therefore had misused his name. According to the third commandment, they were therefore guilty. False prophets are not viewed kindly by God.

The Happy Ending

Deuteronomy 18:20 But a prophet who presumes to speak in my name anything I have not commanded him to say, or a prophet who speaks in the name of other gods, must be put to death."

Therefore, Eliphaz, Bildad, and Zophar deserved death for their folly.

What are some of the things they said that were so wrong? First of all, they had judged Job when they had first seen him. In Chapter 1, we saw that they performed the appropriate ritual in the presence of a blasphemer. They were wrong. Throughout the discourses, they repeatedly restated their creed, which was "God is just and God is omnipotent. Therefore, the righteous prosper and the wicked suffer. Job is suffering, therefore he is wicked." They were wrong. There is no universal connection between sin and suffering. Their observations were often truisms, but were quite inappropriate in Job's case. They had misrepresented God.

To claim to speak for God is a very serious matter. It requires a "calling" and people who are deemed worthy of this "calling" are normally given a title such as rabbi, reverend, or father. A friend of mine once said that he had observed that many preachers had obviously *not* been called...they just "up and went."

I am sure there is a lesson here for all of us when we are tempted to criticize or judge others. It makes God angry when we elevate ourselves as judge and jury. God is the only one who reserves the right to make judgment...and he is always right. Some wag has correctly stated:

Want to get along with God? Don't sit in his chair.

ELIPHAZ, BILDAD, AND ZOPHAR APOLOGIZE

Eliphaz, Bildad, and Zophar are told to go to Job and sacrifice seven bulls and seven rams as a sin offering (see Leviticus 9). God stated that Job would pray for them so that they would not be dealt with according to their folly. Wow! After all they had said about Job with such certainty and conviction, they now must go to him and submit to being prayed for by this man they had so roundly denounced. This must have totally deflated their egos.

Amazingly, they went and did exactly what God had required. On the other hand, they really had no other option. God had commanded them to make a sin offering. Refusing would have only compounded their folly. Note that God didn't instruct Job to pray for his friends. Refusing was one of Job's options, but I believe God knew that Job would forgive.

At the same time, God was beginning the healing of Job. This incident confirms that the best healing for the self-centeredness of a person who is suffering comes when he reaches out to someone else who needs help. Job's

The Absence of Justice

friends came to him asking his help. Rather than slam the door in their faces as some of us would have been inclined to do, he does pray for them and the text says that "...the Lord accepted Job's prayer." Job had the opportunity to prove to his friends that he was sincere in 16:4-5 where he said "...if you were in my place...my mouth would encourage you; comfort from my lips would bring you relief."

JOB'S FAMILY AND FORTUNES ARE RESTORED

Job 42:10-12 After Job had prayed for his friends, the LORD made him prosperous again and gave him twice as much as he had before. ¹¹All his brothers and sisters and everyone who had known him before came and ate with him in his house. They comforted and consoled him over all the trouble the LORD had brought upon him, and each one gave him a piece of silver and a gold ring.
¹²The LORD blessed the latter part of Job's life more than the first. He had fourteen thousand sheep, six thousand camels, a thousand yoke of oxen and a thousand donkeys.

It is significant that it was *after* Job had prayed for his friends that the Lord began the restoration process that resulted in his having twice as much as he had before. It wasn't given back suddenly, but the process began when each of his brothers and sisters, along with everyone who had known him, came to a banquet in Job's house. In the light of all the people Job had helped (see Chapter 29), there must have been quite a crowd. Each brought a piece of silver and a gold ring to help refinance Job & Co. (Perhaps they also brought a covered dish since Job's poverty would have precluded his paying for it out of his own pocket.) I can imagine that many of these people who had been helped by Job were more than happy for the opportunity to help him in return. It is also a sign of Job's character that he could graciously accept help from them. Note that Job had moved back into his house again, so evidently his sores had healed and he was again regarded as "safe" to mingle with society.

Verse 12 tells us that God again blessed Job, but with double the livestock he had owned before. I take it that this means his businesses also doubled in size, making him worth more than $ 22.56 million minimum, and $183.36 million maximum in assets. His gross income could have grown to more than $25.2 billion per year! With Job's other possible investments only hinted at in the book, Job's net worth could have been even greater than the above figures.

Job 42:13-16 And he also had seven sons and three daughters. ¹⁴The first daughter he named Jemimah, the second Keziah and the third Keren-Happuch. ¹⁵Nowhere in all the land were

The Happy Ending

there found women as beautiful as Job's daughters, and their father granted them an inheritance along with their brothers.

¹⁶After this, Job lived a hundred and forty years; he saw his children and their children to the fourth generation.

God also restored to Job a perfect family of seven sons and three daughters. But let us not think for a minute that his new family could ever replace his first one. Those who have lost a child and have borne others after their loss will tell us that nothing will ever replace the lost child. Job surely bore the pain of their loss to his dying day.

However, there was compensation. Nothing brings more joy to the heart of a father, and especially an older father, than his daughters. And Job's were the most beautiful in the land! How they must have brought him joy after his bitter experience. And his beautiful daughters certainly presented him with beautiful grandchildren, and great grandchildren, and great-great grandchildren! Interestingly, his daughters' names are given while his sons' names are not mentioned.

That Job was far ahead of his time is again shown in his handling of his inheritance. He made no distinction between his sons and his daughters. They all received a share.

One could ask if Job's first wife bore him his second family. We're not told. In terms of our modern life span, it seems that his first wife would have been beyond the childbearing age. Someone suggested that surely God, in his goodness, would have given Job a new wife to bear him a new family since his first wife had wished him dead. But we'll never know the answer to this question this side of heaven.

There are commentators who think that the epilogue was added to the story to give us a happy ending. This may be so, because every "Job" in history does not have such a happy ending. Many of them have died in misery. That Job enjoyed prosperity at the end of his ordeal is no guarantee that we will also be restored on this earth after suffering. So it would be wrong to take false hope from this passage. The New Testament book of Hebrews, Chapter 11 gives us the "Hall of Fame of Faith," which gives a partial list of the many Old Testament people who died horrible deaths in misery and suffering because of their faith. A magnificent statement is made of them in verse 38: "The world was not worthy of them." For all of us who trust in God, the final chapter is not written on earth.

CHAPTER 13

THE PROBLEM OF EVIL

While God "answered Job," evidently to a measure of satisfaction for Job, there remains at least one residual, unanswered question for which we do not see the answer in the book. I think that perhaps, somehow not revealed to us, Job may have received insight regarding the residual question(s), but I seriously doubt that Job ever knew the details of what had transpired in the courts of heaven preceding his trials as the reader has been privileged to know.

The residual question(s) asks for a definitive answer about why there is no justice on the earth. *Why*, as a result, do the innocent and righteous suffer? *Why* has God created such a world where justice does *not* rule?

Alan Dershowitz, famous Jewish lawyer, struggles with these problems. "Every time I look at the photographs of Nazi soldiers, with their mocking smiles, taking aim at the babies and women they are about to machine-gun into anonymous mass graves, I imagine those soldiers—now honored businessmen, grandfathers, church leaders—living out their lives in peace. And I think about a world that allowed both the Holocaust and its aftermath to happen." He goes on to say, "I experience a haunting guilt for not having devoted my career to hunting down these killers of my people and bringing them to justice. But I also realize that there was no "justice" to which to bring them."[1]

The issues we are talking about are elements of the problem of evil. This problem has been debated ever since Job's time. Epicures, the Greek philosopher, wrote about it, as have most of the great philosophers since. C. S. Lewis, the Christian apologist, wrote *The Problem of Pain*. Most of the greatest minds in history have wrestled with it and written treatises on the subject. Some of them are listed in the bibliography in the back of this book.

The problem of evil can be stated in several ways:

Hume said it something like this:

> God *wants* to do something about the evil in the world—but he *can't*...
> In which case, he is impotent.
> Or... God *can* do something about the evil in the world—but he won't...
> In which case, he is malevolent.   ...Or both!

C. S. Lewis said it something like this:

The Problem of Evil

If God is good, he will want us to be happy.
If God is all-powerful, he will be able to make us happy.
But...We are not happy!
Therefore, God must not be good...
Or... He must not be all-powerful...Or both!

One way people deal with tragedy and suffering is with humor. Excellent humor has come out of the Jewish experience, and the oppressive regimes of Hitler and communism have generated volumes of humor. The problem of evil has also produced humor.

> The rain, it raineth on the just
> And also on the unjust fella...
> But chiefly on the just, because...
> The unjust steals the just's umbrella.
> Lord Bowen

> Malt does more than Milton can
> To justify God's ways to man.
> Housman

> In this sad vale of toil and sin
> Man's head grows bald, but not his chin!
> Burma Shave

An engineer named William Murphy proposed a law describing the way things always seem to go wrong in this world when they ought to go right. We call this phenomenon Murphy's Law, and while its variations are presented "tongue in cheek" and we laugh at them, we all have a sneaking suspicion that they are more often right than wrong. Hence, the popularity of calendars, mottos, etc., listing them.

Examples of Murphy's Law

Everything that can go wrong, will.
Not only that, but everything will go wrong at the same time.
And if there is the possibility of several things going wrong, the one that does go wrong will be the one that causes the most damage and will be the hardest to track down.
If left alone, things will go from bad to worse.
The perversity of the universe tends toward maximum.
The more work done on a problem, the more confusing it will be.
If everything seems to be going well, something has been overlooked.

O'Toole's Commentary on Murphy's Law

Murphy was an optimist.

The Absence of Justice

Incidently, if God does everything that happens, then God must be Murphy. No! No! No! Our God is not capricious. He does not do everything that happens and he is not Murphy.

Rabbi Bemporad described four ways that man can look at the idea of God. They are pantheism, polytheism, theism and atheism. He said that atheism derives from problems in theism, and specifically, the problem of evil.

I have known several atheists in my lifetime. It is true that the biggest stumbling block to their acceptance of the possibility of the existence of a good God has been the problem of evil. Why do innocent babies suffer such horrible birth defects and diseases? And believers, if they are honest, usually shrug their shoulders and admit that they do not know the answer. Miller[2] says,

"The theologians' inability to supply the skeptic with a straightforward and satisfying answer to this challenge has made evil, no doubt, the biggest stumbling block to belief in a God of love."

The atheists and agnostics along with all thinking people are certainly not willing to accept the philosophy of Elihu (God is great, God is good, don't ask questions).

All thinking people would do well to consider a very interesting observation credited to Prager and Telushkin:

The believer in God must explain one thing: the existence of suffering. The unbeliever, however, must explain the existence of everything else.

Miller[3] asks a penetrating question:

"Why is it any easier to account for goodness without God than it is to account for evil with him?"

Actually, Christians have not fared well in dealing with this problem. I quoted Dr. James Dobson earlier in this book, but what he said has a direct bearing on the subject of this chapter and it will bear repeating: He quotes Dr. R. T. Kendall, pastor of Westminster Chapel in London, as giving his opinion that "one hundred percent of believers eventually go through a period when God seems to let them down. More than ninety percent fail to break through this betrayal barrier after feeling abandoned by God. Our faith is then hindered by a bitter experience that we can't forget." Dobson adds "...where did we get the notion that the Christian life is a piece of cake?"[4]

It is easy to see where people get such notions. If "God is Good," and if "God is in Control" (as the bumper stickers affirm), then we Christians should have it easy and the sinners should be getting their just rewards. Sounds familiar, doesn't it? Yep! It's the philosophy of Eliphaz, Bildad, and Zophar all over again. Bumper stickers also proclaim that "Jesus is Lord," and "Jesus is King."

The Problem of Evil

And the unbeliever in the car behind looks around at the suffering and pain in the world, perhaps his own, and ends up with a very bitter attitude about this "Jesus." He won't be helped much by the platitude that most Christians adopt to try to deal with this "betrayal barrier," which is "We'll understand it better by and by." That is what Zophar tried to pawn off on Job. But I'm with Job! Let's get some answers now! (21:19-21) Actually, many Christians adopt the philosophy of Elihu. They strongly affirm that God is all-powerful and that he is good. But beyond that, they have no answers and often do not even want to discuss the issue. They "cop-out" by saying that it is just a matter of faith. In other words, "God is great, God is good: don't ask questions. Only believe."

Also, it is strange how the philosophy of Eliphaz, Bildad, and Zophar persists to this day. I had a very dear friend, John Kroeker, who was the young pastor of a little country church in Kansas. In my experience I haven't known another man who gave his heart and soul to the ministry to the extent that John did. There were only twenty members in his little church, and there were very few in the community who were not churched. Yet he never spent less than fourteen to twenty hours per week preparing his sermons. In addition, he spent two full evenings a week calling on members of his little flock. They had prayer meeting on Wednesday night and two services on Sunday. This is a reasonably heavy schedule for a minister. But the church couldn't afford to pay him enough to live on, so he worked a part-time job, taking another twenty hours minimum out of his week. Understandably, his people loved him. And then, tragedy struck. A lump on John's neck was diagnosed as Hodgkin's disease. This was before the medical profession had any effective treatment for the disease. John, his wife, Grace, with their two sweet little daughters, and his church were all devastated, because the doctors gave him three years to live. It literally drove them to their knees. We all prayed for them and asked God for a miracle.

An SOS was sent to the denominational headquarters. They promptly put a prominent notice in the periodical published by the denomination requesting prayers and help for this young, dedicated couple. And then the Eliphazs, the Bildads, and the Zophars came out of the woodwork. John and Grace began getting letters telling them if they would just get down on their knees and confess their sins, John would be healed. Obviously, they contended, he was a great sinner because he was being punished. They were accused of having too little faith. The letters were critical and harsh. John's and Grace's hearts were crushed by the criticism, but it drove them closer to the Lord. (Incidently, the letters did *not* express the position of the denomination.) As John became weaker and weaker with the disease, and found he could work less and less, he began traveling all over southwestern Kansas, visiting hospitals. Soon his reputation preceded him, and he would simply go from hospital bed to hospital bed, giving comfort and encouragement with empathy as only a dying man could. He lived only about three years and his grieving widow and family buried him at too early an age. Yet those who lived in southwestern Kansas said that he had more of a ministry in those last three years than most pastors have in a lifetime.

The Absence of Justice

I talked with John's denominational supervisor at the funeral (which was held in the largest church in the community; it was packed). I mentioned the grief those critical letters had caused this dedicated young couple. He responded that he knew of many people who were in the insane asylum because they had held those beliefs when tragedy hit them. They had gone stark raving mad trying to figure out what they had done to deserve punishment.

In his excellent book *When Bad Things Happen to Good People,* Rabbi Harold Kushner[5] cites numerous experiences from his ministry where people held the belief that suffering resulted directly from sins they had committed. I have coined the term "Eliphazism" to describe the beliefs of Eliphaz and his two friends, who held that God is just and God is in control; therefore, the righteous prosper and the wicked suffer. If you are suffering, Eliphazism claims it as proof that you are wicked.

At one time or another in our lifetime, we will all be faced with tragedy, even if it is our own demise. The church has failed to prepare us for these times. "To be forewarned is to be forearmed" is an appropriate maxim for this problem. We need to deal with these issues before they occur, when we can think them through and form a theology or philosophy that will carry us through those times without leaving us struggling to get past the "betrayal barrier."

Like Job, when we are suffering, our whole being is dominated by our emotions. We become introspective and self-centered, often incapable of rational thought. Most of this book (except the last chapter) will be meaningless to the person in the midst of the fire. There is too much rethinking to do and too many readjustments to long-held ideas to be made for someone in the throes of suffering.

On his deathbed, my father made a significant statement. He said, "I'm glad I settled things with God long ago, because I am too sick to pray now." When tragedy strikes, it is too late to try to figure out our theology of suffering. It would be like waiting until the hurricane strikes to furl the sails, batten down the hatches, and cast off the sea anchor. There is great danger of spiritual shipwreck for the person who procrastinates regarding this vital issue.

A devout Christian family we knew many years ago suffered a terrible tragedy when their five-year-old child suddenly died because of an aneurysm in the brain. Over time, the family seemed to recover and they had more children. However, after a move, difficulties in their marriage began to surface which ultimately resulted in divorce. The wife never remarried, but the husband did, resulting in another divorce. When one of their other children, a son, was a teenager, he was killed in a car accident. The last I heard of the father was that he was attending Alcoholics Anonymous. I can only guess, but surely a misconception of God's involvement in his family's tragedies contributed to his turning to liquor for help.

The Problem of Evil

Why *do* the innocent and righteous suffer?

Why doesn't God intervene when they do?

For the answer to these vital questions, we will have to look outside the Book of Job to the rest of Scripture. We will have to back up and try to get a panoramic view of what God was up to when he created man, as I like to think that Job did as God answered him (although we are not told this). Let us continue asking penetrating questions and see how Scripture answers:

Exactly why did God create man? For what purpose did he put us on earth?

God must have a purpose for us on this earth, otherwise, we would not exist. Why are we here? What is our main function as human beings? With all due respect to the Shorter Catechism of the Westminster Confession, which states, "The chief end of man is to glorify God and enjoy him forever," I submit that loving God is prerequisite to glorifying him. It could be argued that loving God is implied in the concept of glorifying God. Perhaps I am "nitpicking," but it seems there are a lot of people who are in the "glorifying God" business for motives other than love. We can "Praise the Lord" all day long, but if we do not love him from the heart, all the sanctimonious verbiage is hollow. The same holds true in our relationships with our fellow humans. Therefore, we have:

Proposition 1. God created us to love both God and our fellow humans.

This proposition is first seen clearly in the Ten Commandments (Exodus 20:1-17). Our first responsibility is toward God as seen in the first four commandments. Moses reiterates the commandments in Deuteronomy 5, and sums up this responsibility in:

> **Deuteronomy 6:4-5 Hear, O Israel: The LORD our God, the LORD is one. ⁵Love the LORD your God with all your heart and with all your soul and with all your strength.**

But there are six more commandments that deal with our relations toward others. Jesus sums up the whole Decalogue in the New Testament:

> **Matthew 22:36-40 "Teacher, which is the greatest commandment in the Law?"**
> **³⁷Jesus replied: "'Love the Lord your God with all your heart and with all your soul and with all your mind.' ³⁸This is the first and greatest commandment. ³⁹And the second is like it: 'Love your neighbor as yourself.' ⁴⁰All the Law and the Prophets hang on these two commandments."**

The Absence of Justice

Note that Jesus mentions "All the Law and the Prophets." So the thread of our purpose of love weaves its way throughout the law and the prophets. It goes throughout the New Testament. We choose one passage from the gospels:

> **John 13:34-35 "A new command I give you: Love one another. As I have loved you, so you must love one another. ³⁵By this all men will know that you are my disciples, if you love one another."**

As we read through the New Testament, we find many passages that repeat this command, "Love one another." Unfortunately, history shows us that many people who have claimed to be Christians have not demonstrated love. According to the standards presented in the New Testament, there is reason to doubt their true commitment to Christ.

Love, defined by our modern culture, refers mostly to bodily functions. God's kind of love, and the love we are instructed to show to others does *not* refer to bodily functions. It is not just a warm, fuzzy feeling either. The love God extends to us is a kind of love that goes on loving, even if and when the beloved is not lovable. He wants us to show that same kind of love to each other. It is obvious if you think about it that God's love is not based on emotion, or even intellect, but on the will. God makes it plain in Deuteronomy 7:6-8 that his choice of Israel was not based on emotion, but was an act of love which was also an act of his will. Not that there is *no* emotion involved with this kind of love; there is, but it is a side effect, not the basis for the love. As a side effect, our physical and emotional love is free to grow stronger and better than if our relationships were built only on emotions. Emotions alone can be a very shaky foundation for a relationship.

This basic proposition concerning our God-given ability to love forms the foundation for all our existence and will be the basis for our understanding of the problem of evil.

Proposition 2: If mankind is to be capable of love, he must have choice.

Choice is absolutely essential to love. There can be no love without it. Robots cannot love. Machines cannot love. We cannot force others to love us by coercion. Love comes only by persuasion. Take the act of physical love for example. In the right context of marriage, the love act can be a most beautiful expression of our feelings and devotion for our spouse. It is truly called "making love." However, taken out of that context, and inserting the elements of deceit, force, and coercion, the same act becomes an ugly thing. We call it rape, and people who do such things deserve to be punished. It no longer has anything to do with love because the victim has no choice.

Pinnock[6] says, "What an astounding way for God to deploy power, in the form of servanthood and self-sacrifice...it reveals that love rather than al-

The Problem of Evil

mighty power is the primary perfection of God. When love says that power will not work in a situation, power is allowed to withdraw in favor of powerlessness. God does not overcome his enemies (for example) by forcing but by loving them. God works, not in order to subject our wills but to transform our hearts. Love and not sheer power overcomes evil—God does not go in for power tactics." Yancey[7] agrees: "I believe God insists on such restraint because no pyrotechnic displays of omnipotence will achieve the response he desires. Although power can force obedience, only love can summon a response of love, which is the one thing God wants from us and the reason he created us."

It is possible to capture and enslave other human beings in order to make them serve you. They can be forced to do manual labor, to serve you in your kitchen, laundry, or even in your bedroom. But you can never force them to love you. Some abusive husbands, wives, and parents still don't get it. While they continually abuse their victims, they don't seem to have a clue about why they are not loved.

Since God's first and basic priority for the human race was to create us with the ability to love, then *he had no other choice but to give us choice.* He obeys his own rules. All other subsequent dealings with mankind are attendant to this primary purpose. In the primordial counsels of God, it was decided that man must be able to love and, therefore, the principle of choice would be inviolable. *Without choice, there cannot be love!*

CHOICE REQUIRES ALTERNATIVES

It then logically follows that if man must have choice, there must be alternatives from which he can choose. Under communist regimes, voters often had only one option on their ballots. Man cannot *choose* between one option. That is nonsense.

When I was a teenager, there was a dumb joke that went around that illustrates the absurdity of choosing with only one option:

"What is the difference between a duck?"
"I don't know."
"Old age pension."
"I don't get it."
"I don't either, I'm not old enough."

As the Decalogue states, one alternative is to love God and our fellow man. The other choice then, by default, is the opposite. God did not create evil as an option. It occurred by default. The possibility of rebellion was a "given," even for God, if man is to have the ability to love. Therefore, we see that there was an element of risk for God when he decided to create a race of people with the ability to love, because there was, from the beginning, the possibility that man would not choose the option that God wanted. If mankind is to be capable of loving God, then he must of necessity also be capable of hating

The Absence of Justice

God and rebelling against him. If mankind is to be capable of loving his fellow man, then he must of necessity also be capable of hating and hurting him. While Adam and Eve faced the choice between good and evil, the distinctions we face today are often not as simple as black and white. So many wrong choices have entered the equation since Adam and Eve that many of us find ourselves deciding not between good and evil, but rather between the lesser of evils.

If God intervened in man's choices, that would constitute coercion, and the result would be anything but love. Yancey[8] says, "God's terrible insistence on human freedom is so absolute that he granted us the power to live as though he did not exist, to spit in his face, to crucify him." However, choice is not the end of the matter.

Proposition 3: Each choice has its own set of consequences.

It is in the nature of things that each choice sets off its own chain of consequences. God made this quite plain when he offered Israel the choice between blessing and cursing at Mounts Gerizim and Ebal (Deut 11:26-28). As we make choices, there may be good consequences resulting from our right choices. I'm glad Dr. Jonas Salk chose to go into medical research. All of us have benefitted, either directly or indirectly, from his discovery of the Salk vaccine for polio. But we all have suffered the incomprehensible consequences of the choices Hitler made. We all are the result of the choices we have made or our ancestors made. Therefore, evil in the world is the result of man's wrong choices—*not* God's decree.

God can no more intervene in the consequences than he could in the choice. Our world would be unpopulated if we were zapped and annihilated the second we made a wrong choice. Or, as Rabbi Bemporad illustrates with the game of darts: What kind of game would it be if God changed the course of every dart so that all of them would hit the bull's-eye no matter which direction you threw the darts? What kind of challenge would there be to life if God altered everything you did, no matter how stupid, to produce success?

While God does not intervene in our choices and their consequences, it cannot be denied that he is continually at work in this world to accomplish his ultimate goals. His workings can be seen much more clearly in retrospect. But while he is accomplishing his ultimate will, he never interferes with our choices in the process. His purposes will be ultimately accomplished without violating our wills. Only God could do that!

Proposition 4: To provide mankind an arena in which his choices could play out, God gave them dominion over the earth.

So that mankind could exercise this wonderful, God-given gift of choice without any hint of coercion from God, they were given responsibility for the earth. C. S. Lewis says, "Perhaps we do not fully realize the problem, so to

The Problem of Evil

call it, of enabling finite free wills to coexist with omnipotence. It seems to involve at every moment almost a sort of divine abdication."[9] While we must agree with the Psalmist:

> **Psalm 24:1 The earth is the LORD's, and everything in it, the world, and all who live in it;**

We cannot ignore what God, the Creator, did with this earth that is his. Scripture states categorically that he gave it to mankind:

> **Genesis 1:26-30 Then God said, "Let us make man in our image, in our likeness, and let them rule over the fish of the sea and the birds of the air, over the livestock, over all the earth, and over all the creatures that move along the ground."**
> **[27]So God created man in his own image, in the image of God he created him; male and female he created them.**
> **[28]God blessed them and said to them, "Be fruitful and increase in number; fill the earth and subdue it. Rule over the fish of the sea and the birds of the air and over every living creature that moves on the ground."**
> **[29]Then God said, "I give you every seed-bearing plant on the face of the whole earth and every tree that has fruit with seed in it. They will be yours for food. [30]And to all the beasts of the earth and all the birds of the air and all the creatures that move on the ground—everything that has the breath of life in it—I give every green plant for food." And it was so.**

> **Psalm 8:6 You made him ruler over the works of your hands; you put everything under his feet:**

> **Psalm 115:16 The highest heavens belong to the LORD, but the earth he has given to man.**

> **Jeremiah 27:5 With my great power and outstretched arm I made the earth and its people and the animals that are on it, and I give it to anyone I please.**

> **Hebrews 2:7-8 You made him a little lower than the angels; you crowned him with glory and honor [8]and put everything under his feet."**
> **In putting everything under him, God left nothing that is not subject to him. Yet at present we do not see everything subject to him.**

So the Lord gave the earth to mankind to rule and subdue. If he gave man the authority to rule on the earth and to master it, he also gave him the abilities to accomplish this. But man has chosen to squander his God-given cun-

The Absence of Justice

ning and intelligence to create machines of destruction rather than fund schemes of good will as we will see in Proposition 5. Because of his wrong choices, man has become less than God intended man to be. Ian Thomas pointedly observes that "Jesus is man as God intended man to be." If we want to see what God intended in man, we only need to look at Jesus. Our world would not be in the mess it is in if we were all like Jesus. It follows then that the evil that happens on earth is man's responsibility, not God's.

Proposition 5: Mankind made the wrong choice.

God placed a certain tree in the Garden of Eden, but instructed man to not eat of its fruit. Why did God put it there in the first place? Remember, without choice there can be no love. God wanted Adam and Eve to love him and each other as they grew into a race of humans. Without the alternative of disobedience, love would be impossible. So there the tree stood...in the middle of the garden. The serpent took advantage of it to tempt Eve into disobeying God. He convinced her that God had an ulterior motive in forbidding her the fruit, and was holding out on her. She took the bait and Adam joined her. In eating the fruit of the tree of knowledge of good and evil, something happened. Man lost his innocence and entered a world for which he was not prepared. He had disobeyed God and the fellowship he had enjoyed with God was now gone. What's more, since God had placed man over the earth, the consequences of Adam and Eve's choice affected the whole planet. Not only man suffers, but the animal kingdom and all nature also suffer. Scripture teaches that the world was cursed as a result of the sin of Adam and Eve (Gen 3:17-19) and therefore this world is fallen, not ideal.

> **Romans 8:22 We know that the whole creation has been groaning as in the pains of childbirth right up to the present time.**

Someone might say, "That's not fair." They're perfectly right. Since Adam and Eve sinned, things have not been "fair" on the earth. That was Job's problem. He said, "I'm not being treated fairly." But if God had established this world based on justice and fairness, then we would all be in trouble because God said:

> **Isaiah 53:6 We all, like sheep, have gone astray, each of us has turned to his own way; and the LORD has laid on him the iniquity of us all.**

> **Psalm 53:2-3 God looks down from heaven on the sons of men to see if there are any who understand, any who seek God.[3] Everyone has turned away, they have together become corrupt; there is no one who does good, not even one.**

> **Romans 3:23 ...for all have sinned and fall short of the glory of God,**

The Problem of Evil

It is no more fair that I should be pardoned for my sins than it is fair that an innocent baby should suffer, as many do. An "unfair" world where my forgiveness and pardon are possible must also be a world where suffering is possible. Instead of justice on the earth, God has offered mercy. Mercy for me in my sin, and mercy and comfort for the innocent one who suffers.

Not only did Adam and Eve make the wrong choice in the garden, we have continued to make wrong choices ever since. We pollute the "good" earth God created. We get drunk and kill innocent children. We go to war and cause mass destruction and suffering. And the list goes on. A report I read in the '80s noted that every minute the world spent $1.3 million on military spending while during that same minute, thirty children died for want of food or cheap vaccines. One new nuclear submarine costs the same as the total education budget for twenty-three developing countries! The wrong choices did not stop with Adam.

From Adam we inherit a sense of "good and evil," a sense of "fair." Every sentient human being has this sense. C. S. Lewis said "...human beings, all over the earth, have this curious idea that they ought to behave in a certain way, and cannot really get rid of it...(but) they do not in fact behave in that way."[10] Each of us will come to the crossroads of good and evil at some time in our life, and perhaps many times. Even if an individual never hears the Gospel or never knows about the true God, there will still be moral grounds on which God can judge him based on which fork of the road he took at the crossroads of good and evil. None of us has taken the right turn every time.

Proposition 6: Since God gave the earth to man, God is no longer in "immediate" control on the earth.

This proposition will probably be the toughest one to swallow for some people. We have been taught since childhood that God rules the earth. The reason Job and his friends were so upset was because they thought God was in control on the earth and therefore was responsible for Job's suffering. This is why so many people never get beyond the "betrayal barrier" in their lives. When pain and suffering come, they go beyond asking God "Why?" and literally shake their fist at God in anger because they see God as the cause of their suffering. It has been said, "If God is good, and if God does everything that happens, then everything that happens is good and the category of evil does not exist."

Thinking people have great difficulty accepting the premise that a benevolent God is in control on the earth when they read of the horrors of the invasion of the Mongol hordes, the brutality of the crusaders, the agonies of the Holocaust under Hitler, and the killing fields of Cambodia, to name only a few atrocities. In fact, God agrees with people who have this problem. Scripture says:

1 John 5:19 We know that we are children of God, and that *the*

The Absence of Justice

whole world is under the control of the evil one. **(emphasis added)**

The *only* place where God is in immediate control on the earth is in the hearts and lives of those who have chosen to make him Lord of their lives. Of course, we hasten to point out that God is in "ultimate" control and will one day take complete, immediate control of the earth as we will see in Proposition 10. Somehow, usually apart from our immediate perceptions, God *is working* toward the ultimate goals of his kingdom. Part of being a believer is the conviction that God's side will ultimately win! We do this by faith, because the eternal victories are not always apparent to us in the present. I believe that it is entirely probable that, from the vantage of heaven, we will be able to look back and trace the finger of God working throughout history. That will be the divine perspective mentioned in Chapter 2. However, today we may feel as Job felt, that we are totally abandoned by God.

A good example of this is found in the history of the establishment of the State of Israel in 1948. I am always thrilled as I read of one unlikely-to-impossible occurrence after another in the events leading up to the establishment of Israel as prophesied throughout the Bible. Abba Eban[11] admitted regarding one of these occurrences that "Against the Cold War atmosphere which prevailed in every other sector of the international arena, there was something almost messianic in this convergence of American and Soviet ideas." In another place he uses the word "miraculous" to describe the way events unfolded regarding Israel's fortunes. God certainly was at work bringing about the fulfillment of the Biblical prophecies. Yet to the early settler in Israel who was enduring constant threats of death at the hands of the Arabs, the hand of God was not obvious. There was nothing but the "fire and blood" promised by the Arabs.

To understand the presence of evil in the world it is essential that we grasp the difference between the two sides of the coin of God's ultimate control and the principle of man's free choice. Dr. Kenn Gangel put it this way: "When we come to Heaven's gate, we will see 'Whosoever will, may come' written over it. But, having passed through, and looking back, we will see 'Chosen in him before the foundation of the world' written on the inside." Such is the distinction (and tension) between man's perspective and God's perspective. Both are there. God's perspective, we accept by faith. But we are responsible for what we can understand from man's perspective.

It follows that if God is not in immediate control of the whole world, then his will is not being done on earth in the immediate sense. If his will is done on earth, why would Jesus teach us to pray...

> **Matthew 6:10 your kingdom come,**
> **your will be done**
> **on earth as it is in heaven.**

The Problem of Evil

...as if it were not? We are also told in the Epistles:

> **2 Peter 3:9 The Lord is not slow in keeping his promise, as some understand slowness. He is patient with you, not wanting anyone to perish, but everyone to come to repentance.**

He doesn't want anyone to perish, yet people are perishing every day. To see this, all we have to do is look at our world. I daresay we won't have to look far. The atrocities, horrible pain, and intense suffering we see should convince us that a good God is not in control and his will is not being done. Rice[12] says, "The will of God, therefore, is not an irresistible, all-determining force. God is not the only actor on the stage of history. Other agents, too, play a role. Creatures who bear the image of God are capable of deciding and acting, and God allows for their decisions and actions as he determines what course to follow."

In the late '80s a terrible accident occurred near a major metropolitan area in the U S. A group of young people from an evangelical church, on their way to camp, were involved in a tragic accident that was not their fault, and some of them were killed. The evening news featured an interview with the church leaders. The spokesman for the church stated sorrowfully, "It was God's will." A salesman who is a nonbeliever called in my office the next day and immediately erupted with indignation regarding this statement that he had viewed on his TV. He had no printable words to express his contempt for this attitude. What should have been an opportunity to proclaim a faith in a loving God who doesn't go around killing innocent young people became instead a statement that produced nothing but contempt for "stupid Christians."

Some have dealt with the dilemma of a good God who is all-powerful coexisting with evil in his world by splitting God's will in two. They define his "directive" will as all the good things he ordains. His "permissive" will is defined as all the evil things that, for some reason or other, he chooses to permit, although they do not necessarily conform to his desires.

I find it hard to conceive that, if God is God, that is, ultimately sovereign, there can be any other will for God than his *will*...period! Something is either his will or it is not his will. An all-powerful God, who for some incomprehensible reason wills evil, although it is defined as his "permissive will," cannot be good! God is not a wimp who permits evil when he really doesn't want to.

A man would not be considered good who would respond in the following ways:

1. Suppose he is standing by a busy highway and a group of young children are playing nearby. Suddenly, their play results in their running, in mass, right past our man and into the busy thoroughfare where they would be badly hurt or killed. Our concept of "good" requires that he stop them

before they come into harm's way. But our man only reaches out and stops two of the children, *permitting* the others to run right by him, out into the street where they are mangled and killed. No court would absolve such criminal negligence!

2. Our man is standing beside a lake when he sees a boat full of people capsize nearby. Obviously, the people cannot swim and have no flotation devices. There is an empty boat pulled up on shore beside him, so he jumps into the boat, rows out to the scene, and pulls two or three floundering people to safety in the boat. Then, although he still has plenty of room in the boat, he ignores the screams of the others, and casually *permits* the rest to drown while he rows back to shore. Such a man would be held in utter contempt by society for his negligence.

If God is all-powerful, he is able to rescue all of us from evil. Since he obviously does not, does this mean that God is not good? It would be criminal negligence on God's part if he could indeed prevent evil, and chose rather to *permit* it.

Someone might observe that God obviously "permits" evil or it would not exist. We will discover as we work our way through this chapter that a better terminology would be that God is self-obligated to "accept" the existence of evil rather than deliberately "permit" it by an act of his "permissive will."

We often hear a variation of this same idea stated another way: "Nothing can touch the believer that hasn't passed through the hand of God." Are we to believe that God puts his stamp of approval on the actions of the drunk driver who kills a car full of innocent people? Are we to believe God put his stamp of approval on the Holocaust? Are we to believe that God approves the actions of a wife-beater who mauls his wife and damages their unborn child?

The Jews in the Nazi concentration camps struggled with God's inaction as they saw millions of innocent people tortured, shot, or gassed. In at least one case, they put God on trial for negligence in keeping his promises of justice and righteousness for his people. He was found guilty. It was stated that between God and Hitler, Hitler could be counted on more to keep his promises than God. Indeed, many of the survivors of the Holocaust came out of their experiences as atheists or agnostics.

I think it makes more sense and is easier to simply believe that evil is not God's will...period. His will is not being done on the earth.

SOMETHING GOD CAN'T DO

Why doesn't God do something about evil in the world? As he revealed to Job, he will. But not yet. In fact, he can't! Describing process theology, Hasker[13] says, "...God does not *permit* the evil, because God could not *prevent* the evils from occurring. All God can do, and what he does do, is attempt to persuade worldly beings to act according to his plan; if they act differently, and evil and suffering are the result, then God suffers along with us." Neither Hasker nor this author subscribes to process theology which teaches that God *lacks* the power to do anything about evil in the world. However, I do subscribe to the above statement by Hasker modified by the proposition that God does not "lack the power," but his prior choice imposes a severe limitation on his power to act in the present situation. Having decided to give man choice so that man could love, he cannot then contravene his own plan. God will do what God will do. And his first and primary will is that man must be able to love, which requires man's autonomy. God has not yet taken back the control of the world. The prophecies of how that will happen are scattered throughout the Prophets and are the subject of the Book of Revelation. But until that time, God has limited himself on the earth so that man can choose to love and exercise his moral freedom.

Anytime we decide to do something, we limit ourselves. If we decide to vacation in Florida, we are severely limited regarding our options of vacationing in California or Arizona at the same time. If I decide to pursue a career in medicine, my choice of an institution of higher learning is limited to those that give medical degrees. Furthermore, I am limited by my choice of specialization, since some colleges specialize in certain disciplines. If I have a limited budget to accomplish my education, then I am also limited to those institutions that give grants or aid. I am also limited in my extracurricular activities during my pre-med, medical college, and residency. I am also limited to those institutions that will accept me as a student. So my initial decision to go into the field of medicine results in severe limitations.

This is true for God also. He has decided, in this age, to deal with the world on the basis of grace. This decision sets limits on God's dealings with mankind. He cannot deal with us on the basis of grace and at the same time take fiery vengeance on wickedness. This is the age of mercy. He cannot dispense mercy and justice simultaneously in the same situation. The age of fiery vengeance will come as God promised Job, but when that time comes, he will no longer be dealing in grace. So even God's options are limited by his decisions.

NONSENSE QUESTIONS

For God to decide to give man the ability to love and choose as described in our propositions thus far, and then renege and intervene is nonsense. It is on the same level as the "nonsense questions." Miller[14] says, "Even an omnipotent God cannot do that which is *logically* impossible; he cannot make a rock so big that he cannot lift it, he cannot make four-sided triangles, he cannot make things both to be and not to be at the same time and in the same respect, and he cannot create something that possesses the full power of being that he himself possesses." Nor can God choose to give man the ability to love by giving him choice and then determine, or interfere with, the choices and consequences. This also would be nonsense. Pinnock[15] says, "To say that

The Absence of Justice

God hates sin while secretly willing it, to say that God warns us not to fall away though it is impossible, to say that God loves the world while excluding most people from an opportunity of salvation, to say that God warmly invites sinners to come knowing all the while that they cannot possibly do so—such things do not deserve to be called mysteries when that is just a euphemism for nonsense."

God is correctly described by theologians as omniscient, omnipresent, and omnipotent, and having foreknowledge. Kushner solves the problem of evil by describing God as finite and not all-powerful,[16] and if we carefully study Scripture we find that all these attributes of God are not fully functional on the earth. Fretheim[17] points out that when God involves himself with man, he injects himself into time, which implies a type of limitation for God. Fretheim goes on to show how this limits God's foreknowledge, his omniscience, his omnipresence, and his omnipotence. Therefore, while God possesses foreknowledge, omniscience, omnipresence, and omnipotence, he limits these manifestations on the earth. Ellul[18] puts it this way, "...the world is going to belong to the autonomy of men, now assured, acquired, precisely by the fact of the decision of God to adopt for the salvation of men the way of nonpower, of incognito, of humility, of the renunciation of his power in order to be nothing more than love."

God has limited his foreknowledge and omniscience on the earth.

Scriptures that support this position are:

> **Genesis 6:6 The LORD was grieved that he had made man on the earth, and his heart was filled with pain.**

> **1 Samuel 15:11 I am grieved that I have made Saul king, because he has turned away from me and has not carried out my instructions." Samuel was troubled, and he cried out to the LORD all that night.**

It is nonsense that God should know in advance exactly what mankind would do, and then be grieved or angry when they do it, to the extent of being sorry that he had even created man. Evidently he did not know in advance, at least in a sense. Hasker[19] says,"...it is logically impossible that God should have foreknowledge of a genuinely free action."

> **Deuteronomy 13:3 you must not listen to the words of that prophet or dreamer. The LORD your God is testing you to find out whether you love him with all your heart and with all your soul.**

Along with Exodus 16:4, Judges 2:21-22, 3:4, and 2 Chron. 32:31, this passage indicates that God has tests to determine man's response to him. It is implied again that without these tests, God doesn't know. Basinger[20]

The Problem of Evil

says,"...God can never know with certainty what will happen in any context involving freedom of choice."

> **Jeremiah 7:31 They have built the high places of Topheth in the Valley of Ben Hinnom to burn their sons and daughters in the fire—something I did not command, <u>nor did it enter my mind.</u> (Underline added)**

This passage along with Jer.19:5 and 32:35 indicates in very strong language that it had never occurred to God that Israel would sin in the way that they did. He didn't know ahead of time.

> **Jeremiah 26:3 Perhaps they will listen and each will turn from his evil way. Then I will relent and not bring on them the disaster I was planning because of the evil they have done.**

Here and in 36:3, God uses the word "perhaps," again indicating that he is not sure how Israel will react.

> **Matthew 24:36 "No one knows about that day or hour, not even the angels in heaven, nor the Son, but only the Father.**

Jesus, being God, is limited regarding his foreknowledge of the day and hour of the end times.

> **Matthew 8:10 When Jesus heard this, he was astonished and said to those following him, "I tell you the truth, I have not found anyone in Israel with such great faith.**

That Jesus, as God, could be "astonished" is inconsistent with the concept of omniscience. He had limited himself in this area.

> **Mark 5:30 At once Jesus realized that power had gone out from him. He turned around in the crowd and asked, "Who touched my clothes?"**

In this passage Jesus asked a question as if he did not know who had touched him. I don't believe he was playing child's games. C. S. Lewis, speaking of Jesus' taking on the human nature with its limitations, says, "And if limitation, and therefore ignorance, was thus taken up, we ought to expect that the ignorance should at some time be actually displayed. It would be difficult, and, to me, repellent, to suppose that Jesus never asked a genuine question; that is, a question to which he did not know the answer. That would make of his humanity something so unlike ours as scarcely to deserve the name. I find it easier to believe that when he said "Who touched me?" he really wanted to know."[21]

<u>God has limited his omnipresence on the earth.</u>

The Absence of Justice

God's presence in all his glory is overwhelming. For man to be able to exercise free choice, it was necessary for God to limit his presence on the earth. Scriptures that support this position are:

> **Genesis 18:20-21 Then the LORD said, "The outcry against Sodom and Gomorrah is so great and their sin so grievous [21]that I will go down and see if what they have done is as bad as the outcry that has reached me. If not, I will know."**

> **Exodus 3:8 So I have come down to rescue them from the hand of the Egyptians and to bring them up out of that land into a good and spacious land, a land flowing with milk and honey the home of the Canaanites, Hittites, Amorites, Perizzites, Hivites and Jebusites.**

> **Acts 7:34 I have indeed seen the oppression of my people in Egypt. I have heard their groaning and have come down to set them free. Now come, I will send you back to Egypt.'**

In all these passages God speaks of "coming down" from heaven. If he is here in his omnipresence, then these verses do not make sense. Note that the Genesis passage indicates that God will come down to determine the extent of their sin, which is another indication of his limitation regarding his omniscience.

> **Job 1:12 The LORD said to Satan, "Very well, then, everything he has is in your hands, but on the man himself do not lay a finger."**
> **Then Satan went out from the presence of the LORD.**

When Satan went out from the presence of the Lord in this verse (and 2:7), where did he go? He came to earth to afflict Job. So while God's presence was in heaven, it was not on the earth (at least in the same sense).[22]

> **Exodus 33:14 The LORD replied, "My Presence will go with you, and I will give you rest."**

If God's presence is everywhere, why would it be necessary for him to promise that he would go with them?

> **2 Kings 17:22-23 The Israelites persisted in all the sins of Jeroboam and did not turn away from them [23]until the LORD removed them from his presence, as he had warned through all his servants the prophets. So the people of Israel were taken from their homeland into exile in Assyria, and they are still there.**

The Problem of Evil

When Israel went into exile, this passage says they were removed from God's presence.

> **Luke 5:17 One day as he was teaching, Pharisees and teachers of the law, who had come from every village of Galilee and from Judea and Jerusalem, were sitting there. And the power of the Lord was present for him to heal the sick.**

Evidently, God's power to heal was not always present, even for Jesus.

> **Matthew 1:23 "The virgin will be with child and will give birth to a son, and they will call him Immanuel" which means, "God with us."**

This name for Jesus means "God with us," which implies that when Jesus was on the earth, God was present in a sense that was not true before Jesus had come. So we see here another different aspect of the presence of God.

Also, since he was in a human body, he was thereby limited to being in only one place at one time.

God has limited his omnipotence on earth

Compared to anything we know on earth, God's power unlimited would be overwhelming. I'm sure that is an understatement of understatements. Therefore, to establish an environment where man could choose without being overwhelmed, God limited himself on the earth in this area also. Scriptures that support this position are:

> **Jeremiah 5:22-25 Should you not fear me?" declares the LORD.**
> **"Should you not tremble in my presence?**
> **I made the sand a boundary for the sea,**
> **an everlasting barrier it cannot cross.**
> **The waves may roll, but they cannot prevail;**
> **they may roar, but they cannot cross it.**
> **²³But these people have stubborn and rebellious hearts;**
> **they have turned aside and gone away.**
> **²⁴They do not say to themselves,**
> **'Let us fear the LORD our God,**
> **who gives autumn and spring rains in season,**
> **who assures us of the regular weeks of harvest.'**
> **²⁵Your wrongdoings have kept these away;**
> **your sins have deprived you of good.**

God describes his awesome power in this passage. "Shouldn't Israel recognize it and tremble with fear?" God asks. But his power yields to this stubborn and rebellious people's disdain. God's power yields to man's sinful will...for now.

The Absence of Justice

> **Daniel 10:11-14** He said, "Daniel, you who are highly esteemed, consider carefully the words I am about to speak to you, and stand up, for I have now been sent to you." And when he said this to me, I stood up trembling.
> ¹²Then he continued, "Do not be afraid, Daniel. Since the first day that you set your mind to gain understanding and to humble yourself before your God, your words were heard, and I have come in response to them. ¹³But the prince of the Persian kingdom resisted me twenty-one days. Then Michael, one of the chief princes, came to help me, because I was detained there with the king of Persia. ¹⁴Now I have come to explain to you what will happen to your people in the future, for the vision concerns a time yet to come."

This passage, like the prologue in Job, gives us insight into the spirit world that may explain many delayed answers to prayer. Actually, it is a bit scary, especially if we have taken demon forces lightly. Daniel had prayed. God had heard, and had acted immediately by sending an angel in response to Daniel's prayer. However, the angel, who had come from the very presence of God, ran into trouble. He was held up by an evil power called "The Prince of the Persian Kingdom" for twenty-one days! He was not able to break away to carry out God's command until the Archangel Michael came to help.

In the context of our discussion here, we notice several things. The controlling "power" of Persia was evidently stronger than the angel. And obviously, God's power was not present or the angel would have gotten through immediately. It took the angel plus Michael to break loose from this power to get through to Daniel. This passage strongly supports the notion that God's omnipotence is limited on the earth.

> **Mark 6:5** He could not do any miracles there, except lay his hands on a few sick people and heal them.

Jesus was in Nazareth, his hometown. Familiarity breeds contempt and these people who had watched Jesus grow up would not believe that he would ever amount to anything. (Hometown people are like that.) Because of their unbelief, God's omnipotence was not there, although he was able to heal a few people.

> **Luke 5:17** One day as he was teaching, Pharisees and teachers of the law, who had come from every village of Galilee and from Judea and Jerusalem, were sitting there. And the power of the Lord was present for him to heal the sick.

In contrast to the passage above, here we find a situation where the "power of the Lord was present..." The implication is that this power is not always present.

The Problem of Evil

The concept of God limiting himself on the earth may be new to some readers. A pointed and descriptive passage that teaches this is in Philippians.

> **Philippians 2:5-8** Your attitude should be the same as that of Christ Jesus:
> [6]Who, being in very nature God,
> did not consider equality with God something to be grasped,
> [7]but made himself nothing,
> taking the very nature of a servant,
> being made in human likeness.
> [8]And being found in appearance as a man,
> he humbled himself
> and became obedient to death—
> even death on a cross!

Jesus Christ, although he was God, made himself nothing. He limited himself severely when he took on human flesh. He submitted to the point of being executed as a common criminal so that we might reign with him in the heavenly kingdom, and so that we might have the option of choosing God's way. Matt 24:36 also reveals that God knew something of which Jesus in his earthly form was ignorant when Jesus claimed ignorance regarding the time of his return. He said that was something only God the Father knows.

The view of a self-limited God that we have just described in Proposition 6 has been presented in a book titled *The Openness of God* by Clark Pinnnock, Richard Rice, John Sanders, William Hasker, and David Basinger. They call this view of God "free will theism." Comparing this view of God with other views, Hasker[23] says, "Free will theism is...in a better position...to deal with the problem of evil." He goes on to say, "According to free will theism...God knows that evils will occur, but he has not for the most part specifically decreed or incorporated into his plan the individual instances of evil. Rather, God governs the world according to *general strategies* which are, as a whole, ordered for the good of the creation but whose detailed consequences are not forseen or intended by God prior to the decision to adopt them. As a result, we are able to abandon the difficult doctrine of 'meticulous providence' and to admit the presence in the world of particular evils God's permission of which is not the means of bringing about any greater good or preventing any equal or greater evil."

At this point it is proper that we point out again that Scripture is very precise in affirming that God is indeed *ultimately* sovereign. But in his sovereignty he chose to give man the ability to love, which therefore limited his own ability to interfere in man's choices.

Proposition 7: Since man listened to Satan regarding his choice, Satan took control of the earth by default.

The Absence of Justice

There are several references in Scripture other than 1 Jn 5:19 about the power and control that Satan wields over the earth. It seems his power is considerable, and nothing to be tampered with by mere human beings. (However, the weakest Christian has the option of resisting him in the strength provided by the Lord. Satan may be in control on this earth, but we need not be *under* his control.)

> John 16:11 and in regard to judgment, because the <u>prince of this world</u> now stands condemned. (Underline added)
>
> 2 Corinthians 4:4 The <u>god of this age</u> has blinded the minds of unbelievers, so that they cannot see the light of the gospel of the glory of Christ, who is the image of God. (Underline added)
>
> 2 Corinthians 11:14 And no wonder, for Satan himself masquerades as an angel of light.
>
> Ephesians 2:2 in which you used to live when you followed the ways of this world and of <u>the ruler of the kingdom of the air</u>, the spirit who is now at work in those who are disobedient. (Underline added)
>
> Ephesians 6:12 For our struggle is not against flesh and blood, but against the <u>rulers</u>, against the <u>authorities</u>, against the <u>powers of this dark world</u> and against the <u>spiritual forces of evil</u> in the heavenly realms. (Underline added)

We also note that when Jesus was in the wilderness being tempted, he was offered the kingdoms of the world by the devil. Jesus did not respond by challenging Satan's right to make such an offer. This implies that the kingdoms of the world were under Satan's control as stated in 1 John 5:19.

> Matthew 4:8-10 Again, the devil took him to a very high mountain and showed him all the kingdoms of the world and their splendor. ⁹"All this I will give you," he said, "if you will bow down and worship me."
> ¹⁰Jesus said to him, "Away from me, Satan! For it is written: 'Worship the Lord your God, and serve him only.'"

Proposition 8: Man wasted his opportunity by making the wrong choice. But God quickly reestablished the principle of choice.

The position in which man found himself after he had sinned in the garden was hopeless. He had made his choice and it had been wrong. He was now doomed to spiritual death. He was on the wrong side of the fence and couldn't get back over. So God in his mercy made a promise that made all the difference. It is a bit obscure, but many theologians believe this verse is the first promise of a messiah.

The Problem of Evil

> **Genesis 3:15 And I will put enmity between you and the woman, and between your offspring and hers; he will crush your head, and you will strike his heel."**

Immediately after Adam and Eve had sinned, God came to them with a ray of hope. He promised that there would be a redeemer who would crush the head (power) of the serpent. Subsequently, more promises were given about this coming redeemer. All that was required was that the believer in the Old Testament look forward to this savior much as we look back to him. Their faith that he would somehow pay the debt for their transgressions was imputed to them as righteousness. (Heb 11)

Based on this promise, Adam, Eve, and their descendants once again have the privilege to choose, which means that they still have the ability to love. But they now are choosing from the other side of the fence. They are choosing from a fallen state to be reinstated into a love relationship once again with God. Based on this promise, God calls men to repentance:

> **Matthew 11:28-29 "Come to me, all you who are weary and burdened, and I will give you rest. ²⁹Take my yoke upon you and learn from me, for I am gentle and humble in heart, and you will find rest for your souls.**
>
> **Acts 17:30 In the past God overlooked such ignorance, but now he commands all people everywhere to repent.**

Having fallen, man is now "dead in trespasses and sin" (Eph 2:1) and finds himself helpless to save himself unless God "draws him" (John 6:44). This would imply that there is to be a continuous intervening in man's choices by the very act of God "drawing him." However, Jesus made it plain that inherent in God's plan to redeem man was a "drawing" provision that applies to all men:

> **John 12:32 But I, when I am lifted up from the earth, will draw all men to myself."**

Therefore, all men once more have a free choice to make...a choice of fellowship with God or to remain independent from God, a choice to love him or hate him (either overtly or by ignoring him).

Proposition 9: God will not interfere with man's choices on the earth, but man has the privilege of asking God to intervene in this world.

As we have mentioned previously, God cannot intervene in man's choices on the earth 1) because he gave it to man and he respects man's autonomy,

The Absence of Justice

and 2) because he cannot intervene in man's choices and still achieve his first priority for man, which is love. But when man loves God, he will talk with him and ask his help. When man, who was given this earth, asks God's help, then God, having been invited to intervene, can do so, and the petitioner is assured that he will receive God's help. Job's continuing communication with God was vital to his spiritual survival during his ordeal.

> **Matthew 7:7-11 "Ask and it will be given to you; seek and you will find; knock and the door will be opened to you. ⁸For everyone who asks receives; he who seeks finds; and to him who knocks, the door will be opened.**
> **⁹"Which of you, if his son asks for bread, will give him a stone? ¹⁰Or if he asks for a fish, will give him a snake? ¹¹If you, then, though you are evil, know how to give good gifts to your children, how much more will your Father in heaven give good gifts to those who ask him!**

When we ask God to intervene in this world on our behalf or for the sake of the kingdom of God, he responds willingly to the pleas of his children. This is called prayer. God may or may not give his child what he asks. Nevertheless, he does hear and respond and that child can rest, knowing that his Heavenly Father has now been given control of the situation. Basinger[24] says, "But we all agree that it is, at the very least, quite reasonable to view petitionary prayer as a means whereby we grant God the permission to influence our noncognitive states of mind and/or share with us those cognitive insights concerning ourselves and others that will help us better live out our Christian commitment in this world."

Someone may object to this proposition by pointing out that God was intervening in the world in Job's case when he erected a hedge around Job. Doesn't he also intervene when he protects all of his children from Satan?

The intervention we are discussing deals with man's choices and their consequences. The activity of God in protecting his children is more of a "restraining" of evil rather than an interference in the realm of our choices. That he is working in this world, restraining evil is clearly taught in the Scripture:

> **2 Thessalonians 2:6-8 And now you know what is holding him (the man of lawlessness) back, so that he may be revealed at the proper time. ⁷For the secret power of lawlessness is already at work; but the one who now holds it back will continue to do so till he is taken out of the way. ⁸And then the lawless one will be revealed, whom the Lord Jesus will overthrow with the breath of his mouth and destroy by the splendor of his coming.** (Parentheses added for clarity.)

"The one who now holds it back" is not clearly identified, but most evangelical scholars identify this "one" as the Holy Spirit who was sent to the

The Problem of Evil

earth when Jesus ascended to the Father. His functions here are many, but none of them is coercive. He is here to persuade, convict, and convince people of their sin and their need of a savior. He is also here to help believers and stand by their side to support them, no matter what circumstances they may face in this world dominated by the evil one. His is the power that enables us to live in this evil world.

> **2 Corinthians 5:20a We are therefore Christ's ambassadors, as though God were making his appeal through us.**

The Holy Spirit empowers us with a sort of "diplomatic immunity" in this world that is hostile to God. As ambassadors, we have diplomatic status. Ambassadors have their citizenship and loyalty elsewhere. They enjoy limited freedom in the country where they serve, but they are also subject to its laws...to a point. We live in a world that is fallen and are subject to the consequences of the fall. But our citizenship and real home is in heaven, where the laws of sin and death cannot reach us.

Proposition 10: God plans to invade this unjust world and reestablish justice.

We found in Chapter 11 that the establishment of justice on the earth is man's task, not God's responsibility. But when we review history and note the increase and prevalence of evil in this fallen world, the probability that man will be able to accomplish the task of establishing justice on the earth, before we destroy each other and the world, looks doubtful at best. Both Jews and Christians look forward to the coming of the Messiah who will direct the process of the establishment of true justice here on earth.

From Genesis 3:15 (the first promise of a redeemer) throughout the Bible, there are hundreds of references to that day when God will establish justice on the earth. They are woven through Scriptures in the Pentateuch, the Psalms, the Prophets, the Gospels, the Epistles, and Revelation. The promises that these prophecies contain constitute the blessed hope of the believer.

> **Isaiah 40:10 See, the Sovereign LORD comes with power,**
>   **and his arm rules for him.**
> **See, his reward is with him,**
>   **and his recompense accompanies him.**
>
> **Isaiah 66:15-16 See, the LORD is coming with fire,**
>   **and his chariots are like a whirlwind;**
> **he will bring down his anger with fury,**
>   **and his rebuke with flames of fire.**
> **[16]For with fire and with his sword**
>   **the LORD will execute judgment upon all men,**
>   **and many will be those slain by the LORD.**

The Absence of Justice

> **2 Thessalonians 1:6-10** God is just: He will pay back trouble to those who trouble you ⁷and give relief to you who are troubled, and to us as well. This will happen when the Lord Jesus is revealed from heaven in blazing fire with his powerful angels. ⁸He will punish those who do not know God and do not obey the gospel of our Lord Jesus. ⁹They will be punished with everlasting destruction and shut out from the presence of the Lord and from the majesty of his power ¹⁰on the day he comes to be glorified in his holy people and to be marveled at among all those who have believed. This includes you, because you believed our testimony to you.

There is a question suggested here for those who may still be wrestling with the idea that God is not in immediate control on the earth. If God is already in control here, why will it be necessary for him to come back and take control?

Proposition 11: Meanwhile, we have the option of being a part of the problem or part of the solution.

Just as Job was commissioned to establish justice in every area of his influence, so believers are not only commissioned to do the same, but also to preach the Gospel to all the world. That is, believers are to tell mankind that the wrong choice we made in the garden of Eden can be remedied, starting with the acceptance of the gift of salvation God offers us. This gift is made possible because God became man in the person of Jesus, who paid the just penalty for our wrong choices. In turn, he offers us his righteousness.

> **John 3:16** "For God so loved the world that he gave his one and only Son, that whoever believes in him shall not perish but have eternal life.

> **Matthew 28:18-20a** Then Jesus came to them and said, "All authority in heaven and on earth has been given to me. ¹⁹Therefore go and make disciples of all nations, baptizing them in the name of the Father and of the Son and of the Holy Spirit, ²⁰and teaching them to obey everything I have commanded you..."

It might be questioned that if "All authority in heaven and on earth" has been given to Jesus, how can it be said that he is not in control? Hebrews 2:8 confirms this, but indicates that his full control will be accomplished at that future time promised to Job.

In Proposition 4, we showed how God gave man the earth along with the commission to subdue it. He also gave man the ability to do this, but man has chosen to utilize most of his choices in the wrong ways. However, it is still an option to choose to use our own personal abilities to do good, to relieve suffering, to ease pain, to find cures, and to subdue nature.

The Problem of Evil

So we have the option of remaining in the rebellion begun in the Garden of Eden that has resulted in the consequences of pain, suffering, and death that we see all around us in this world. Or we can choose to join the counter rebellion started by Jesus Christ and made possible by his death in our behalf and his subsequent resurrection. We can remain a part of the problem or join in on the solution.

Proposition 12: God has not abandoned us.

God has promised to establish justice at some future date. That sounds exciting, especially as we realize that day is drawing near. But what about today? Are we to be left out in the cold until that day dawns? The answer is an emphatic "no!" God is working in our world today though there are times when it is not apparent. He providentially protects his children with "hedges" against evil. He providentially feeds and clothes us. His providence is evident everywhere to those who are sensitive to his workings. And as we note his providence working in this fallen world, our faith is increased to believe in God's ultimate triumph over evil.

I believe the near tragedy of the Apollo 13 mission demonstrates God's providence. I think it was providential that Ken Mattingly was cut from the mission because of a possible exposure to measles. While he was terribly disappointed at first, when the problems arose during the flight, he performed a crucial function on the ground as the most qualified person to put together a procedure that would safely bring back the crew with their severely limited resources.

I also firmly believe that our men returned safely because the whole nation cried out to God on their behalf. The Russian cosmonauts, part of an atheistic system, did not have that resource, and men were lost in space.

On the other hand, our Columbia astronauts were lost, even though several of them claimed to be devout believers in God. The commander even prayed with his crew before they lifted off. That was a first for our space program. Yet they were lost. So we cannot make a hard case for or against God's providence...or judgment. It may be the disaster happened to give America a wake-up call.

Ravi Zacharias tells of a young Christian interpreter who traveled with him throughout Southeast Asia during the Vietnam war. After the U. S. left and the communists took over, he was arrested and sent to a concentration camp for reeducation. The communists seemed to delight in humiliating Christians by putting them in degrading situations, and he was therefore assigned to latrine duty. It was horrible work. Eventually, the propaganda forced on him day after day began to take hold. He began to wonder if there really was a God after all. Had his friend Ravi Zacharias really lied to him all along as his captors contended?

The Absence of Justice

Then one day as he went about his duties in the latrine, he spotted a printed piece of paper that had been used as toilet tissue. He was about to shovel it out with the rest of the excrement when his eyes spotted the heading on the page. It was a page from the Book of Romans. He eagerly fished it out of the filth and laid it aside, later washing and drying it out. From this time on, he eagerly went to his work and, eventually salvaged almost the whole Book of Romans in this way. Someone was desecrating God's Word in a most ignoble way, but God was using the "wrath of man" to providentially speak to his faltering child. The young man's faith was renewed, and his captors saw such a sweet change in his spirit that they questioned him. He was eventually released, and he made his way to the United States.

Proposition 13: God is in the business of salvaging good out of a bad situation.

As we look around us in a world filled with crime, hate, wars, disease, suffering, and pain, we must confess that we are in a bad situation that is of our own (mankind's) making. It wouldn't have to be this bad. God told Job (and mankind) that if we establish justice in every area of our influence, we would enjoy peace, prosperity, tranquility, and security. Instead, we have spread rebellion, violence, and hatred. We've got a dragon by the tail and we don't know what to do about it...and we can't let go!

When God warned Adam about disobeying and eating of the forbidden fruit, he specified that the consequence would be death. That is, spiritual death, and then eventually physical death. We have been battling this enemy ever since. The final indignity of our bad situation is that we are going to die. Even if we make jokes about death and taxes, they don't go away; we are going to die (and they'll get our taxes from our estate if we haven't paid up beforehand). Death is our worst and final enemy. But look what God has done with death. By sending his Son to die in our place, he has turned our worst enemy into mankind's greatest hope. Miller[25] says, "The crucifixion of God's Son was at once both the epitome of evil and the occasion of God's greatest blessing on men." By trusting in Jesus' death to pay the penalty for our sins, we can be reconciled to God and receive forgiveness.

> **1 Peter 2:24 He himself bore our sins in his body on the tree, so that we might die to sins and live for righteousness;**
>
> **1 Corinthians 15:54b-57 "...Death has been swallowed up in victory."**
> **55"Where, O death, is your victory?**
> **Where, O death, is your sting?"**
> **56The sting of death is sin, and the power of sin is the law. 57But thanks be to God! He gives us the victory through our Lord Jesus Christ.**

The Problem of Evil

If God can salvage good out of the worst of situations we face, namely death, then there is no bad situation that can occur in our lives out of which he is unable to salvage good. That is very good news. The conditions, though, are that we have to make that choice that he offers us: to sign on for his remedy for the bad situation on the earth. That is, we must choose to accept God's son as our savior and allow him to make our lives a part of the solution rather than a part of the problem.

David suffered much affliction in his lifetime. He had this to say about it:

Psalm 119:71 It was good for me to be afflicted so that I might learn your decrees.

Note that he did not say that the affliction was good. I do not believe there is any merit in seeking suffering. Nor does God initiate suffering or evil to produce a good result. The end does not justify the means, even for God. But David, having been afflicted, could see that he had learned from it and that God had worked in him to salvage good from bad situations. From these situations David could also observe:

Psalm 76:10 For the wrath of man shall praise Thee; (NAS)

Which is another observation that God salvages good, even out of man's wrath.

Proposition 14: The final chapter for us is not written in this world.

It is true that there are some people who, unlike Job, will not be restored here in this life such as my friend John Kroeker and the Columbia astronauts. Job had little understanding about what comes after death. We cannot claim ignorance on this subject because Scripture is very clear on it.

Hebrews 9:27b...man is destined to die once, and after that to face judgment,

Titus 2:11-14 For the grace of God that brings salvation has appeared to all men. [12]It teaches us to say "No" to ungodliness and worldly passions, and to live self- controlled, upright and godly lives in this present age, [13]while we wait for the blessed hope—the glorious appearing of our great God and Savior, Jesus Christ, [14]who gave himself for us to redeem us from all wickedness and to purify for himself a people that are his very own, eager to do what is good.

Blu Greenberg defines the necessity of "something else beyond this moment of time."[26] "If God is omniscient, omnipresent, omnipotent, there has to be something else beyond this moment in time. Hitler now in his grave and Jewish children now born to the second generation are not enough. Hitler deserves something more terrible than inert death, and the second-generation parents' one hundred cousins who didn't survive deserve something more than our memory of their truncated, traumatic lives. Nice guys should never finish last. And I have seen righteous people neglected and their children begging for bread, and I know something is terribly amiss."

But, more about this in the final chapter.

Summary

The solution to the problem of evil in a nutshell

God *is* good. But since his first priority on earth is to have a race of people capable of love, and since love requires choice, God must limit his foreknowledge, omniscience, omnipresence, and omnipotence *on the earth* for now. Tennant[27] says "...there is no moral goodness apart from autonomy and the possibility of evil. Thus free will is requisite to man (the moral being) as well as the full possibility of his misuse of that freedom resulting in sin." The alternative would be a world without love!

In response to Hume's statement of the problem of evil, we can now state the following:

God *wants* to do something about evil in the world, but he can't...yet...
  Not because he is impotent, but because his prior purpose for man is moral freedom enabling him to love...which requires choice.
Or...God *can* do something about the evil in the world, but he won't.
  Not because he is malevolent, but because to do so would deprive man of the moral freedom enabling him to love...which requires choice.
And...God *will* do something about the evil in this world...at the right time.

A number of years ago, Rabbi Jack Bemporad made an insightful statement about the problem of evil on his radio show, "The Jewish Perspective." I close this chapter with his quote.

"The problem of evil is not a problem with God. It is a problem with man. Not why does God permit evil, but why does man persist in doing evil...evil that leads to his own destruction...that brings pain and suffering in a world God created for our good and enjoyment?"

1. Dershowitz, Alan M. *Chutzpah.* Boston: Little, Brown & Co., 1991. p. 131
2. Miller, Ed L. *God and Reason.* New York: Macmillan, 1972. p. 139
3. Ibid, p. 143
4. Dobson, James. *When God Doesn't Make Sense.* Wheaton, Ill.: Tyndale House, 1993. pgs 26, 28 & 40
5. Kushner, Harold S. *When Bad Things Happen To Good People.* New York: Schocken Books, 1981.

The Problem of Evil

6. Pinnock, et al. *The Openness of God.* Downers Grove, Ill.: Inter-Varsity Press, 1994. p. 114
7. Yancey, Philip. *The Jesus I Never Knew.* Grand Rapids: Zondervan Publishing, 1995. p.78
8. Ibid, p. 78
9. Lewis, C. S. *The World's Last Night.* New York: Harcourt Brace, 1952. p. 9
10. ─────────── *Mere Christianity.* New York: Macmillan, 1943. p. 21
11. Eban, Abba. *Personal Witness.* New York: G. P. Putnam's Sons, 1992. p. 112
12. Pinnock, et al. *The Openness of God.* Downer's Grove, Ill.: Inter-Varsity Press, 1994. p. 38
13. Ibid, p. 139
14. Miller, Ed L. *God and Reason.* New York: Macmillan, 1972. p. 144
15. Pinnock, et al. *The Openness of God.* Downer's Grove, Ill.: Inter-Varsity Press, 1944. p. 115
16. Kushner, Harold. *When Bad Things Happen to Good People.* New York: Schocken Books, 1981.
17. Fretheim, Terrence E. *The Suffering of God.* Philadelphia: Fortress Press, 1984. p. 44
18. Ellul, Jacques. *Apocalypse: The Book of Revelation.* New York: Seabury Press, 1977. p. 79
19. Pinnock, et al. *The Openness of God.* Downer's Grove, Ill.: Inter-Varsity Press, 1994. p. 148
20. Ibid, p. 163
21. Lewis, C. S. *The World's Last Night.* New York: Harcourt Brace, 1952. p. 100
22. Scripture teaches us that there are various "senses" in which God is present. I would not want any readers to presume that they could get away with sinning just because God is not "present" and therefore wouldn't know.
23. Pinnock, et al. *The Openness of God.* Downer's Grove, Ill.: Inter-Varsity Press, 1994. p. 152
24. Ibid, p. 162
25. Miller, Ed L. *God and Reason.* New York: Macmillan, 1972. p. 148
26. Reimer, Jack, ed. *Jewish Insights on Death and Mourning.* New York: Schocken Books, 1995. p. 325
27. Tennant, F. R. *Philosophical Theology.* Cambridge, England: University Press, 1928.

CHAPTER 14

THERE IS A BALM[1]

For thirteen chapters we have wrestled with the ideas of a sovereign, good God and his relationship to suffering righteous people. In this chapter we move from ideas to feelings. How will I react when someone I care deeply about is suffering? How will I react when I find myself confronted with undeserved suffering and pain? What can I do to help others and myself in such situations?

Everyone who experiences tragedy and suffering in his or her life comes face to face with the question of God's existence. Most of us in the Judeo-Christian culture have been taught from our childhood that God is good and that he is kind, generous, and compassionate. Tragedy and suffering usually prompt us to critically examine those beliefs, since what we are experiencing is not in accord with what we had always expected from a good God. Sadly, many people turn away from God at this point. Many Holocaust survivors have done just that. Failing to make any sense out of the horror they saw and endured, they conclude that God does not exist. This conclusion is a position of deep despair.

If God does not exist...

If there is no power apart from ours and no standard apart from what we may establish on a whim, then everything is random and meaningless, even our feelings of injustice and hurt. Our sense of how things "ought to be" is a cruel joke of evolution. In fact, *nothing matters*. There is no distinction between right and wrong. The Nazi killers were just as "moral" as their "innocent victims," since there is no final authority or standard, and therefore no accountability beyond what we may feel at the moment from peer pressure...and peer pressure is only the result of the biased thinking of people who are just as confused as we.

Kushner asks, [2] "What sort of world would it be if there were no God?—Without God, it would be a world where no one was outraged by crime or cruelty, and no one was inspired to put an end to them. It would be a world where, if we were the victims of crime or misfortune, we would curse our bad luck, and if someone near us was a victim, we would merely feel relief that it happened to her and not to us. But we would have no reason to feel 'this is not the way the world is supposed to work'..." Blu Greenberg[3] also explores this concept. "In this world, justice is not only delayed but all too often denied. In this world, the motto that drives people is do unto others before they do it unto you. In this world, bad things happen to good people

There Is a Balm

and good things happen to bad people. The only answer is that this is not the only world.

But perhaps there really is nothing. Stare for a moment into the terror of nihilism, which is the only coherent alternative to this belief of Judaism. Looking at nothingness is a necessary spiritual exercise before you can firmly accept a belief in the world-to-come.

"...Let us examine the possibility that death is the true and final end of us in every way—no heaven, no hell, no soul, no eternal life, no God. Just blackness and nothingness. Let us consider this charming, heartwarming, hope-inducing prospect—and then ask yourself just one question in response: 'Can I live with this?'"

On the other hand...

If there is indeed a God who is ultimately sovereign, who will someday establish justice as he has promised, then there is hope, although we cannot understand the "why" of our suffering. No one, the author of this book included, can answer all the whys of suffering and pain. There will always be loose ends in the fabric of our reasoning. But if there is a God, we can rest assured that an answer does exist.

There are people who seem to have no problem accepting the fact that God is higher than we, and his ways are beyond our understanding, and therefore there is no need to delve any deeper into the question of evil. Many of these people may not have yet personally entered fully into the vale of suffering. When they do, they too will be compelled to reexamine their beliefs to find out if they still make sense.

Just because God is greater than we provides no excuse for us to stop learning and searching for truth. I belong to the category of people who find it hard to accept dogma by blind faith. There are a lot of us out here who cannot accept pat answers in defense of God when things go wrong. Job was one of us. What had happened to him simply did not square with the belief system that he and his friends had held. His friends urged him to repent and quit asking questions. In the final analysis, Job was the one who enjoyed the favor of God, not Eliphaz, Bildad, or Zophar, who were so zealous in their attempts to defend God against Job's charges.

It is obvious from the Book of Job that God welcomes our questions, and even our challenges. He will not zap us if we are honest with him. However, Eliphaz, Bildad, and Zophar were recipients of God's anger, although they were fierce in their defense of God. Why? I believe that they were wrong because they had adopted a creed and substituted it for a personal relationship with God...and their creed turned out to be wrong! Job demonstrated his personal relationship with his God by talking with him continually throughout the discourses, although God did not respond for a long time. Through the process, Job eventually came to see things as God saw them.

The Absence of Justice

This is our task, as we live our lives on this earth—not to blindly accept a creed or an idea of God and then stagnate, but to continue seeking answers by getting to know God more intimately. From the Book of Job, we see that God delights in being sought out, and rewards those who diligently seek him. He is evidently not angered by our hard questions. God has promised to reward our seeking (Deut 4:29-31). Then, as we find him, we are able to reach out to help others, fulfilling God's purposes regarding justice, compassion, mercy, and love on the earth.

Some readers may still be asking the very same questions Job and Jeremiah asked. Is there no hope? Why is there no healing? I want to assure you that there is a balm. There is hope. There is healing. But God does not always give it like we want it and when we want it, as we saw in the Book of Job. Sometimes the relief from suffering comes in the form of death, which is really the only perfect and permanent healing for the believer. Until the healing comes, God never abandons us, although we, like Job, may feel that he has. In the first thirteen chapters, I have tried to look at Job's dilemma and the problem of evil objectively and logically. Now we will deal with suffering from a personal or subjective approach.

We have seen how Job dealt with suffering. In this chapter, I will illustrate how others have reacted to extreme suffering, and how God worked in their lives to bring spiritual healing. Like Job, some people experience physical healing, but God's priorities are spiritual. Physical healing, if it occurs, will last only the allotted four score years at best. Our spiritual healing will last throughout eternity.

When others hurt...

The church has failed to train us to minister to people who are suffering. We go to comfort the hurting as Eliphazs, Bildads, and Zophars, bearing our pat answers. Harold Kushner[4] describes and illustrates from his experiences the most common pat answers used in attempts to bring comfort.

1. We get what we deserve.
2. God has a reason we do not know.
3. Thornton Wilder's tapestry: God is weaving a beautiful tapestry. It may look terrible from down here, but when we see the other side, it will be beautiful.
4. God is trying to tell us something. Suffering is educational.
5. God means it for our good.
6. God is testing us.
7. It will be worth it all when we get to heaven.

There are surely others. We note that they all assume that God causes suffering and they try to explain why it is that God would want us to suffer. But when we find ourselves in the bed of affliction, we will find out that suffering people don't want pat answers. They want sympathy and love. They want to know that

There Is a Balm

someone cares. Their emotions have taken over in their pain, and only emotion (love and caring) can communicate with and minister to them. Eliphaz, Bildad, and Zophar started out OK, that is, until they opened their big mouths.

One of the lessons of the Book of Job is that we need to be very cautious as comforters. The person to whom we are ministering may well be one of God's chosen servants, as Job was. We will always do well if we love much and say little. However, most of us feel profoundly embarrassed in the presence of great suffering. Some of us react to this embarrassment by opening our mouths before our brains are in gear. It is then that we join the ranks of Eliphaz, Bildad, and Zophar as miserable comforters.

When tragedy strikes me...

We usually learn that the church has also failed to prepare us to face tragedy when it hits us personally. There are too many people with shattered faith because they really believe that God sent the suffering to them and they do not understand why. "Why?" is the big question that always comes to mind when we hurt deeply. As we learned when we studied Elihu's speech, *it is not wrong to ask why.* Suffering saints and suffering sinners have all asked this question from the beginning of time. Even Jesus asked "why" as he hung on the cross, feeling forsaken by God.

There are many reasons why someone might be suffering.

1. We may have brought it on ourselves.
   Suffering may result from sin such as substance abuse or dissipated living or even carelessness.

2. We may have inherited it from our ancestors.
   Our ancestors may have passed on the consequences of sin, or the genes of our parents may have carried some unfortunate flaw.

3. We may be the victims of another's abuse.
   For instance, an alcoholic's spouse and children certainly suffer.

4. We may be the victims of a dread disease, or war, or violence with which we had nothing to do.

5. It may be prejudice or intolerance that brings suffering.

6. We may suffer as the result of natural disasters.

7. We may suffer as the result of Satanic oppression.

If a person's suffering is brought on by his own sin, he is invited to confess that sin to God and plead for his mercy:

The Absence of Justice

1 John 1:9 If we confess our sins, he is faithful and just and will forgive us our sins and purify us from all unrighteousness.

Note that we have God's promise that we will be forgiven and cleansed. But if that sin has caused disease or disability, he has not promised to heal or reverse the ravages of that sin, although that, too, sometimes happens.

Pain and suffering most often come because of no apparent fault of our own. It is at these times that we become introspective and self-centered as Job did as we try to figure out what we did to deserve this pain.

If we have learned one thing in the Book of Job, it should be that we can rarely identify a cause and effect relationship between a specific sin and the pain we are feeling. That is because there usually *is* no cause and effect relationship to be found. Job, Eliphaz, Bildad, and Zophar all sought diligently for the sinister reason for Job's suffering, and in the end God agreed with Job's conclusion that the reason for his suffering did not lie with Job. Jesus dealt with the same thinking in his day.

Luke 13:1-5 Now there were some present at that time who told Jesus about the Galileans whose blood Pilate had mixed with their sacrifices. ²Jesus answered, "Do you think that these Galileans were worse sinners than all the other Galileans because they suffered this way? ³I tell you, no! But unless you repent, you too will all perish. ⁴Or those eighteen who died when the tower in Siloam fell on them—do you think they were more guilty than all the others living in Jerusalem? ⁵I tell you, no! But unless you repent, you too will all perish."

John 9:2-3 His disciples asked him, "Rabbi, who sinned, this man or his parents, that he was born blind?"

³"Neither this man nor his parents sinned," said Jesus, "but this happened so that the work of God might be displayed in his life."

Many people add to their suffering and hinder healing by blaming themselves.

God has better things to do than to zap us for every nasty thought or word. In fact, he doesn't have to do anything. Wrongs we may have committed often carry their own consequences. If we know (or think we know) what sin or sins have caused our suffering, then we should confess them; according to 1 Jn 1:9, he forgives and cleanses. The Old Testament prophets say:

**Micah 7:19 You will again have compassion on us;
you will tread our sins underfoot
and hurl all our iniquities into the depths of the sea.**

There Is a Balm

Someone has appropriately added: "...and God has posted a 'no fishing' sign."

> **Isaiah 38:17b you have put all my sins behind your back.**
>
> **Isaiah 43:25 "I, even I, am he who blots out your transgressions, for my own sake, and remembers your sins no more.**

If God doesn't remember them after they have been confessed, neither should we. And if God has forgiven us as he promised, who do we think we are when we won't forgive ourselves!

God in his great mercy has made a wonderful provision for us to start over with a clean slate. This provision was pictured in the Old Testament economy in the Day of Atonement...that singular day in the year when sacrifices were offered and past sins were forgiven. Christians believe this looked forward to the day when Jesus would become the sacrifice for us, cleaning the slate for a new start when we choose to follow him.

> **2 Corinthians 5:17-19 Therefore, if anyone is in Christ, he is a new creation; the old has gone, the new has come! [18]All this is from God, who reconciled us to himself through Christ and gave us the ministry of reconciliation: [19]that God was reconciling the world to himself in Christ, not counting men's sins against them.**

Unfortunately, it often happens that someone else will promptly remind us of our forgiven faults just about the time we thought we had put them behind us. It is well to keep in mind that it is not in Satan's best interests to let us accept God's forgiveness. His agenda includes keeping us under bondage for as long as he can. So when this occurs, we must do as Jesus did and refuse to be influenced by Satan. God's promise to forgive and forget should take precedence over Satan's subtle innuendos.

Many people add to their suffering and hinder healing by blaming others.

It is quite easy to fall into this trap. When we don't feel well, it is easy to become irritable and hypercritical. It often happens that we invent wrongs much as Eliphaz, Bildad, and Zophar did in trying to get to the root of Job's problem. But with forgiveness comes healing. There have been "miraculous" recoveries resulting from forgiveness; if not physical, then spiritual and emotional...but often all three! Jesus taught us to pray:

> **Matthew 6:12 Forgive us our debts, as we also have forgiven our debtors.**

The Absence of Justice

This verse is frightening when we think of the grudges we often bear. If we are honest, we will admit that when we bear ill feelings, they usually accomplish exactly the opposite from what we would wish. Instead of hurting the object of our ill will, the hostile feelings fester and boil up in us, causing all kinds of suffering, often physical and spiritual. How many hospital beds would empty if we could get people to forgive?

There is a growing trend toward blaming our parents for our problems. The current fad is to blame our parents for abuse of all kinds, but especially sexual abuse. Some of this abuse really happened, but a lot of it is generated by either an overactive imagination, or an overzealous, greedy therapist.

A widow I once knew raised her two children alone, even sending them to college. Her son earned his doctorate and landed a prestigious position in a well-known research company. But he and his sister compared notes, deciding that their mother had failed miserably in raising them, and criticized her for it. Their blame and insensitivity caused this dear, sweet mother untold grief and lonely suffering.

What we don't seem to realize is that as our children watch our relations with our parents, they are learning by example exactly how to treat us in just a few years! And then the suffering will multiply in our own lives. How much simpler and happier to forgive, recognizing that our parents (or anyone we might be inclined to blame) probably did the best they could under the circumstances. Even if they were at fault, we usually cause ourselves more pain through bitterness than we inflict on the objects of our blame.

The truth is that we all bear our own share of the responsibility for the mess we are in. It will do no good to point our fingers at others, though they may clearly be in the wrong. Dr. Gerhardt Dierks, the father of the modern computer memory, told of his sense of guilt for the Nazi atrocities that took place during the second world war. He was a scientist in Germany at the time. His "offenses," which he freely acknowledged, consisted of his failure to complain to the authorities when he witnessed the *Kristallnacht* riots against the Jews, and his failure to stand and offer his seat on the bus to an aged Jewish woman when it had become politically incorrect to do so. He could have blamed Hitler or his henchmen, but instead, he shouldered his own responsibilities for the Holocaust. We bear the responsibility, if not for the actions of others, then for our reactions.

Many people add to their suffering and hinder healing by blaming God.

Job came perilously close to doing this. He had eliminated all the possible causes for his suffering, and God was the only one left to blame. Fortunately he stopped just short of this charge. We know he stopped short because he didn't give up on God. He continued to speak to him, though some of his words became harsh. Had he conclusively decided that God was to blame, he undoubtedly would have stopped praying and would have turned his back on him.

As we have learned, God is not responsible for the suffering and pain on the earth. We (the human race) are. God cannot stop our choices to hurt others any more than he can force us to help others without violating our ability to choose and, therefore, to love. Love is the bottom line which God will not violate. Blaming God will not shame him into doing something about my personal pain today. It only makes me bitter and less capable of joyfully accepting, by faith, God's ultimate dealing with evil in the world.

Yet there is that pervasive belief that God does everything that happens. If we look carefully at Job's affliction, we will find that what happened to Job was not God's idea. It was Satan's futile attempt to induce Job to turn against God and curse him. I think it is somewhat like blasphemy to blame God for Satan's work, something like attributing Jesus' works to the devil (see Matt 12:24-32).

James 1:17 Every good and perfect gift is from above, coming down from the Father of the heavenly lights, who does not change like shifting shadows.

We are beings who gained a rational sense of "good and evil" when we partook of the fruit of the tree in the garden. In any rational or logical sense, it is nonsense to call war and suffering and hatred and prejudice and disease "perfect gifts." They are not God's doings! We are right to be angry about them. But our anger should be directed constructively to doing something about them, and not directed toward God.

WHERE THE RUBBER MEETS THE ROAD

We can theorize about pain and suffering without end. However, suffering takes on a new dimension when tragedy strikes at home—in our own lives—and it will in some form sooner or later. None of us will continue to live our lives in tranquility forever.

What can we do when it hits us? How can we cope? I would like to submit eight suggestions that may be helpful as we face suffering in our lives. Doubtless those who have suffered victoriously could add to our suggestions, so this should be considered an "open ended" list.

STEPS TO DEALING WITH PAIN AND SUFFERING

1. Remember that God suffers with us when we are hurting.

While God cannot intervene in our choices or change the consequences of our choices, it does not follow that he is unaffected by our pain and suffering.

The Absence of Justice

God, being a person, has emotions as well as a mind and a will. His emotions are very much tied into his creation. Scripture speaks of his grief, his sorrow, his frustrations, as well as his compassion, his joy, and his love.

In his book *The Suffering of God,* Terrence Fretheim compiles Old Testament metaphors which describe how God suffers *because* of the condition we are in and how he suffers *with* the people. In the New Testament we see Jesus suffering *for* us. He describes the same picture in the lives of the prophets who spoke and acted for God among the people. The lives of Isaiah, Jeremiah, and Hosea, for example, are pictures of God's suffering.

Part of the reason for the coming of Jesus was to communicate to us how much God loves us (John 3:16). He was called "a man of sorrows, familiar with suffering" (Isa 53:3). Hebrews 2:17-18 says that because he became human and experienced the suffering and pain of being human, he is able to sympathize with us and help us in our pain. Because God suffers with us, we can be sure he cares and understands and will help us cope.

2. Become part of the solution; refuse to be part of the problem.

There are those who choose to become very bitter through suffering. In doing so, they usually make things worse. They not only make themselves miserable, but they succeed in making everyone around them miserable also.

When God was ready to reverse Job's miserable fortunes, he ordained that the first step should be made by Job. When Eliphaz, Bildad, and Zophar came humbly to Job asking for his forgiveness, and asking him to pray for them, Job could have taken the opportunity to give them a piece of his mind and kick them out. He could have tried to "get even." But he didn't. He prayed for them. I would like to have been there. Surely it was a highly-charged emotional renewal of old friendships. I imagine there were tears of repentance and then tears of joy as the old fellowship was restored. To reach out to help someone else in kindness and sympathy, even while we ourselves are suffering, is the best therapy there is for our own pain. My friend John Kroeker found it so, and in so doing, he ministered in a way that has long outlasted his short life. In fact, I believe his works will follow him throughout eternity. (Rev 14:13)

> **2 Corinthians 1:3-7 Praise be to the God and Father of our Lord Jesus Christ, the Father of compassion and the God of all comfort, ⁴who comforts us in all our troubles, so that we can comfort those in any trouble with the comfort we ourselves have received from God. ⁵For just as the sufferings of Christ flow over into our lives, so also through Christ our comfort overflows. ⁶If we are distressed, it is for your comfort and salvation; if we are comforted, it is for your comfort, which produces in you patient endurance of the same sufferings we suffer. ⁷And our hope for you is firm, because we know that**

There Is a Balm

just as you share in our sufferings, so also you share in our comfort.

Though we may be suffering greatly, one of the greatest joys we can know can be found in reaching out to comfort others just as God has comforted us. And it is true that he comforts us as we comfort others. God doesn't *send* troubles so that we can then be comforted and comfort others. But when troubles come as troubles will in this fallen world, God can move in and bring comfort and help. In the process, the body of believers is drawn closer together in love and fellowship. God provides for us in this way to assure us that we are not alone in our suffering.

My best friend lost his wife tragically when she was in her early twenties. She had been pregnant with twins and was in her seventh month when she suddenly died. They tried, but were unable to save the babies. It was heart rending to see her lying in her casket with a tiny bundle in each arm. Something happened when my father walked into the funeral parlor to comfort my friend. Dad had lost his first wife too. Dad never said a word. He gripped my friend's hand and put his other hand on my friend's shoulder and just looked into his eyes. From halfway across the room, I sensed something. I can't explain it, but somehow Dad had comforted my friend more than I could in a lifetime. Somehow, my friend knew that Dad knew.

Scripture doesn't give details about Job's life after the ordeal he went through. But judging from others who have had similar experiences, I strongly suspect that while Job had been generous, kind, and thoughtful before his affliction (Job 29), he was even more so after his recovery. Suffering will never leave us in the same place it has found us. We will always be better because of it, or we will become bitter.

Dr. Ken Opperman, missionary statesman with the Christian and Missionary Alliance, tells a particularly touching story. He met a pastor of a Chinese home church who had been raised in a Christian home. His father also had been a pastor. They had sent their son to college and he had been trained as a medical doctor. Then the communists came and took his parents away, never to be seen by him again. They took him and put him in a prison camp with ten thousand other political refugees. Because he was a Christian and a doctor, they chose to humiliate him by putting him on latrine duty.

The latrine was three meters deep, six meters wide, and ten meters long. Ten thousand people used it every day. His duty was to clean out the pit every night. So now, this Christian man whose hands had been trained to heal, found himself, night after night, shoveling excrement. As time went on, he developed a burning hatred for his guards. This went on for ten years! He was kept in solitary confinement. Besides, others couldn't tolerate the odor that continually clung to his body.

But after ten years, he had an experience with his Lord. Remembering

The Absence of Justice

what his father had preached and taught, he yielded his life anew and afresh to Christ. That night, as he shoveled the excrement, he found himself singing a song his mother had sung:

> I come to the garden alone, while the dew is still on the roses
> And the voice I hear falling on my ear, the Son of God discloses,
> And he walks with me and he talks with me, and he tells me I am his own
> And the joy we share as we tarry there, none other has ever known.

He went on singing at his horrible task, night after night, for another seven years!

Finally the Chinese guards said they could stand it no longer. They announced to the whole camp that anyone who sang that song again would go to their death before a firing squad. The only consolation he had was now being taken away. When he went down into the pit again that night, determined to save his life, something overtook him. He found he could not hold it in, so he threw back his head and started to sing that song at the top of his voice. While he was singing, he heard what he thought were the voices of angels and he stopped. All over the camp he heard voices singing...people he had never seen were singing with him the song that he had taught them for almost seven years!

The next morning they took him out and stood him against the wall. The guns were readied when once again, throughout the entire camp, they heard voices singing that song—and they knew they'd have to shoot the whole camp. They backed down. He found out later that some seven thousand of those prisoners had come to know Christ through his song. Even in the worst of situations, we have choices and the right choice will invite God to enter the situation and salvage good from it.

3. Get the whole picture in mind.

Pain was designed by our Creator to focus our attention on something that is wrong. In reality, pain is a blessing albeit an unwelcome blessing. But while it focuses our attention on our problem, it can make us terribly introspective and self-centered. Being introspective and self-centered to excess can have a negative effect if not corrected. Hurting people are often found encased in their own little world of suffering and they become oblivious to what is going on in the world around them. They get tunnel vision, spiritually. Like Job, they need to get a vision of God's wonderful program, realizing that even in their pain, they can have a significant part in it. They need to realize that "This too, shall pass."

While the Apostle Paul was suffering in prison, he wrote this to the Philippians:

Philippians 1:12-14 Now I want you to know, brothers, that what

There Is a Balm

has happened to me has really served to advance the gospel. ¹³As a result, it has become clear throughout the whole palace guard and to everyone else that I am in chains for Christ. ¹⁴Because of my chains, most of the brothers in the Lord have been encouraged to speak the word of God more courageously and fearlessly.

Instead of complaining about the prison conditions and the poor food (they may have fed him pork!), he is focused on the advance of the gospel and the witness for Jesus Christ throughout the palace guard that his imprisonment had enabled. Rather than complain, he rejoiced! And God can work the same thing in each of us in the worst of situations—if we will just open our eyes to the big picture.

Martha Snell Nicholson spent many years immobile on a bed of pain with rheumatoid arthritis. Instead of focusing on her suffering body, she made it a point to pray for everyone she knew every day. Since she knew of many missionaries, she prayed for them...around the world...every day! She left us with a legacy of beautiful poetry that mirrored the beauty in her heart, although her body cried out with pain at the slightest movement.

Eavesdropping
Martha Snell Nicholson

My sickroom windows open out
Above a busy street.
How can I help it if all day
Words not intended for my ears
Come drifting up to me?

Footsteps and voices,
Passing all day long!
Where do they go,
These hurrying feet?
I wonder if they know.

All day they pass,
And never guess
Their few chance words
Reveal so much.

All day they go,
And never know
That in an upper room
Someone has prayed for them!

When we get the "big picture" in mind, it also includes our ultimate destination.

The Absence of Justice

Dr. Malcolm Cronk tells of the time when he was a young preacher attending a service where Dr. Paul Rees was preaching about heaven. He said that Dr. Rees had just about gotten them to the gates of glory, when a short, poorly dressed woman with a funny little hat sitting in the third row suddenly jumped to her feet. Grabbing her hat, she threw it up in the air and shouted "Yippee!!!" Then she quietly sat down again.

Dr. Cronk said that he was indignant, and told Dr. Rees as much after the service. Dr. Rees said, "Son, son, that woman has scars all over her body where her drunken husband has beaten her. He doesn't know it, but he's got the most wonderful wife a man could ask for. If anyone has the right to get excited about going to heaven, she does. I wouldn't deny her her 'yippee' for anything!"

For those who suffer greatly, heaven takes on a very special meaning. The more we suffer, the more real heaven can become for us.

> **Romans 8:18 I consider that our present sufferings are not worth comparing with the glory that will be revealed in us.**
>
> **1 Peter 1:3-6 Praise be to the God and Father of our Lord Jesus Christ! In his great mercy he has given us new birth into a living hope through the resurrection of Jesus Christ from the dead, ⁴and into an inheritance that can never perish, spoil or fade—kept in heaven for you, ⁵who through faith are shielded by God's power until the coming of the salvation that is ready to be revealed in the last time. ⁶In this you greatly rejoice, though now for a little while you may have had to suffer grief in all kinds of trials.**

4. Accept and act on God's promises.

As we have explained, God cannot remove us from the consequences of living in a fallen world until he removes us from the world. But there are a lot of things he can do and many promises he has given to help us through the troubles of this world.

A. He has promised that we would not be tempted beyond our strength.

> **1 Corinthians 10:13 No temptation has seized you except what is common to man. And God is faithful; he will not let you be tempted beyond what you can bear. But when you are tempted, he will also provide a way out so that you can stand up under it.**

There is a difference between temptation, testing, and trials. But the above promise applies to all three because in every trial and test, there is the temptation to give in or run. But God has promised that we will never be driven to

There Is a Balm

the point where giving in or running is the only option. The best option is to "give in" and to "run" to Jesus, who has promised help.

> **Hebrews 4:16 Let us then approach the throne of grace with confidence, so that we may receive mercy and find grace to help us in our time of need.**

There were many native Christians in Vietnam during the Vietnam War, and they suffered terribly. What gripped the hearts of the missionaries as they worked among these dear people were their prayers. Not one of them had been untouched by the grief of war. But instead of praying to be delivered from suffering, they fell on their knees, with tears streaming down their faces, begging help from God so that when times of tribulation would come, they would have strength to endure and stay true to their savior.

B. He will be with us in every circumstance of life.

> **Matthew 28:20b And surely I am with you always, to the very end of the age."**

Job experienced a time when God seemed very far away. It was this distance that made his suffering so excruciating because he felt abandoned by God. In the '60s I had the opportunity to attend the Southland Keswick in Dallas. One of the speakers was Dr. Alan Redpath from England. He had just recovered from a serious illness and was rather weak. He told us that while he was in the hospital, his friend Dr. Martyn Lloyd-Jones, pastor of Westminster Chapel in London, came to visit him. Redpath confided to his friend that during this illness, the heavens seemed like brass and he couldn't pray. Dr. Lloyd-Jones assured him that in times like these it was not his task to pray, but the task of his friends to pray for him. Dr. Redpath said that on the occasion of his first sermon after his recovery, a lady came down the aisle with tears streaming down her face. She said "Dr. Redpath, the old fire is gone!" Then she continued, "But in its place, there is a love, and a tenderness I have never before seen in your ministry!"

Though Job had felt abandoned, from our vantage point it is obvious that God was indeed very close to Job. He never forsook him. Although there was silence, he was there. We have the advantage of being able to read the Word of God and see how God does not abandon us, though we may feel that he has. Where feelings leave us wanting, faith takes over. Faith and feelings do not always mix. If we base our faith on our feelings, our faith can be subject to as trivial a thing as a bad piece of pizza or a malfunctioning gland. We need to base our feelings on our faith, and our faith on the Word of God (both the written Word and the living Word). With God's help, we *can* act independently of our feelings.

C. Jesus has promised to pray for us.

The Absence of Justice

Jesus is seated at the very right hand of the Father (Acts 2:33), and there he prays for us:

> **Hebrews 7:25 Therefore he is able to save completely those who come to God through him, because he always lives to intercede for them.**

We are even covered when we don't know how or what to pray!

> **Romans 8:26-27 In the same way, the Spirit helps us in our weakness. We do not know what we ought to pray for, but the Spirit himself intercedes for us with groans that words cannot express. [27]And he who searches our hearts knows the mind of the Spirit, because the Spirit intercedes for the saints in accordance with God's will.**

If Jesus and the Holy Spirit are interceding for us, and God is for us, that's a majority!

D. He feels for us in our weakness and suffering.

One aspect of Jesus' incarnation was that he learned what it was like to be human.

> **Hebrews 5:8 Although he was a son, he learned obedience from what he suffered.**

Scripture says that Jesus experienced whatever we may be going through, yet without sin.

> **Hebrews 4:15-16 For we do not have a high priest who is unable to sympathize with our weaknesses, but we have one who has been tempted in every way, just as we are yet was without sin. [16]Let us then approach the throne of grace with confidence, so that we may receive mercy and find grace to help us in our time of need.**

Moreover, we are told that he sympathizes with our weaknesses and that we have a ready access to the throne of grace to get help whenever we need it.

E. He has promised to set things right in the end.

This is a promise that only Almighty God could make. How it is possible to pay back the sins of an Adolph Hitler boggles the mind, but that is exactly what Scriptures promise:

> **2 Thessalonians 1:6-7 God is just: He will pay back trouble to those who trouble you [7]and give relief to you who are troubled,**

There Is a Balm

and to us as well. This will happen when the Lord Jesus is revealed from heaven in blazing fire with his powerful angels.

5. Don't spend much time seeking divine healing.

The emphasis here should be on the word "much." I have heard of people who have literally spent their whole lives (and livelihoods) running from one faith healer to another faith healer seeking that "special touch" that would mean the end of their suffering. I suspect that praying for others in times of distress is more effective than praying for ourselves. And yet, God has told us to seek healing if we are sick. But he was specific in how it should be done:

> **James 5:14-15 Is any one of you sick? He should call the elders of the church to pray over him and anoint him with oil in the name of the Lord. ¹⁵And the prayer offered in faith will make the sick person well; the Lord will raise him up. If he has sinned, he will be forgiven.**

Someone may ask, "Does that work today?" I have known people who have been healed in this way and I have known people who have not been healed. Evidently healing is not for everyone during this lifetime. We prayed for my friend John Kroeker and he was not healed. However, he came to realize that he *would* be healed perfectly when the Lord took him home. If we ask to be healed, and the Lord answers us perfectly and permanently, he will take us home to heaven, where we will never more experience pain or death. The Apostle Paul prayed for healing and was not healed in his lifetime:

> **2 Corinthians 12:7-9 To keep me from becoming conceited because of these surpassingly great revelations, there was given me a thorn in my flesh, a messenger of Satan, to torment me. ⁸Three times I pleaded with the Lord to take it away from me. ⁹But he said to me, "My grace is sufficient for you, for my power is made perfect in weakness." Therefore I will boast all the more gladly about my weaknesses, so that Christ's power may rest on me.**

From this passage I take the "rule of thumb" to ask God three times. If he says no, then accept the grace to bear the pain in such a way that God will be glorified. From this passage I also see that the child of God can expect either healing or the grace to bear the suffering. In Philippians 2:27, Paul writes that Epaphroditus had been so ill that he almost died, and Paul had been quite alarmed about his illness. Evidently he had not been "healed instantaneously," but had "toughed out" the illness and finally recovered.

Also, from these passages it is obvious that "working up" enough faith to be healed is nonsense, although faith was indeed involved in some of the instances where Jesus healed. I think that if "working up" enough faith is essential to healing, and if the giant of the faith, the Apostle Paul, couldn't do it, then we are all in trouble.

And still, we are told to ask. But after asking, and if God says "no," it seems to me a waste of time to continually seek for something which God in his wisdom has decided is not for me at this time.

6. Commit your whole self to God for his use and for his glory.

Paul is again our example as he suffered in prison and was coming to the end of his life. Rather than complaining, he was rejoicing!

> **Philippians 1:18b-21** ...Yes, and I will continue to rejoice, **¹⁹**for I know that through your prayers and the help given by the Spirit of Jesus Christ, what has happened to me will turn out for my deliverance. **²⁰**I eagerly expect and hope that I will in no way be ashamed, but will have sufficient courage so that now as always Christ will be exalted in my body, whether by life or by death. **²¹**For to me, to live is Christ and to die is gain.

As we read through the Book of Philippians, we see that Paul had learned to trust his Lord. We can too. He is trustworthy! Trust him with your life. Trust him with your health (or even your lack of it). Trust him with your wealth (or lack of it). Trust him with your future. He is trustworthy! Trust him!

7. Join with God in his program of salvaging good out of a bad situation.

One of the "pat answers" we Christians get when well-meaning friends try to comfort us in times of trouble is Romans 8:28. It is usually quoted in the sense that "Everything is going to turn out all right." However, let's look closely at this well-known passage.

> **Romans 8:28** And we know that in all things God works for the good of those who love him, who have been called according to his purpose.

First, we notice that this promise is for a specific group of people only. Everything is not going to work out all right for everyone in the world! God only works for the good of certain people. These are "those who love him, and have been called." What are the characteristics of these people? I submit that they are the kind of people who do not shake their fist at God when tragedy or trouble strikes. Their attitude is more like that of the Apostle Paul, whose aim was to glorify God either in life or in death.

I believe that this verse is talking about people who, when tragedy or trouble strikes, look up to God and say something like this: "God, I'm in pain. This hurts a lot. But I know this does not come from you. It is the result of living in a sinful, fallen world. How can I work with you to salvage good out of this bad situation?" Trust him! God will take you up on your offer!

I would recommend a simple discipline that could accomplish a complete change of attitude regarding God's working in this fallen world. It works for me. It consists of simply (but sincerely) committing the day to God upon arising. Ask him to intervene in your world for his glory. Give him control of your life, including your decisions and even your thought processes. Express your willingness to do his will, and ask him to direct you. Then go to work, trusting him to take control of your life for that day. In the evening, before retiring, review your day. You will find that your original schedule has not always worked out. Sometimes good things enter the picture that were not expected. Sometimes there are unfortunate intrusions in your schedule. Then, look for the things that happened to you that day that cannot be explained in any way other than God's intervention, things for which you can in no way take credit. I do not believe many days will go by before you begin to gain a new sensitivity to God's working in the daily affairs of your life, and your faith and trust in him will grow. It also takes a lot of pressure off our own backs when we turn our burdens over to him. This is what he wants. He wants us to trust him. He wants us to rest in confidence that he is working all things in our lives for our good. Unfortunately, all too often we insist on staying at the controls...to our detriment.

8. A word about Satanic oppression

Satanic oppression can account for considerable suffering, especially for those who are on the front lines, battling for the souls of men. C. S. Lewis made an insightful observation regarding devils.[5] He said, "There are two equal and opposite errors into which our race can fall about the devils. One is to disbelieve in their existence. The other is to believe, and to feel an excessive and unhealthy interest in them." So while we need to be aware of Satan's oppression, caution is advised lest we become obsessed about him and his cohorts.

Missionaries have often been led to the conclusion that a certain affliction was caused by Satan. Satan does not give ground willingly. Where he has held sway in a culture for years, and then someone comes bringing the Gospel, he can get very ugly and vindictive. We need to pray that God will strengthen the "hedge" around his people. When such prayers are offered, the date and time have often been confirmed as the exact time when deliverance has come. We need to be aware that suffering sometimes comes from this source and that believers need not submit passively. Scripture states that Satan will flee when we resist him and claim the victory Jesus won through the shedding of his blood on the cross.

It is also true that Satanism is on the rise in America. We do not wish to delve into this subject extensively in this book except to identify Satanic oppression as a source of suffering and pain, and to assure the believer that

The Absence of Justice

Jesus' sacrifice on the cross accomplished the defeat of Satan. We can appropriate this victory by claiming it by faith and asking God for deliverance. Too often in the realm of Satanic activity "we have not because we ask not" as James indicated. (Jas 4:2) For those who wish to read more on this subject, may I recommend *Christian Counseling and Occultism* by Kurt Koch. There are certainly many other good books on this subject available in Christian bookstores.

The other side of Lewis' observation deals with those who become so obsessed with the devils that they seem to see them behind every corner and bush. They live in constant fear of them. I recommend memorizing the following Scriptures for those who fear Satan and his tactics:

> **2 Timothy 1:7 For God did not give us a spirit of timidity, but a spirit of power, of love and of self-discipline.**

Other translations use "fear" instead of timidity.

> **1 John 4:4 You, dear children, are from God and have overcome them, because the one who is in you is greater than the one who is in the world.**

Pain, suffering, and trouble can come to us because of Satanic oppression. He is our enemy. He is a "murderer from the beginning." God and Satan are engaged in a colossal battle that is being fought over our souls. God loves nothing more than to turn Satan's tricks around into good. Our choices determine whether Satan wins or God wins in a particular situation.

CONCLUSION

While we all will be confronted by, or will confront, tragedy and suffering in our lifetimes, God has given us an arsenal of resources to help us deal with such experiences victoriously. The list I have given can surely be expanded. God's Word is full of help for every circumstance of life. We need to become very familiar with God's Word so that his Spirit can minister to and through us when we face tragedy. Note that Romans 8:28 says that God works *good*, not the *best*. As a race of people, we gave up the "best" in the Garden of Eden. So although we may experience terrible pain and suffering here, we can choose to give them to God and cooperate with him as he works to turn them into good. God has promised to see his children through! As we have learned, deliverance will not always happen in this life, but ultimately God will keep his promises.

There Is a Balm

PASSING THROUGH
Annie Johnson Flint

"When thou passest through the waters, they shall not overflow thee." (Isa. 43:2)

> "When thou passest through the waters,"—
>   Deep the waves may be, and cold,
> But Jehovah is our refuge
>   And His promise is our hold;
> For the Lord Himself hath said it,
>   He the faithful God and true:—
> "When thou comest to the waters,
>   Thou shalt *not go down,* but *through.*"
>
> Seas of sorrow, seas of trial,
>   Bitterest anguish, fiercest pain,
> Rolling surges of temptation
>   Sweeping over heart and brain,—
> They shall never overflow us,
>   For we know His Word is true;
> All His waves and all His billows
>   He will *lead us safely through.*
>
> Threatening breakers of destruction,
>   Doubt's insidious undertow,
> Shall not sink us, shall not drag us
>   Out to ocean depths of woe;
> For His promise shall sustain us,—
>   Praise the Lord, Whose Word is true!
> We shall not go down, nor under,
>   He hath said, *"Thou passest through."*

1. The title of this chapter was suggested by Jeremiah 8:20-22. The Book of Jeremiah is laced with the pathos of a suffering prophet ministering to a suffering people. The question Jeremiah asks in verse 22 voices the agony of his heart. Is there no hope? Why is there no healing?
2. Kushner, Harold S. *Who Needs God?* New York: Summit Books, 1989. p. 205
3. Reimer, Jack, ed. *Jewish Insights on Death and Mourning.* New York: Schocken Books, 1995. p. 331
4. Kushner, Harold S. *When Bad Things Happen To Good People.* New York: Schocken Books, 1981.
5. Lewis, C. S. *The Screwtape Letters.* New York: Macmillan, 1961. p. 3

APPENDIX

JOB & CO. ASSETS AND INCOME

7000 Sheep

What does one do with 7000 sheep? Sheep are bred to produce either wool or mutton. Wool-producing sheep are not usually used for mutton, and mutton sheep do not produce as much wool. If we assume Job's flocks consisted of equal parts of wool and mutton sheep, the average wool yield for Job's flocks at 8 pounds per animal would be 56,000 pounds per year! Today, wool is worth only about 25 cents per pound. This low price is undoubtedly due to all the synthetics we are wearing today. Since wool was most likely the prime fiber used for clothing (31:20), rugs, felt, and other uses, its value would have been much greater in Job's day. Certainly it would have been worth at least the equivalent of $2.50/lb., which would earn Job $140,000.00 per year for wool.

Since sheep usually bear twin lambs, it would be possible to slaughter 70 percent of his mutton flock each year. At 80 lbs. per carcass x 3500 x .7 yields 196,000 lbs. of mutton per year! At $2.90/lb., that would be $568,400.00 income per year for mutton. There would also be an annual yield of 2450 sheep skins. Tanned and combed, they fetch anywhere from $25.00 to $75.00 each at roadside stands in the west. At $25.00 each, that would be an additional $61,250.00 per year. Since clothing made from wool was common in that day, this figure is probably grossly underestimated.

How many men would be required to do all this work? In the American West, there are herds of 1000 sheep or more managed by one or two shepherds with the aid of sheep dogs. We learn that Job did indeed utilize sheep dogs (Chapter 30, verse 1). So the herding operation could have been accomplished with as few as 7 to 15 full time shepherds. However, the shearing and butchering operations were another matter. It is possible for one man with an electric shear to shear 100 sheep per day but Job did not have electric shears. If we assume that with primitive shears one man could shear 40 sheep per day, and the shearing was to be accomplished within a 2-week period, it would take at least 15 shearers working 6 days/wk to accomplish the task. It would take dozens more to round up the sheep, hold them, and begin the processing of the wool. Job had the manpower to accomplish this, as we will see.

Since 10 sheep can be pastured on one acre of good land, Job would have had to have 700 acres of pasture for his sheep alone.

Appendix

If we value his sheep at $100.00/head, his flock would have been worth $700,000.00.

3000 Camels

What did Job do with 3000 camels? Camels were principally used as beasts of burden. The *Encyclopedia Americana* states that Arabian camels can carry 400 - 600 lbs. of freight for 12 hours/day, day after day. Bactrian camels can carry 600 - 800 lbs. If we use an average of 500 lbs. of freight per camel, and assume that each camel made one trip per year, the total freight that could have been imported and exported would be 750 tons each way! It is reasonable that Job would have been in the export/import business. Camel caravans in ancient times ranged all the way to China and India trading goods. Job could have exported finished woolen goods, olive oil, grain, or even salt if he was near enough to the sea. He could have imported silks, spices, ivory and jewelry from the Orient. If indeed Job exported salt, and if salt was literally worth its weight in gold (as it often was in ancient times), 750 tons of salt would have been worth 750 tons of gold! At a current price of $350.00/troy oz x 12 oz/lb x 2000 lbs/ton x 750 tons, we come up with $6.3 billion income from his salt trade. For the return trip he could have traded for the silks, spices, etc., and since a good business man would have tried to double his money, his income for the year based on one round trip could have maxed out at $12.6 billion.

Manpower to attend to a 25-camel caravan would be at least 10 men including guards against bandits and marauders (such as Chaldeans) and perhaps a camp cook. That would entail at least 1220 men involved in Job's import/export business.

It would be entirely possible that Job simply bred and raised camels for sale. If so, he would have needed men to herd his camels. Perhaps this would have required fewer men than the above, but camels are not as docile as sheep and would have required more herders and caretakers than the sheep. Let's put the number at a minimum of 500.

Working horses require at least 4 acres of land to sustain them in pasture and grain. If Job was just raising and selling his camels, perhaps 2 acres of land would be enough for these purposes, but this would then require at least 6000 acres of pasture for the camels alone! It is likely that the caravans did not travel in winter, so if Job were in the shipping business he still would need the pasture available for when the caravans were at home.

What are camels worth? In the USA they are rare animals and fetch fabulous prices. An exotic animal farm in East Texas reported that a 5-year-old female camel would fetch a price of $8000.00 here in the States. I suspect that they would be worth at least as much as an ox in an African nation which would be $715.00 each. If we use that figure, Job's camels were worth about $2.15 million.

The Absence of Justice

500 yoke of oxen

What does one do with oxen? Job obviously cultivated the land and raised crops... possibly wheat and barley. But 500 yoke of oxen? *The Whole Earth Catalog* states that a 1/4 section farm (160 acres) can be worked with 6 horses. That is 26.6 acres per horse. I asked a farmer to give me his opinion about how oxen would compare with draft horses for plowing and cultivation. His response was that the draft horses might be faster than the oxen in the morning, but that the great endurance of oxen would balance the scale during the afternoon. It was his opinion that the work that horses could accomplish vs. oxen would be about equal. That would make it possible for Job to cultivate 26,600 acres with his 500 yoke of oxen! Using a conservative 40 bushels per acre (some areas of the United States produce over 100 bushels/acre), we can see that Job could have produced 1,064,000 bushels of grain per year! At $3.50/bu for wheat, Job's gross income from wheat alone could have been $3.724 million per year (in today's dollars).

Pasture required for 1000 oxen would be similar to that needed for draft horses, which is 4 acres per animal. This means that Job would have needed at least 4000 acres devoted to pasturing his oxen.

What about manpower? Each team of oxen would have required a driver, so there are 500 men to start with. Certainly there were cattle herders and caretakers also. Harvesting the grain would have been accomplished by hand with scythes. One man can harvest 4 acres per day with a scythe. If the harvest were to be completed within a month's time, then it would take 6650 man-days to harvest 26,600 acres of grain, or 240 cutters working 6-day weeks. But there would have to be grain stackers, and threshers, and donkey handlers...probably totaling more than 1000 people.

We don't buy and sell many oxen in the United States today, so I asked a missionary what oxen were worth in the African nation where he served. He told me a good ox was worth about $715.00. That would make Job's herd worth $715,000.00.

500 donkeys

These animals were probably used at harvest time to haul the grain from the field to the threshing floors. They were also probably used for transportation.

When the raid by the Sabeans took place, the donkeys had been feeding while the oxen were plowing, so the cultivated land was used part of the year for pasture. However, there must have been pasture provided for them when the crops were growing, so there would have been at least 250 to 500 acres for donkey pasture.

Appendix

During harvest, there would have been a driver for each donkey and also year-round herders. So the manpower needed for the donkeys would have been at least 500.

My missionary friend also estimated that a donkey in Africa would be worth about $230.00, making a total of $115,000.00 worth of donkeys.

Eleven houses

We are told that each of Job's children lived in their own house. With as big an operation as Job's and considering their lifestyle, it is easy to conceive that each child lived in what today would be at least a half-million dollar house. Job would certainly have lived in at least a 2 million-dollar house. This gives a total of $7 million worth of housing.

Dairy operation and olive orchard

We have only hints about this part of Job's business, but it is certain that if Job had oxen, he also had cows to keep his herd replenished. Since he mentions an abundance of cream in 29:6, it is reasonable that they milked the cows for cream and butter.

His mention of oil is also incidental in 29:6 and could be a poetic reference to his olive orchards producing "streams of oil" from the earth.

Weaving and tanning operations

An enterprising man such as Job surely would have been in these businesses also since his operation produced the raw materials in abundance. And he possessed the financial assets to take advantage of these business opportunities.

Land for these operations

In 31:38 Job speaks of "his land," so he obviously owned the land for the cultivation of his crops and the pasturing of his animals. Adding up the numbers, we get about 11,000 acres of pasture minimum and 27,000 acres under cultivation, making a total of 39,000 acres! Add to this the additional land needed for the dairy herd, the male donkeys, and his olive orchards, his woolen mills and warehouses for his imported and exported merchandise, and we could come up with a respectable ranch of 50,000 acres.

The *Wall Street Journal* advertises large ranches in the west and their value per acre varies from as low as $125.00/acre to $1500.00/acre. At $125.00/acre, his land would have been worth at least $6.25 million. Using the maximum figure of $1,500.00/acre yields a land value of $75 million.

From these numbers, we can assume a minimum and maximum net worth

The Absence of Justice

for Job and Company not counting the income from his orchards, weaving and tanning operations (if he had them). His total number of employees could have been more than 2000 people. No doubt most of his servants were multi-functional. Many could have been seasonal employees. It is also probable that some of their pay consisted of housing, clothing, food, and necessities, which were abundantly provided by Job.

Minimum (Assets Only)

Using only the minimum values of his assets and not factoring in any of his profits we have:

7000 Sheep	$700,000.00
1000 Oxen	715,000.00
500 Donkeys	115,000.00
3000 Camels	2,150,000.00
Land, (50,000 acres @ $125/acre)	6,500,000.00
11 Houses @ $100,000.00 ea	1,100,000.00
Total	$11,280,000.00

However, I cannot be convinced that Job was just operating a gigantic petting zoo. He was in business for profit and would try to maximize those profits. Nor can I believe he and his children lived in middle-class houses.

Maximum Assets

7000 Sheep	$700,000.00
1000 Oxen	715,000.00
500 Donkeys	115,000.00
3000 Camels	2,150,000.00
Land, (50,000 acres @ $1,500/acre)	75,000,000.00
Job's house	3,000,000.00
Children's homes x 10	10,000,000.00
Total	$91,680,000.00

Gross Income

Wool	$140,000.00
Mutton	568,400.00
Hides	61,250.00
Grain	3,724,000.00
Export/import business	12,600,000,000.00
Total	$12,604,493,650.00

Appendix

Wages

Job was a generous man as described in Chapters 29 and 31. I believe he paid his servants well.

    2000 employees @ $50,000/yr average $ 100,000,000.00

It is impossible to guess what his other expenses would have been, but it is easy to see that Job would have enjoyed a very substantial profit.

BIBLIOGRAPHY

Albert, Denise Peterfreund. *Great Traditions in Ethics.* New York: Van Nostrand Co., 1980.

Andersen, Francis I. *Job.* London: Inter-Varsity Press, 1976.

Bemporad, Jack. *Essays in Honor of Rabbi Levi A. Olan.* New York: Ktav Publishing, 1977.

Boa, Kenneth. *God, I Don't Understand.* Wheaton, Ill.: Victor Books, 1975.

Buber, Martin. *Good and Evil.* New York: Charles Scribner's Sons, 1952.

———. *I and Thou.* New York: Charles Scribner's Sons, 1970.

Chartock, Roselle K., and Jack Spencer, eds. *Can It Happen Again?* New York: Black Dog & Leventhal, 1995.

Cheney, Margaret. *Tesla.* New York: Macmillan, 1970.

Dawidowicz, Lucy S. *The War Against the Jews.* New York: Holt, Rinehart and Winston, 1975.

Dershowitz, Alan M. *Chutzpah.* Boston: Little, Brown & Co., 1991.

Dhorme, Edouard. *A Commentary on the Book of Job.* Translated by Harold Knight. Nashville: Thomas Nelson, 1984.

Dobson, James. *When God Doesn't Make Sense.* Wheaton, Ill.: Tyndale House, 1993.

Durant, Will. *The Story of Philosophy.* New York: Simon & Schuster, 1926.

Eban, Abba. *Personal Witness.* New York: G.P. Putnam's Sons, 1992.

Ellul, Jacques. *Apocalypse: The Book of Revelation.* New York: The Seabury Press, 1977.

Fretheim, Terence E. *The Suffering of God.* Philadelphia: Fortress Press, 1984.

Gangel, Kenneth O. *Thus Spake Qoheleth.* Camp Hill, Pa.: Christian Publications, Inc., 1983.

Gerstenberger, E.S. and W. Schrage. *Suffering.* Translated by John E. Steeley. Nashville: Abingdon, 1980.

Hawking, Steven W. *A Brief History of Time.* New York: Bantam Books, 1988.

Hobbes, Thomas. *Leviathan.* New York: Penguin, 1985.

Jastrow, Robert. *God and the Astronomers.* New York: W.W. Norton & Co., 1978.

———. *Until the Sun Dies.* New York: W.W. Norton & Co., 1977.

Jensen, Irving L. *Job.* Chicago: Moody Press, 1975.

Jueneman, Frederick. "Innovative Notebook," *Industrial Research.* February 1974.

Kilby, Clyde S., ed. *A Mind Awake: An Anthology of C.S. Lewis.* New York: Harcourt Brace & World, 1968.

Koch, Kurt. *Between Christ and Satan.* Grand Rapids: Kregel, 1961.

———. *Christian Counseling and Occultism.* Grand Rapids: Kregel, 1965.

Kushner, Harold. *When All You've Ever Wanted Isn't Enough.* New York: Summit Books, 1986.

———. *When Bad Things Happen to Good People.* New York: Schocken Books, 1981.

———. *Who Needs God?* New York: Summit Books, 1989.

LeMaire, T. R. *Stones From the Stars.* New York: Prentice Hall, 1980.

Leupold, H.C. *Exposition of Ecclesiastes.* Grand Rapids: Baker Book House, 1952.

Lewis, C. S. *Christian Reflections.* Grand Rapids: Wm. B. Eerdmans, 1967.

———. *Mere Christianity.* New York: Macmillan, 1943.

Bibliography

———. *The Problem of Pain*. New York: Macmillan, 1962.
———. *The Screwtape Letters*. New York: Macmillan, 1961.
———. *The World's Last Night*. New York: Harcourt Brace, 1952.
Levenson, Jon D. *Creation and the Persistence of Evil*. HarperSanFrancisco, 1988.
Marshall, Catherine, ed. *The Prayers of Peter Marshall*. Lincoln, Va.: Chosen Books, 1949.
Martin, Bernard, ed. *Great 20th Century Jewish Philosophers*. New York: Macmillan, 1970.
Miller, Ed L. *God and Reason*. New York: Macmillan, 1972.
Mitchell, Stephen. *The Book of Job*. San Francisco: North Point Press, 1987.
Mitton, Simon, ed. *The Cambridge Encyclopedia of Astronomy*. New York: Crown Publishers, 1977.
Moody, Raymond A. *Life After Life*. Atlanta: Mockingbird Books, 1975.
Morgan, G. Campbell. *The Answers of Jesus to Job*. Grand Rapids: Baker Books, 1973.
Pinnock, Clark, Richard Rice, John Sanders, William Hasker, and David Basinger. *The Openness of God*. Downers Grove, Ill.: Inter-Varsity Press, 1994.
Prescott, William H. *The Conquest of Peru*. New York: Mentor, 1961.
Reimer, Jack, ed. *Jewish Insights on Death and Mourning*. New York: Schocken Books, 1995.
Ridout, Samuel. *The Book of Job*. Neptune, N. J.: Loizeaux Brothers, 1919.
Safire, William. *The First Dissident*. New York: Random House, 1992.
Sagan, Carl. *Cosmos*. New York: Random House, 1980.
Schaeffer, Edith. *Affliction*. Old Tappan, N. J.: Fleming H. Revell Company, 1978.
Shirer, William L. *The Rise and Fall of the Third Reich*. New York: Simon & Schuster, 1960.
Skinner, Fred Gladstone. *Myths and Legends of the Ancient Near East*. New York: Barnes & Noble, 1993.
Tennant, F. R. *Philosophical Theology*. Cambridge, England: University Press, 1928.
Tsevat, Matitiahu. *The Meaning of the Book of Job and Other Biblical Studies*. New York: Ktav, 1980.
Wiesel, Elie. *Memoirs*. New York: Knopf, 1995.
———. *Night*. New York: Hill & Wang, 1960.
Yancey, Philip. *The Jesus I Never Knew*. Grand Rapids: Zondervan Publishing, 1995.
———. *Disappointment With God*. Grand Rapids: Zondervan Publishing, 1988.
Zuck, Roy. *Job*. Chicago: Moody Press, 1978.